Excel 97
Further Skills

A progressive course for users

Jim Muir

Senior Lecturer in Business Computing
at Bournemouth University

Letts

1997

Acknowledgements

The computer program Microsoft Excel is copyrighted by the Microsoft Corporation, all rights reserved. Screen displays from Microsoft Excel are reprinted with permission. Microsoft Excel, Excel 97 and Windows 95 are registered trademarks of the Microsoft Corporation.

A CIP record for this book is available from the British Library.

ISBN 1 85805 218 1

Editorial and production services: Genesys Editorial

Typeset by Goodfellow & Egan Ltd, Cambridge

Printed in Great Britain by Ashford Colour Press, Gosport

Contents

Contents

About this book

A note on the new Excel Further Skills edition

Each new version of Excel includes more and more features; it is no longer feasible to do them justice in a single, budget-price volume. To keep the size and cost of the publication within acceptable limits, the best solution is to divide the material into 'simple' and 'further skills' books. This will benefit experienced users of Excel, who can cover the more advanced material in greater detail and omit much of the introductory material. However, some of the more elementary features of Excel are still included, and there is also some overlap between the two volumes. This is desirable for the following reasons:

- Certain material falls into both introductory and further skills categories, and it seems arbitrary to omit it, e.g. simple macros.

- A more experienced user may often need a brief introduction or 'refresher' on basic skills (e.g. creating charts) before undertaking more advanced ones. This is especially true if the operations or user interface have changed significantly from previous versions of Excel.

- Experience has shown that even experienced Excel users may only have used quite a narrow range of its total features, e.g. they may have used functions extensively but be unfamiliar with charting and have never used the database features. Many users especially have fought shy of using macros to automate their workbooks, believing (mistakenly) that it involves advanced programming techniques.

I have therefore attempted to fill in these gaps as far as possible with some introductory material, but without the need for step-by-step instructions at every stage.

Who should use this book?

This book is intended for users of Excel 97 who have a good working knowledge of the package. It is equally suitable for students in the classroom or open-learning workshop, or for home study. It therefore assumes (with the reservations stated above) previous experience of Excel or other spreadsheet packages. This implies, in particular, some familiarity with the following:

- creating simple spreadsheet models and amending them
- displaying worksheet data as graphs or charts
- using some Excel functions
- linking worksheets together
- creating and searching databases.

Using macros to automate Excel and develop custom applications is covered in some detail and from first principles. The examples used have mainly a business flavour, but the author has avoided biasing the examples towards areas where specialised numeric or accountancy skills are required.

Structure

Excel features are introduced in the context of practical business activities and problems to be solved, with the opportunity for further practice and consolidation.

This material has been organised into 17 units, each taking about 1 hour to complete. Every unit has the following features:

1 a list of the skills covered in the unit and the prior skills needed to tackle it successfully

2 tasks for acquiring and practising the skills in the context of practical problems

3 Excel screens to help you check your learning

4 summaries of commands and functions

5 solutions, where appropriate, in the appendices.

The units are mainly designed to be worked through in sequence, as often activities build on the skills acquired in earlier units, and may use spreadsheets and charts created in previous activities.

Conventions

Typographical conventions

Menu items and Dialog boxes are shows as: File

Buttons are shown as: Save

Keys on the keyboard are shown as: *Ctrl* /*Home*

Filenames are shown as: **SUMMARY 1**

Typed text is shown as: *=B9+B11*

(Note that text can be typed in upper or lower case.)

Functions and macro statements are shown as: *SUM( )*

(d.) indicates text that gives a definition of a term. Note that all definitions are also included in the Glossary.

indicates a tip providing a helpful hint or short-cut method.

(!) indicates a cautionary note.

indicates a cross reference.

indicates a feature that is new in Excel 97.

What's new in the Excel 97 edition

 The 'New in 97' icon indicates a feature that is either new or significantly changed in Excel 97.

- **The Office Assistant**. The Office Assistant is new to Excel 97 and supplements other Help features by answering questions typed in ordinary English.

- **The Range Finder**. When you edit a formula the Range Finder feature highlights the cell range in colour.

- **Indenting, rotating and aligning text** in cells is now possible.

- **Conditional formatting**. You can format cells whose values lie outside specified limits.

- **New functions**. The functions *AVERAGEA, MINA, MAXA,* and *STDEVA* work the same as the normal functions *AVERAGE, MIN, MAX* and *STDEV,* but include in their calculations cells that contain text and the logical values True and False.

- **Highlighting changes**. You can keep track of any changes to a workbook that you or other users may have made. As this feature is primarily designed to record changes made by users sharing workbooks on a network you must also turn on sharing features.

- **Validating workbook data**. Various types of data entry check can be made, e.g. mandatory entry, range/limit and format checks.

- **Macro virus protection**. A dialog box displays a warning message whenever you try to open a workbook that uses macros and gives you the option of quitting or opening the workbook with the macros either enabled or disabled.

What's changed in the Excel 97 edition

- **Multiple Undo**. You can undo up to your last 16 actions.

- **Chart Wizard**. The Chart Wizard allows you to create charts using four guided steps. These steps have been changed in Excel 97.

- **Paste Function**. Replaces the Function Wizard.

- **Toolbars and menus**. The distinction between a toolbar and a menu has been dropped. Command bars can contain both toolbar buttons and menu items. They can either be 'docked' on the edge of a window or 'float' anywhere in the window. A custom menu is now created using the Customize dialog box rather than the Menu Editor.

- **The Application Development Environment**. Some of the Visual Basic commands have changed and some new development features are included. These are briefly as follows:

  - Generally all the Microsoft Office products – Excel, Access, Word etc. – have been given a common interface, similar to that of Microsoft's standalone Visual Basic version 5.0.

  - Every workbook has an associated project that keeps track of all the worksheets, forms, macros etc.

  - The Project Explorer helps you keep track of these elements.

  - Macro sheets are accessible via an improved Visual Basic Editor; they are no longer stored in a special macro sheet.

  - The Properties window allows you to set the properties of objects used in the application, e.g. menus, buttons or text boxes.

  - New utilities replace the Menu and Dialog Editors.

Extra material in this edition

Extra material has been included on PivotTables, data maps, Excel 7 Advanced Search, and the **FORECAST** and **TREND** functions.

A note to lecturers and students

A photocopiable resource pack is available covering material in both the *Introductory* and *Further Skills* books (call 0181 740 2266 for details of the cost and terms of an institutional site licence). A disk containing the work achieved at the end of units is available free of charge to lecturers using the book as a course text.

Jim Muir

July 1997

Developments in Excel

Excel is produced by Microsoft Corporation, the US software company. It is specifically designed to operate using Windows, Microsoft's graphical operating environment.

Excel was first launched in 1987. The version prior to Excel 97 (Excel 7) was introduced in 1995 specifically to operate with Windows 95.

Excel 97 was launched in January 1997 and, at the time of writing, is still operating under Windows 95. By the time you are using this book, however, Excel may also be running under Windows 97, the proposed update to Windows 95.

Earlier versions of both Excel and Windows are still widely used, however, especially in education. If you have used a previous version of Excel you will find that for standard operations the basic Excel menus, commands and screen layouts remain very similar and new features of later versions form natural add-ons.

Spreadsheet terminology

In this book the following terms are used:

- A **spreadsheet** is a grid of vertical columns and horizontal rows.

- Where a column and a row intersect is a **box** or **cell**.

- The **cell reference** or **address** consists of two coordinates – the column letter followed by the row number (as in a street map).

- Certain cells can contain **formulae** which tell the spreadsheet to perform calculations, e.g. add the values in a column or work out a percentage. These formulae ensure that totals are automatically recalculated when the values in the spreadsheet are changed.

(Excel uses the term 'worksheet' for its spreadsheets, so I shall use it too from Unit 1 onwards.)

Creating a workbook

What you will learn in this unit

By the end of this unit you will be able to:

- retrieve or open a workbook
- save a workbook
- change the window size
- move windows
- add and subtract the contents of cells
- clear cell data
- select cells
- copy and paste cell data
- edit cell data
- enlarge rows
- widen columns
- use the Fill Right feature
- use formulae
- use help
- use keyboard commands
- use the Office Assistant
- use the SUM function
- use the spell checker
- undo an operation
- use the **AutoCalculate** feature
- use the **AutoCorrect** feature
- use the **AutoFill** feature
- use the **AutoSum** feature
- exit from Excel.

What you should know already

This unit assumes that you have some familiarity with the main features of Windows 95/97 and a grasp of basic spreadsheet concepts and operations.

Introduction

This unit assumes that you already know how to start up Excel and find your way around the worksheet screen. The first task, which introduces the various features of the Excel window, is therefore brief. You are advised to 'skim' it rather than skip it completely, however, especially if you have not used a recent (Windows 95 or later) version of Excel. You will similarly find Task 2, where you create your first worksheet, fairly straightforward, but you will probably discover useful new features of Excel 97. You should create this worksheet as you will need it for later tasks.

Task 1: The worksheet screen

1 Overview and terminology

An Excel workbook consists of one or more worksheets, like pages in a book, named initially **SHEET1**, **SHEET2** etc. Looking at the Excel screen shown in FIGURE 1.1, you will see that it actually consists of two windows:

■ Around the outside is the *Application Window*, which carries all of the Excel commands – menus, toolbars etc.

■ Within the Application window is the *Document Window*, i.e. the worksheet itself.

2 Before you start using the keyboard make sure that you recognise the main components of the Excel screen. Keep referring to the labelled diagram in FIGURE 1.1.

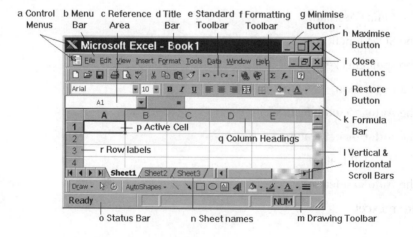

FIGURE 1.1

3   a   The **Control Menu** boxes. These offer commands such as resizing and closing the window.

    b   The **Menu Bar**. The Menu Bar at the top of the screen shows the usual options – File, Edit, View etc.

    c   The **Reference Area**. This shows the row and column number of the active cell – see Page 2.

    d   The **Title Bar**. Whenever a new workbook is opened Excel gives it a temporary or default name, Book1, Book2 etc.

    e and f   The **Toolbars**. There are two standard toolbars immediately below the menu bar. The **Standard Toolbar** offers options such as opening and closing files, cutting and pasting, printing etc. The **Formatting Toolbar** allows you to alter the appearance and alignment of data in your workbook.

In these units we concentrate mainly on the menu versions of commands, rather than using buttons. A key to these two toolbars is included at the end of this unit.

    g–j   At the top right of the screen are the usual groups of three buttons which control the size of the worksheet window. One set is for the whole application window and one for the inner cell area – the document window.

    g   **Minimize buttons** (a line). These either reduce Excel to a button on the Taskbar or the document window to a small icon within the application window.

    h   **Maximize buttons** (a square). These either increase the size of the Excel application window to fill the screen or increase the size of the document window so that it fills the whole of the application window.

    i   **Close buttons** (an 'X'). These close either Excel or one of the workbooks. If you click one of these buttons by mistake you will need to open Excel and/or your workbook(s) again.

    j   **Restore buttons** (overlapping squares). These restore the individual windows to their original sizes.

    k   The **Formula Bar**. This shows whatever is entered in the active cell – see Page 2. This is a new workbook, so all the cells are blank.

    l   The vertical and horizontal **Scroll Bars**.

    m   The **Drawing Toolbar**. This allows you to draw a variety of shapes on your worksheet – circles, rectangles, arrows etc. It also allows you to add colour and text effects. A key to this Toolbar is included at the end of this unit.

    n   **Sheet names**. Each sheet is marked with a name tab – the name in bold indicates which sheet is currently selected or 'active'.

    o   The **Status Bar**. Displays information about the current command; no command has been issued yet, so it reads 'Ready'.

    p   The **Active Cell**. At the moment the top left cell A1 is the active cell – the one currently selected and shown by a heavy border. In Excel 97 a cell can contain up to 32,000 characters.

q and r **Column and Row Headings**. These contain the column references (letters) and the row references (numbers). Jointly they give the cell reference or address, e.g. A1, D5.

4 Now that we've identified the basic screen components let's try some of them out; keep referring to FIGURE 1.1 if necessary. First we will experiment with the window size; this often causes problems when you're starting out.

5 Minimising the window size. As explained in Step 1 there are two windows in the Excel screen; each of these can be resized independently of the other window.

Move the screen pointer (the arrow) onto the topmost Minimize button at the top right of the screen.

Click the left mouse button once. The whole workbook disappears, and you return to the Windows Desktop.

On the Taskbar at the bottom of the screen is a button marked Microsoft Excel; this represents the minimised worksheet – the Excel application is still running, but cannot be used until it is restored to normal size.

Move the screen pointer onto this button and click the left mouse button once.

The Excel window reappears – try again if it doesn't.

6 **Troubleshooting**: if you can't locate the Excel icon hold down the *Alt* key then press the *Tab* key. Continue to keep *Alt* pressed down and press the *Tab* key – Windows runs through all your open applications until it finds Excel.

At this point release the *Tab* key and the *Alt* key and you are returned to Excel.

7 **Maximising and restoring the window size**. Check that you can do this for both the outer application window and the inner document window.

8 **Adjusting the window size**. Try altering the size of the workbook windows by dragging the sides in the usual way. If you can't see the sides then you may need to click the Restore button first.

Restore both windows to a workable size by reversing this dragging process.

Remember that the sides of a window can be dragged in order to adjust the window size vertically or horizontally.

9 **Moving a window**. First make sure that neither the application window nor the document window is maximised – click the Restore buttons if they are.

Try moving each window independently of the other by dragging the title bars of the windows.

10 **Keyboard commands**. You may not know the following keyboard commands, which are useful in changing the screen position quickly. Try these:

- Hold down the *Ctrl* key and press the *Home* key – you are returned to the top of the worksheet – cell A1 is the active cell.

- Hold down the *Ctrl* key and press the down arrow key on the keyboard – you are taken to the last row of the worksheet. (if the worksheet is not empty you are moved to the last row containing an entry).

- Now hold down the *Ctrl* key and press the right arrow key. You are taken to the last column of the worksheet.

- Now try out the following key combinations:

  Ctrl/left arrow

  Ctrl/up arrow

  You will return to the top of the worksheet again.

- The *Page Up* and *Page Down* keys can also be used to move quickly around the worksheet.

11 **Selecting groups of cells**. Make sure that you can select groups or *ranges* of cells – check that you are happy with the following:

- Move to cell A1, hold down the left mouse button, and drag the screen pointer down and across to cell D6. Release the mouse button and 24 cells should be selected in all. A1, the first cell selected, remains white while the others go dark. The cell and column labels (A–D and 1–6) are also shown in bold.

- Deselect this cell range by clicking anywhere on the worksheet.

- Now try selecting a whole column – click on the column heading for column A (called the *column designator*). The whole column is selected.

- Several columns can be selected by dragging across the column designators with the mouse pointer – try this for rows too.

Selecting or 'highlighting' cells is an essential first step in many operations; it requires a little practice to select the precise range of cells.

12 **Calling up Help**. Excel provides a comprehensive online help and tutorial facility. The **Help** menu options have changed from earlier versions of Excel, so try the following:

Move the screen pointer onto the Menu Bar and click the **Help** menu.

Select the second menu option, **Contents and Index** – a dialog box opens.

Look at the top left-hand corner of the dialog box. Three choices are shown as tabs – **Content** , **Index** and **Find** . Click the **Contents** and **Index** tabs in turn and a new dialog box appears.

13 **Help Contents**. Finally, click the **Contents** tab. The Help contents are divided into topics, represented as chapters in a book.

Double click on the topic **Getting Help** (i.e. click the mouse button twice in quick succession). The icon changes to an open book showing a series of subtopics. Read a few of these subtopics, returning to the Contents dialog box by clicking the **Back** or **Help Topics** buttons.

Finally, double-click the **Getting Help** topic to close it – the icon changes from an open to a closed book.

14 **The Help Index**. Click the **Index** tab at the top of the **Help** dialog box.

All the **Help** topics are listed alphabetically. Provided you are fairly sure of what your topic is called this feature can be easier to use than the **Contents** option, which, as we have seen, involves negotiating several levels of contents.

Scroll down to the topic **menus, customizing** and click it to select it.

Click the **Display** button at the bottom of the dialog box and the Help text is displayed.

When you have read it click the **Help Topics** button to return to the dialog box.

15 **Keying in a Help topic**. A quicker way of scrolling through a long list is to type in the name of the topic. The top part of the **Index** dialog box allows you to do this – try it for the topic **worksheets**.

16 **Independent activity**. Excel offers another way of getting help – **Find**. This is offered as third tab option on the dialog box. Take some time to explore it.

17 **Exiting Help**. Click either the **Close** or the **Cancel** button. You are returned to the workbook.

 18 **Using the** **Office Assistant**. The Office Assistant is new to Excel 97 and supplements other **Help** features by answering questions typed in ordinary English.

Look at the Standard toolbar at the top of the screen. The Office Assistant button is marked with a question mark – see the key to the toolbar at the end of this unit. If it is not in view then you may need to maximise the application window.

Click the **Office Assistant** button once; the Office Assistant window opens, asking you the question: 'What would you like to do?'.

Using FIGURE 1.2 as a guide, type **close a window** as shown and click the **Search** button.

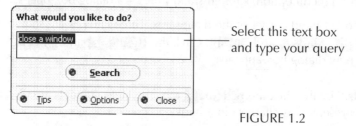

Select this text box
and type your query

FIGURE 1.2

The Office Assistant displays a list of relevant topics – choose one by clicking it and the relevant help window appears. When you have read it close the window – you are returned to the Office Assistant logo (an animated paperclip by default). Click it once to display the Office Assistant window again.

This time click the **Tips** button – a screen tip appears. You can use the **Back** and **Next** buttons to display further tips when available.

Click the **Close** button on the Tips window. You are returned to the Office Assistant logo. Close it.

19 **The** 'What's This?' feature offers 'context-sensitive' tips, i.e. tips specific to the Excel feature that you are currently using.

Open the **Help** menu and select the **What's This?** option. Move the screen cursor around the window; every time that it changes to a '?' shape you can click to get help on this feature.

Now move the screen pointer (after choosing **What's This?**) onto an Excel feature, e.g. open one of the menus and then select an option. A 'ScreenTip' window opens explaining its function. Simply click again to remove the screen tip. You can use ScreenTips whenever you're not sure what a particular Excel item does.

20 **Help on the Toolbars**. For a brief description of each button's purpose simply move the mouse pointer on top of it.

For a more detailed description use the **'What's This?'** option again.

21 Exiting from Excel. Click the File option on the Menu Bar. The File menu opens. Click the Exit option at the bottom of the menu and you will leave Excel. As you have entered no data in the worksheet you should not be prompted to save it. If you are offered this option click the **No** button.

Task 2: Entering data into a worksheet

Now that you know your way around the Excel screen you can create your first worksheet. We'll choose a simple example – managing your personal finances.

Look at FIGURE 1.3. The worksheet is based around a student's income and expenditure.

	A	B	C	D	E	F
1			PERSONAL FINANCES - TERM 1			
2	INCOME		Week 1			
3	Opening Bals.		0			
4	Grant		500			
5	Loan		400			
6	Parents		300			
7	Total Income					
8						
9	EXPENDITURE					
10	Accomodation		60			
11	Food		30			
12	Books		75			
13	Other		20			
14	Total Expenditure					
15						

FIGURE 1.3

Later on you can adapt it if you like to suit your own circumstances; for the moment enter the data exactly as shown here. As entering and editing data is straightforward I will keep instructions to the minimum.

1 First enlarge the worksheet and make sure that **SHEET1** is the active sheet.

2 **Entering titles and labels**. Enter the data shown in FIGURE 1.3. It displays in the Formula Bar as you type it. Include the wrong spelling of the word 'Accomodation'.

 Remember that whenever you enter or change a cell's contents you need to complete the entry. There are several ways to do this:

■ press *Enter*

■ click the next cell

■ press one of the arrow keys on the keyboard

■ click the green 'tick' box that appears next to the Formula Bar.

Text is automatically aligned to the left of the cell. Forgetting to complete the entry causes a number of problems, e.g. menu options being dimmed and unavailable.

Always check this if your next command fails to execute.

3 **Checking spelling**. First click cell A1; now click the **Spelling** button on the Standard toolbar; it is marked with a tick and 'ABC'.

After you click the button, Excel compares all the text in the selected cells with its dictionary. A dialog box opens, telling you, for example, that the abbreviation 'Bals' is not in the dictionary – click the **Ignore** button.

The label 'Accomodation' is selected; it has been misspelt with only one 'm'. Excel suggests the correct spelling. Click the **Change** button.

Continue until a dialog box informs you that all the text is checked, then click the **OK** button.

Spell checkers will not recognise most abbreviations and proper names unless you add them to the dictionary. An **Add** button is provided to do this.

4 **AutoCorrect**. Open the **Tools** menu and select the option **AutoCorrect**. A dialog box appears. Commonly misspelt words and other common errors shown in the dialog box can be corrected as you type.

Click the **OK** button if you wish to use this feature. It can be turned off by selecting **AutoCorrect** again and then clicking the option box 'Replace text as you type' to remove the 'X'.

5 **Editing cell contents using the Formula Bar**. Let's alter the text in cell A5 from **Loan** to **Bank Loan**.

First click cell A5 to activate it. The text appears in the Formula Bar at the top of the screen.

Now move the mouse pointer in front of the first letter of **Loan** in the Formula Bar (*not* the cell) – the pointer changes to a vertical bar.

Click once to place a flashing cursor there – this marks the insertion point – see FIGURE 1.4.

locate cursor here
and click

	A	B	C
		▼ X ✓ =	Loan
1			PERSONA
2	INCOME		Week1
3	Opening Bals		0
4	Grant		500
5	Loan		400
6	Parents		300
7	Total Income		1200
8			

FIGURE 1.4

Type the word **Bank** and press *Enter*. The cell is amended.

6 **In-cell editing**. You can also edit cell contents directly without using the Formula Bar. Let's alter the label **Food** in cell A11 to **Food and Travel**.

Move the screen pointer to cell A11 and *double* click the space after the word **Food**. A flashing cursor marking the insertion point should be placed there – if not, keep trying!

Amend the label to **Food and Travel** and press *Enter*.

7 **Information only – deleting**. If you need to delete any character, you must place the insertion point in the same way as in Steps 5 and 6, then use the *Delete* key to delete to the right of the insertion point or the *Backspace* key to delete to the left of the insertion point. To overtype the contents of a cell, just click the cell once to select it and start typing. There is no need to delete the contents first.

8 **Widening columns**. Some of the labels in Column A are too wide for their cells. Try out these alternative methods:

■ Locate the screen pointer on the vertical line that separates column heading A from column heading B. The pointer changes to a double-headed arrow.

Now press down the left mouse button and drag the column to the right until its width is about **16.00**. The width is given in the Reference Area.

■ Click the column designator, i.e. the 'A' in the column heading. The whole column is selected.

Click on the **Format** menu to open it.

Select the **Column** option, followed by **Width** from the next menu that appears. A dialog box is displayed.

Enter the new width as *15*, and click the **OK** button.

■ Click the column designator A again to select the column if necessary.

Open the **Format** menu and select the **Column** option then **AutoFit Selection**. The width is automatically adjusted to fit the longest entry.

9 **Altering the row height**. We will now make row 1 taller to emphasise the title.

Locate the screen pointer on the horizontal line that separates row designator 1 from row designator 2.

Drag the row down until the height is **15.00** (you can also select the row by clicking the row designator, then using the **Row** option on the **Format** menu to achieve the same result).

10 **Entering numeric data**. Make sure that you enter the number 0 and not the letter O (a common source of error).

Complete the other income and expenditure items as shown in FIGURE 1.3; use the *Enter* key or down arrow key to complete each entry.

 Don't calculate the totals yet.

 If the number entered is too wide for the column Excel alerts you to this by a row of hash signs (####). You must then widen the column.

11 **Optional**: if you are not proceeding to the next Task then save and close the workbook. Saving is covered in detail in the next unit. For the moment proceed as follows (I am assuming throughout these units that you wish to save your work to a diskette. If not then substitute the appropriate drive letter for A drive.)

Open the **File** menu (click **File** on the Menu Bar) and select the **Save As** option. A dialog box appears.

At the moment the workbook has the default name **BOOK1.XLS** – see the **File name** box at the bottom of the dialog box.

First make sure that you have a suitable, formatted floppy disk in the disk drive.

Click the █down arrow█ button on the **Save in:** box and select 3¹/₂ **Floppy (A:)** from the list offered.

Click the **File name** box to select it and amend the file name to **TERMS** (upper- or lower-case).

If you have made a mistake click the █Cancel█ button and start again; otherwise, click the █Save█ button and the name of the workbook, **TERMS.XLS**, is displayed in the title bar.

To quit Excel, open the **File** menu and select **Exit**. You will be returned to the Windows 95 desktop.

If you wish to exit Windows 95 then click the █Start█ button on the Taskbar and select **Shut Down**.

Task 3: Using formulae

Formulae are used to perform a variety of operations, such as calculations.

A formula is placed in a cell in the same way as text or numbers. It can be very simple, such as adding the contents of two cells, or complex, containing mathematical or financial functions.

You must always start a formula with an equal (=) sign; this tells Excel that you are about to apply a formula to a cell.

 If you are not continuing from the previous activity then you will need to open the workbook **TERMS**. Make sure that **SHEET1** is the active sheet.

1 **Addition**. We will calculate the first week's income and expenditure figures.

Enter the formula *=SUM(C3:C6)* in cell C7 – functions and formulae may be typed in upper- or lower-case.

Click the tick button next to the formula (or press *Enter*). The results of the formula are displayed in cell C7 – the income total of 1200.

 Notes on the *SUM* function: The *SUM* function is a lot quicker than typing the full formula *=C3+C4+C5+C6*. *SUM* is also expandable – if another row were to be inserted into this range of four cells at a later stage, say between rows 4 and 5, the new cell would automatically be included in the range. This would not be the case if one were to type the formula out in full using the + sign.

2 **Adding up columns – shortcuts**. We will now use a formula to add up the total expenditure.

Activate cell C14 and type *=SUM(*

Move the screen pointer to the first expenditure item, cell C10.

Hold down the mouse button and drag the pointer to cell C13. Four cells are enclosed by a dotted box.

The formula bar should read *=SUM(C10:C13*

(If you have made a mistake then click the cross (X) box on the formula bar and start again.)

Click the tick box and the result of the formula – 185 – is displayed – there is no need to type the final bracket.

3   **Amending formulae – error messages**. Try the following:

Activate cell C7 and move the pointer onto the Formula Bar; it reads **=SUM(C3:C6)**

Alter the formula to **=SUM(C3:C7)** and click the tick box to execute the new formula. An error dialog box appears. As C7 is the 'destination' cell – the cell containing the formula – it cannot also be one of the cells to be summed, as this is 'circular'.

Click the **Cancel** button on the dialog box.

Correct the formula to its original **SUM(C3:C6)** and execute it again.

When you edit a formula, the 'Range Finder' feature highlights the cell range in colour, both for the formula and for the cells in the worksheet.

4   Excel has a range of error messages. We'll look at one more for the moment.

Activate cell C14 and amend **SUM** to **SIM** in the Formula Bar.

Execute this formula (use the *Enter* key or tick box). The error message **#NAME?** appears in the cell. Make sure that the cell is still selected, but don't correct it just yet.

5   **Clearing cell contents**. Open the **Edit** menu and select the **Clear** option followed by the **All** option. The cell is cleared (you can use the *Delete* key instead of the **Clear** command).

6   **Adding columns – the AutoSum button**.

The **AutoSum** button offers the quickest way of adding a column of figures. It is on the Standard toolbar and is marked with the Greek letter sigma (Σ).

We need to add the expenditure cells again; use the dragging technique used in Step 2 to select the cell range C10 to C14 (see note below).

Click the **AutoSum** button once and the **SUM** formula is executed; the total of 185 appears in cell C14.

A note on AutoCalculate Whenever you select a range of cells holding numeric data Excel will automatically tell you the sum of their values in the bottom right-hand corner of the window. This is for information only, and is not executed until you enter a **SUM** formula.

7 **Subtraction formulae.** We now need to subtract total expenditure from total income to find the closing balance for week 1.

First enter the cell label in cell A16 – see FIGURE 1.5.

	A	B	C	D	E	F
	File Edit View Insert Format Tools Data Window Help					
1			PERSONAL FINANCES - TERM 1			
2	INCOME		Week 1			
3	Opening Bals.		0			
4	Grant		500			
5	Loan		400			
6	Parents		300			
7	Total Income		1200			
8						
9	EXPENDITURE					
10	Accomodation		60			
11	Food		30			
12	Books		75			
13	Other		20			
14	Total Expenditure		185			
15						
16	CLOSING BALS		1015			

FIGURE 1.5

Activate cell C16 and type the formula *=C7-C14*

Execute the formula as before and the closing balance for week 1 (1015) appears in cell C16. Your worksheet should now be the same as FIGURE 1.5.

Task 4: Saving your workbook

In these units I make the assumption that you will want to save your work on a floppy disk (A drive) not on the computer's hard disk. All future references assume this.

If you have already saved the workbook as **TERMS** *then open the* **File** *menu and select* **Save** *(not* **Save As***) to save the present version and continue with the next activity. (You can also use the* ▆Save▆ *button on the Standard toolbar to save.)*

1 Open the **File** menu (click **File** on the Menu Bar) and select the **Save As** option. A dialog box appears.

2 At the moment the workbook has the default name **BOOK1.XLS** – see the File name box. **.XLS** is an extension automatically assigned to all Excel workbook files, but we want to save it under a more meaningful name than **BOOK1**.

A filename can be up to 218 characters long, and can consist of any combination of letters, numbers and certain special characters (including spaces, dashes and underscores), but not the following: \ / < > * ? " ; *or* :

3   First make sure that you have a suitable formatted floppy disk in the disk drive.

Click the down arrow button on the **Save in:** box and select 3¹/₂ **Floppy (A:)** from the list offered.

Amend the file name to **TERMS** (double click the **File name** box to select it if necessary and type over the top).

If you have made a mistake click the **Cancel** button and start again; otherwise click the **Save** button.

4   When you return to your workbook you will see the name of the workbook, **TERMS.XLS**, displayed in the title bar.

5   At this point use the **File** menu and select **Exit** to exit from Excel. (If you are familiar with closing and opening files then skip this operation and go on to the next task.)

Task 5: Loading an existing workbook (optional)

Your workbook **TERMS** has been saved to disk as an Excel file on the A drive. To work on it again you must use this name to retrieve it from disk and load it into main memory.

1   Start Excel again. A new blank workbook appears with the default name **BOOK1**. We will close it as we want to work on an existing workbook.

Open the **File** menu and select the **Close** option (not **Exit**). The document window goes blank, as no workbook is in use.

2   If you saved your **TERMS** workbook to a disk then obviously the first step is to ensure that this disk is in drive A.

Open the **File** menu and select **Open**. A dialog box appears. It is similar to the **Save As** dialog box used in the last activity.

3   **Retrieving a file by typing the name**. If you are sure of the file name and the drive (as you should be on this occasion) then simply type them in the **File name** box – it is already selected.

Type *A:\TERMS* and click the **Open** button.

The file will load from disk and appear on screen.

If it does not appear, check your spelling (especially the colon and the backslash) and that you are using the correct disk.

Open the **File** menu and select the **Close** option again.

4   **Retrieving a file from the file list**. Alternatively you can open a file by choosing it from a list. Open the **File** menu and select the **Open** option. The **Open** dialog box opens again. This time we may need to select the drive.

Move the screen pointer onto the **Look in:** box and click the down arrow button. Select the 3¹/₂ **Floppy (A:)** drive icon. The workbook **TERMS.XLS** is listed in the dialog box.

Click it to select it if necessary, then click the **Open** button again. The file will load from disk and appear on screen.

5 **Independent activity**. Close the workbook as before. Open the **File** menu again and look at the bottom of the menu. You should see the workbook listed near the bottom of the menu. Click it to load the workbook again. Excel remembers the last four workbooks that you (or another user of the application) have used.

Task 6: Copying cells and deleting data

At the moment we only have data for one week. We are going to copy these data into adjacent columns to create data for week 2 onwards, and modify certain cells. We will then experiment with a number of ways to move, copy and delete cells. They are all useful in certain contexts, so if you are not familiar with them make sure that you try out all these tasks.

1 **Copying**. First select all the cells containing the Week 1 data; move the screen pointer onto cell C2 and drag down to column C16.

If you select the wrong cells then merely click anywhere on the worksheet to remove the selection and try again.

Open the **Edit** menu and select **Copy** (not **Cut**). The selected area is now enclosed by a flowing dotted line – called the **marquee**.

2 **Pasting**. Next we must indicate where the cells are to be copied to.

Activate cell D2 – the cell where you want to start pasting from.

Open the **Edit** menu and select **Paste**. The cells are copied to a new location, and the dotted area remains around the area that you copied, allowing you to paste it again if you wish.

Remove the dotted area by pressing the *Esc* key on the keyboard.

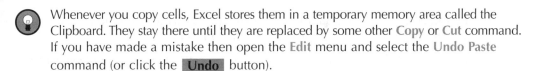

Whenever you copy cells, Excel stores them in a temporary memory area called the Clipboard. They stay there until they are replaced by some other **Copy** or **Cut** command. If you have made a mistake then open the **Edit** menu and select the **Undo Paste** command (or click the **Undo** button).

You can undo up to your last 16 actions.

3 Notice that not only the data but also the formulae are copied. Excel automatically adjusts the cell references in the formulae to refer to their new location in column D. For this reason they are called *relative references*. Click the cells D7, D14 and D16 and check their formulae in the Formula Bar.

4 **Cutting and pasting.** Cutting cells physically removes them from their original location so that they can be pasted to a new one. This is a similar operation to copying.

Select the cells for week 2 now, i.e. cell range D2 to D16.

Open the **Edit** menu and select the **Cut** option; (not **Copy**) the cells are surrounded by the marquee as before.

Activate cell E2, then open the **Edit** menu and select **Paste**. This time the column is moved a column to the right, leaving column D blank.

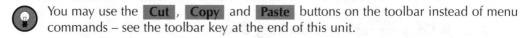

You may use the **Cut**, **Copy** and **Paste** buttons on the toolbar instead of menu commands – see the toolbar key at the end of this unit.

5 **Clearing ranges of cells.** Let's now clear the copied column – in the next section you will learn a better way of copying columns using the **Fill** command.

Select the cells in column E again if necessary, then open the **Edit** menu and select **Clear** followed by **All**.

As before you can use the **Edit-Undo** command to restore deleted data. You can undo up to your last 16 actions.

6 **Copying cells using fill right.** Move the screen pointer onto cell C2.

Hold down the mouse button and drag down the column to cell C16.

Keeping the mouse button pressed down, drag the screen pointer across to select the same number of cells in the next column. Now let go.

You should now have selected two columns.

7 Now open the **Edit** menu and select **Fill** followed by **Right**. The contents of column C – data and formulae – are copied to column D.

(If the copying is incorrect then open the **Edit** menu again and select **Undo Fill Right**.)

Select cell D2 and amend the column label to *Week 2*.

8 The values in cells D4–D6 for Grant, Loan and Parents will need to be deleted; they are 'one-off' income items only applying to week 1.

Drag from D4 down to D6 to select these three cells, then press the *Delete* key. Notice how the totals in column D are automatically recalculated. (If you have cleared the wrong cells, open the **Edit** menu again and select **Undo Clear**.)

Notice also that your closing balance for week 2 is now a negative amount, an insolvent –185 in cell D16. However, this is because we have not yet carried forward the closing balance of 1015 from week 1 to the opening balance for week 2. Let's do this with a formula.

9 We want the value in cell D3, the opening balance for week 2, to equal C16, the closing balance for week 1.

Activate cell D3 and type **=C16**.

Click the tick button to execute the formula and the week 2 totals are recalculated – your closing balance for week 2 is now a healthy 830.

10 Now make the following amendments to week 2:

Food and Travel	35
Books	15

The closing balance is now 885.

11 We can now use week 2 as our model for the next three weeks.

First select the week 2 values and the three adjacent columns, i.e. four columns in all, cells D3–G16.

Then use the **Edit-Fill-Right** command as before. The contents of column D (week 2) are copied into columns E, F and G.

The closing balance at the end of week 5 should be 495 in cell G16 – see FIGURE 1.6.

	A	B	C	D	E	F	G
1			PERSONAL FINANCES - TERM 1				
2	INCOME		Week 1	Week 2			
3	Opening Bals		0	1015	885	755	625
4	Grant		500				
5	Bank Loan		400				
6	Parents		300				
7	Total Income		1200	1015	885	755	625
8							
9	EXPENDITURE						
10	Accommodation		60	60	60	60	60
11	Food and Travel		30	35	35	35	35
12	Books		75	15	15	15	15
13	Other		20	20	20	20	20
14	Total Expenditure		185	130	130	130	130
15							
16	CLOSING BALS.		1015	885	755	625	495

FIGURE 1.6

 Use the **Undo** command as before if you make a mistake.

Remember to save the changes that you have made – use **Save** (not **Save As**) on the **File** menu.

12 **Using AutoFill to complete a series**. Rather than typing in week numbers 3–5 in cells D3–F3 we can use **AutoFill** to complete the series.

Click cell D2 to select it. Notice that in the bottom right-hand corner of the cell there is a small 'handle'.

Move the mouse pointer onto the handle and it becomes cross-shaped (a '+' sign).

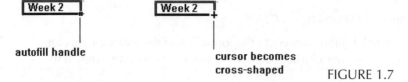

autofill handle

cursor becomes
cross-shaped   FIGURE 1.7

Now drag the cursor to enclose cells D2–G2 as well. When you release the mouse button these cells are correctly labelled.

13 If you are not continuing with the next unit then save and close the workbook.

Summary of commands and functions

Menu commands show the menu name first, followed by the command to choose from the menu, e.g. **Edit-Clear** means open the **Edit** menu and select the **Clear** command.

Keyboard commands

Ctrl/Home	Go to cell A1
Ctrl/Down Arrow key	Go to last row of the worksheet
Ctrl/Right Arrow key	Go to last column of worksheet

Menu commands

Edit-Clear	Clear cell contents
Edit-Copy	Copy selected cells
Edit-Cut	Remove selected cells
Edit-Delete	Delete selected rows or columns
Edit-Delete Sheet	Delete selected worksheet
Edit-Fill-Right	Copy selected cells into selected right-hand columns
Edit-Paste	Insert cut or copied cells at a specified location
Edit-Undo	Undo previous operation(s)
File-Close	Close current workbook
File-Exit	Exit Excel
File-New	Open new blank workbook
File-Open	Retrieve an existing workbook
File-Save As	Save and name a new workbook
File-Save	Save an existing workbook
Help	Select Help
Tools-Autocorrect	Correct misspelled words automatically

Functions

=SUM()   Add a range of cells

Standard Toolbar

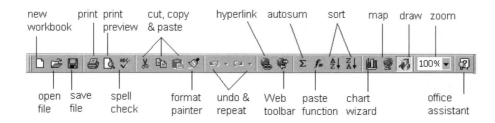

Formatting Toolbar

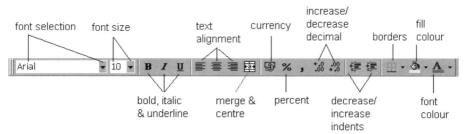

The Drawing Toolbar

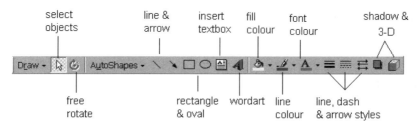

Formatting, printing and copying

What you will learn in this unit

By the end of this unit you will be able to:

- add blocks of text
- add drawing objects
- align cell data
- apply cell borders
- calculate averages
- calculate percentages
- centre titles
- change character size
- change headers and footers
- copy and delete worksheets
- copy formatting
- delete and insert columns
- delete and insert rows
- embolden text
- format cells
- freeze titles and labels
- indent, rotate and align text
- name or rename a workbook
- print a worksheet
- remove gridlines
- select fonts
- select number and currency formats
- use automatic and conditional formatting
- use the page setup feature
- use the print preview feature
- use relative and absolute addressing
- view the worksheet on the full screen.

What you should know already

Before you start this unit, make sure that you can do the following:

Skill	Covered in
Use the basic features of Excel	Unit 1

What you need

To complete this unit you will need:

■ The workbook **TERMS** created in Unit 1

Introduction

This unit reviews worksheet formatting, including type size and style and text alignment. It also covers the use of printer and page settings.

If you don't have the workbook **TERMS** created in Unit 1 then any worksheet will do, though you will have to adjust any cell references.

Task 1: Formatting the worksheet

If you are not continuing from the previous unit then you will need to open the workbook **TERMS** created in Unit 1. You will be formatting it so that it looks like FIGURE 2.1.

	A	B	C	D	E	F
1			PERSONAL FINANCES - TERM 1			
2						
3	INCOME	Week 1	Week 2	Week 3	Week 4	Week 5
4	Opening Bals	£ -	£ 1,015.00	£ 885.00	£ 755.00	£ 625.00
5	Grant	£ 500.00				
6	Bank Loan	£ 400.00				
7	Parents	£ 300.00				
8	Total Income	£1,200.00	£ 1,015.00	£ 885.00	£ 755.00	£ 625.00
9						
10	EXPENDITURE					
11	Accommodation	£ 60.00	£ 60.00	£ 60.00	£ 60.00	£ 60.00
12	Food and Travel	£ 30.00	£ 35.00	£ 35.00	£ 35.00	£ 35.00
13	Books	£ 75.00	£ 15.00	£ 15.00	£ 15.00	£ 15.00
14	Other	£ 20.00	£ 20.00	£ 20.00	£ 20.00	£ 20.00
15	Total Expenditure	£ 185.00	£ 130.00	£ 130.00	£ 130.00	£ 130.00
16						
17	CLOSING BALS.	£1,015.00	£ 885.00	£ 755.00	£ 625.00	£ 495.00

FIGURE 2.1

1 **Emboldening**. First we will put the title and cell labels in bold.

Drag to select the title and the column headings – cells A1–G2.

Click the **Bold** button on the Formatting Toolbar – marked with a capital B. The cells are emboldened. (You may also wish to use the **Italic** or **Underline** buttons, marked with a capital I or U).

Now select the row labels in column A and embolden them in the same way – you may need to widen column A now, in which case open the **Format** menu and select the **Column** and then **AutoFit Selection** options.

Repeat this operation to embolden the closing balances in row **16.**

2 **Character size and fonts**. Select all the row labels in column A again.

Click the **Font Size** button – see FIGURE 2.2.

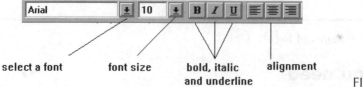

select a font   font size   bold, italic   alignment
                                          and underline   FIGURE 2.2

At the moment, all the characters on the worksheet are the default size of 10 points.

Select **8** – you may need to scroll it into view – the row labels in column A are now in a smaller font.

You may also like to experiment with different fonts or typefaces using the **Font** button.

3 **Alignment**. At the moment the numeric values are aligned to the right of the cells, which is the default for numbers. It can look neater to centre them under the column headings.

Select all the cells containing numeric data, i.e. cells C3–G16.

On the Formatting Toolbar are a group of three alignment buttons, showing left, centre and right alignment – see FIGURE 2.2.

Click the **Centre** button. The values in cells C3–G16 are now centred within each cell.

4 **Number and currency formats**. Let's alter the way numeric values are displayed. Select all the numeric cells again if necessary (C3–G16).

Open the **Format** menu and select the **Cells** option; the **Format Cells** dialog box is displayed.

Select the **Number** tab if necessary.

Select the **Accounting** option from the **Category** list, then select two decimal places and the £ currency symbol.

Click the **OK** button and the cells are reformatted.

 You may need to widen some columns if a row of hash (#) symbols is shown – see Task 2, Step 8 of Unit 1.

 Always use the **Format-Cells** option to add currency symbols and other types of number formatting. If you enter currency symbols directly Excel will regard the values as text, not numbers, and will be unable to use them in calculations.

5 **Inserting and deleting columns and rows**. Click the column designator at the top of column **B** (i.e. the capital B); this selects the whole column.

Open the **Edit** menu and select **Delete**. Column B is deleted and subsequent columns are shifted to the left. All the cell references and formulae are automatically adjusted to reflect their new positions.

 Removing a blank column should cause no problems, but removing a column containing data and formulae obviously could. You can select **Undo** from the **Edit** menu if you delete the wrong column or row.

Now let's insert an extra row; click the row designator for Row 2 – the whole row is selected.

Open the **Insert** menu and choose **Rows**. A new blank row is inserted. The worksheet now has a neater and more balanced appearance.

6 **Centring the title**. It would look neater to centre the title across columns B to F – the area of the worksheet that will eventually be printed.

Select cell range B1–F1.

Click the **Merge and Centre** button on the Formatting Toolbar, which is marked with a small 'a' – see key at the end of this unit. The title is centred across the columns selected – however, the cell range B1–F1 is now treated as one merged cell and cannot be selected individually. If this causes a problem then you will need to remove the centring – see notes below.

 If you decide to widen the worksheet later you will need to re-centre the title.

To restore the default alignment, select the cells, open the **Format** menu and select the **Cells** option, then click the **Alignment** tab. Click the **Merge Cells** box to deselect it.

7 **Adding borders**. Borders can be used to mark off various sections of the worksheet and make the worksheet easier to read – see FIGURE 2.1.

First let us draw a single line to mark off different sections of the worksheet.

Select cells A9–F9.

Open the **Format** menu and select **Cells**.

The **Format Cells** dialog box opens. Click the **Border** tab and new options are shown – see FIGURE 2.3 for the options to select.

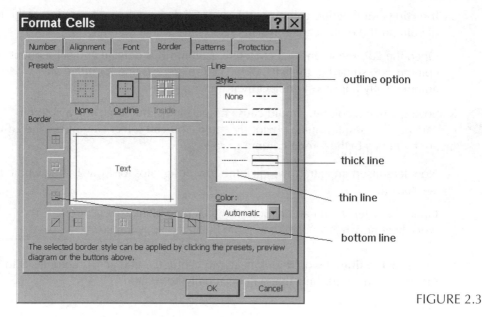

FIGURE 2.3

Select the **Outline** option from the **Presets** section.

Select the thin line option from the **Style** box.

Click on the top, left and right recessed boxes in the **Border** section so that only the bottom box is selected. The white box marked 'Text' in the centre should show a line at the bottom only.

Click the **OK** button – this places a single line at the bottom of row 9. Click to remove the highlight from the cells.

8 Next we will put a thicker line around all the worksheet data.

Select cell **A1** and drag the screen pointer down to cell **F17**.

Open the **Format** menu again and select **Cells**.

The **Format Cells** dialog box appears. Click the **Border** tab if necessary.

Select the **Outline** option from the **Presets** section.

Select the thick line button in the **Style** box – see FIGURE 2.3.

Make sure that the box marked 'Text' shows thick lines on each side by clicking the top, bottom, left and right buttons as necessary.

Finally click the **OK** button – you are returned to the worksheet.

Click to remove the highlight from the cells – the worksheet is enclosed in a thick line.

To remove unwanted borders, use the same commands, i.e. select the relevant cells and then select **Cells** from the **Format** menu. Then click the relevant style button to deselect the unwanted border.

9 **Independent activity**. The Formatting Toolbar supplies a **Borders** button. Identify it and click the down arrow button; use it to:

- draw a single line under cells A16–F16.

- give the cells in column A a single right-hand border. Remember that you can use the **Edit-Undo** command to undo any formatting.

10 **Gridline display**. The gridlines marking the cell boundaries can be turned off to emphasise the borders that we have drawn.

Open the **Tools** menu and choose **Options**. A dialog box opens.

Make sure that the **View** tab is selected.

Click the **Gridlines** button – the tick disappears as this option is deselected.

Click the **OK** button and the gridlines disappear (this will not prevent the gridlines displaying when the worksheet is printed).

Your worksheet should now look like FIGURE 2.1.

11 **Freezing titles and labels**. We will add a note to the bottom of the worksheet. This may mean (depending on your computer's display) that the worksheet will become too large to view all at once. Before one scrolls to another part of the worksheet it is possible to 'freeze' both the titles and the column and row labels so that they are always in view, and so keep a track of what each row or column represents.

Click cell B4, then open the **Window** menu and select the **Freeze Panes** option. All cells above and to the left of this cell are frozen.

Try scrolling across and down; the column A and rows 1–3 stay fixed as a constant reference when you scroll.

To unfreeze panes, open the **Window** menu and select **Unfreeze Panes**.

12 **Entering and justifying blocks of text**. Although Excel does not offer full word-processing facilities, blocks of text, such as brief notes, can be added to worksheets.

Click the **Text Box** button on the Drawing Toolbar, which is at the bottom of the window (see key at the end of this unit) – if it is not displayed then open the **View** menu and select the **Toolbars** option.

Now move the screen pointer to cell C19.

Drag to draw a text box large enough to hold the text shown in FIGURE 2.4.

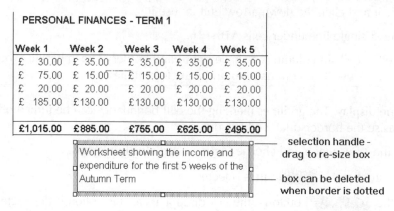

PERSONAL FINANCES - TERM 1

Week 1	Week 2	Week 3	Week 4	Week 5
£ 30.00	£ 35.00	£ 35.00	£ 35.00	£ 35.00
£ 75.00	£ 15.00	£ 15.00	£ 15.00	£ 15.00
£ 20.00	£ 20.00	£ 20.00	£ 20.00	£ 20.00
£ 185.00	£130.00	£130.00	£130.00	£130.00
£1,015.00	£885.00	£755.00	£625.00	£495.00

Worksheet showing the income and expenditure for the first 5 weeks of the Autumn Term

selection handle - drag to re-size box

box can be deleted when border is dotted

FIGURE 2.4

Type in the text – it is aligned within the text box.

If the text box is selected, it may be:

■ moved by dragging the border

■ resized by dragging one of the small selection handles

■ deleted provided that the border is dotted, rather than diagonal lines (see FIGURE 2.4) by pressing the *Delete* key.

Text within the box can be edited, emboldened etc in the usual ways.

13 **Adding arrows and shapes to a worksheet**. You can also emphasise a key point in your worksheet by circling it or using an arrow to point to it. Let's try this, using FIGURE 2.5 as a guide.

	A	B	C	D	E	F
1		PERSONAL FINANCES - TERM 1				
2						
3	INCOME	Week 1	Week 2	Week 3	Week 4	Week 5
13	Books	£ 75.00	£ 15.00	£ 15.00	£ 15.00	£ 15.00
14	Other	£ 20.00	£ 20.00	£ 20.00	£ 20.00	£ 20.00
15	Total Expenditure	£ 185.00	£ 130.00	£130.00	£130.00	£130.00
16						
17	CLOSING BALS.	£1,015.00	£ 885.00	£755.00	£625.00	£495.00
18						
19		Worksheet showing the				
20		income and expenditure for the				
21		first 5 weeks of the Autumn			On Target!	
22		Term				

FIGURE 2.5

Click the **Oval** button on the Drawing Toolbar – if the toolbar is not displayed then open the **View** menu and select the **Toolbars** option.

Use the mouse pointer to encircle cell F17. (If the cell becomes invisible don't worry – see below.)

Click the **Arrow** button and draw the arrow.

Finally, use the `Text Box` button to draw a text box large enough to hold the text shown in FIGURE 2.5.

Now scroll the worksheet; you should find that the objects that you have drawn are attached to their underlying cells and move with them. If the cell is invisible then click the oval object to select it, then open the **Format** menu and choose the **AutoShape** option. Choose the `Colors and Lines` tab. In the dialog box that appears, click the down arrow button on the **Fill-Color** box and select **No Fill** followed by `OK`.

14 **Viewing the full screen**. Open the **View** menu and select **Full Screen**. This enlarges the worksheet to its fullest extent, allowing you to see the maximum number of rows. However, other useful components, such as the Toolbars and the Taskbar are hidden. Issue the command again to reinstate them.

Task 2: Printing a worksheet

To print a worksheet you must give Excel instructions on what and how to print – which cells, number of copies and so on.

1 **Selecting the print area**. First select the entire worksheet area that you want to print – cells A1–G22. You may find it easier to select a large range of cells as follows:

- Click cell A1 – the top left of the area that you want to select.

- Scroll down the worksheet using the keyboard while holding down the *Shift* key.

- Select cell G22 – the bottom right of the range that you want to select. The whole cell range is selected.

2 **Setting the print area**. Open the **File** menu and select the **Print Area** option followed by the **Set Print Area** option. The print area is surrounded by a dotted line. If no print area has been set then the default area is the same size as a printed page, e.g. an A4 page.

3 **Printing**. Open the **File** menu and select **Print** – the **Print** dialog box appears.

Click the `Active sheet(s)` button in the **Print what** section – the print area of the selected worksheet will be printed, not any blank areas outside it. This is important when the worksheet becomes larger.

Before you print, click the `Preview` button, which shows how the worksheet will look when printed on an A4 page.

Now click the `Setup` button at the top of the **Preview** window.

4 **Page Setup**. The **Page Setup** dialog box appears – make sure that the **Sheet** option is displayed.

Make sure that two boxes **Row and Column Headings** and **Gridlines** are both unchecked, i.e. there is no tick in either of them. (It is usual to print a worksheet without the row and column headings and gridlines if it is not too large or detailed.)

5 **Other page settings**. Next click the ▐Page▌ tab on the **Page Setup** dialog box – a new set of options is displayed. Your printer might or might not offer the following settings. If it does, they will appear in black rather than pale grey. Check the following:

- **Orientation**: **Portrait** or **Landscape**

- **Paper size**: Choose the size of paper in your printer

- **Scaling**: You can adjust the size of the printed area to fit the paper size.

- **Fit to**: Adjusts the size of the printed area to fit on one or more pages.

6 Margins and alignment. Now click the ▐Margins▌ tab – a new set of options is displayed. Click the **Horizontally** and **Vertically** boxes. They will centre the printout on the page.

7 **Headers and footers**. Now click the ▐Header/Footer▌ tab. Headers and footers can be added to the top and bottom of every printed page. You can choose from among the predefined headers and footers available in the dialog box, or you can create your own. Let's add the date and your name.

Click the ▐Custom Header▌ button and a further dialog box appears. This is divided into three sections – left, right and centre aligned.

Select the left section and type in your name.

Select the right section and click the ▐Date▌ button – use the ▐Help▌ button (marked with a ?) if you need to identify it. Click ▐OK▌.

Now click the ▐Custom Footer▌ button. Insert the page number in the centre section. Click ▐OK▌.

You are returned to the main **Page Setup** dialog box, Click ▐OK▌ again.

8 **The printer**. Make sure that the printer:

- is switched on

- is set online – check the switch and warning light

- is connected via cable to your computer

- has paper in it.

Check each of these in turn if the next step does not produce a printout.

9 **Print Preview**. Open **Print Preview** again if necessary. The **Print Preview** screen appears. You can now see the headers and footers. There are various options along the top of the screen. Do not use any of these options for now; they are for information only.

- **Next** and **Previous** are for multi-page worksheets.

- **Margins** displays the current margin settings.

- **Page Break Preview** allows you to reset both the print area and the page breaks simply by dragging them. You can also cut and paste between different printed pages. Excel will then automatically re-scale the cells to fit.

- **Print** and **Setup** allow you either to proceed with printing or to go back to the **Page Setup** menus.

Now move the screen pointer over the printed area – it changes to a magnifying glass shape. Click and the area under the pointer is enlarged.

You can scroll around to look at other parts of the worksheet.

The **Zoom** button will return you to the full-page view.

Now, if you are happy with the print preview, click the **Print** button at the top of the screen. (If you are not happy then the **Close** button will cancel printing.)

Click **OK** on the **Print** dialog box if necessary. The worksheet should start printing now.

 If your worksheet won't print check the previous stages again.

10 Finally check that the correct printer is selected as follows:

- Open the **File** menu and select the **Print** option again.

- Check in the **Printer** section that the correct printer is selected.

- If the print area is incorrect then you will need to remove it and reset it by selecting the menu options **File-Print Area-Clear Print Area**. The dotted print area line reverts to the page default – see Step 2.

11 Save and close the workbook.

Task 3: Consolidation – check your progress

You are now going to extend the worksheet to cover a 10 week term.

1 Retrieve the **TERMS** workbook if necessary.

Make sure that **SHEET1** is selected

First select the week 5 column, i.e. cells F3–F17, and drag across the worksheet to select the next five columns, G to K.

These will hold the data for weeks 6–10.

2 Now use the **Edit-Fill-Right** command to copy the data across.

Remember that you can always use the **Undo** command if you make a mistake.

3 Some minor amendments need to be made next.

- Amend the week numbers for weeks 6–10.

- Select each oval shape in turn in cells G18–K18, so that the oval is enclosed in a selection rectangle. Use the *Delete* key to remove it.

29

Use **Edit-Undo** if you delete the wrong data.

■ Amend the note at the bottom of the worksheet.

■ Use the **Format-Cells** menu to remove or change unwanted cell borders.

 Weeks 6–10 are reproduced as Appendix 3 – check your version against this.

 4 You will see that by the end of week 10 you are £155 in debt. Task 5 will show you how to try to solve this!

Task 4: Copying a worksheet

We are going to copy the worksheet **SHEET1** and then modify the copy.

1 Make sure that the Sheet1 tab is still selected.

Hold down the *Ctrl* key, place the cursor on the Sheet1 tab and drag with the mouse. The cursor changes to represent a copy of the worksheet, marked with a '+' sign.

2 Drag the cursor onto the Sheet2 tab.

Release the mouse button and then the *Ctrl* key. Excel copies **SHEET1**, renaming it **SHEET1 (2)**.

3 Click the tab for Sheet1 (2) if necessary. It opens, becoming the active worksheet; it is a replica of **SHEET1**.

If you forgot to hold down the *Ctrl* key, or released it too soon, then you may have merely moved **SHEET1** to a new position rather than copied it. In this case use the mouse to drag it back to its original position and try again.

Task 5: Testing assumptions – what if?

1 Make the following two changes to **SHEET1 (2)** for weeks 6–10: The easiest way is to amend the relevant value for week 6, then **Fill-Right**.

■ Reduce the amount spent on books to zero.

■ Spend £5 less on food and travel per week.

However, you still end the term with a £55 overdraft!

Save the worksheet at this point.

2 Let's assume that you find a part-time job at £20 a week from week 7 onwards. This involves inserting an extra row to hold this new income category.

First select the row designator for row 7.

Open the **Insert** menu and select **Rows**.

A new row is inserted – label it ***Part Time Job***.

Now insert *20* for weeks 7–10.

If entered correctly, this extra income means that you end the term with £25. This is obviously only a simple example of building alternative models, based on different assumptions. In later units you will use more sophisticated analysis tools.

Task 6: Naming a worksheet

At the moment our workbook **TERMS** contains two worksheets with the default names **SHEET1** and **SHEET1 (2)**. We will give them the more meaningful names 'pessimistic model' and 'optimistic model'.

 A sheet name can be up to 31 characters long. It can contain spaces, but the following special characters cannot be used: *[ ], /, \, ?* and *

1   Make sure that **SHEET1** is selected as the active sheet (click the ▐ Sheet ▐ tab).

Open the **Format** menu and select **Sheet** followed by **Rename**. The sheet's tab is highlighted.

2   Type the new name ***pessimistic model***.

Press *Enter* – the sheet name appears as the name tab.

3   Repeat this operation for **SHEET1 (2)**, naming it ***optimistic model***.

 Renaming worksheets makes the name tabs larger. This may mean that not all name tabs are visible at the same time. If so you will need to use the arrow buttons to the left of the sheet tabs to find the sheet that you need. You can also select the sheet tab for renaming by double-clicking it.

Task 7: Consolidation – check your progress

Copy the sheet optimistic model (hold down the *Ctrl* key and drag the sheet by its tab), renaming it ***Spring Term***. Then make the following changes to this sheet.

1   From week 3 onwards, 'Accommodation' rises to £65 a week.

2   Your parents send you £30 for your birthday in week 8.

3   You want to go to an end of term celebration in week 10.

Modify the value in the 'Other' category for week 10 so that you end the Spring Term with £5.

 4   Save these changes and use Appendix 4 to check your calculations.

Task 8: Deleting a worksheet from a workbook

You now have three worksheets in the workbook **TERM1.XLS** – **PESSIMISTIC MODEL**, **OPTIMISTIC MODEL** and **SPRING TERM**. Let's assume that the first sheet, **PESSIMISTIC MODEL**, was an original cash flow forecast that is no longer needed.

Click the name tab **pessimistic model** to activate it.

Open the **Edit** menu and select the **Delete Sheet** option.

A dialog box appears, warning you that the sheet will be permanently deleted.

Make sure that you are deleting the correct sheet, then click the **OK** button.

Task 9: Independent activities

1 Copy the worksheet **SPRING TERM** under the new name **SUMMER TERM** (see Task 4).

2 Modify the income and expenditure categories and amounts to fit your own financial situation.

3 Print out the **SUMMER TERM** worksheet using the **File** menu or the **Print** button.

Here are some additional tips on the use of the **Print** options under the **File** menu.

Use the **Print Area** command to change the print area to include all the worksheet data

Select **Page Setup** and use the **Page** tab to print in Landscape (widthways).

In the **Print Preview** option check the appearance of your sheet before you print (use the **Zoom** button too).

Select the **Print** option followed by the **Active Sheets** option to print the whole sheet.

Task 10: Consolidation – averages and percentages

In this task we will recap on some of the skills that you have learned and also find out how to calculate averages and percentages. We will create a new workbook for this activity.

1 Open a new workbook. If you have started a new Excel session then one is provided; otherwise save and close the present workbook, open the **File** menu and select **New**.

2 Now create the worksheet shown in FIGURE 2.6 as follows:

	A	B	C	D	E
1		Insurance Sales - First Quarter			
2					
3		Motor	Life	Property	Total
4	Jan	1465	1243	2456	
5	Feb	1345	1456	1987	
6	Mar	1132	2310	1598	
7					
8	Quarterly Average				
9	Quarterly Total				
10	% of Total				
11					

FIGURE 2.6

Format the worksheet as shown:

■ title centred across columns A–E

■ cell labels in bold

■ column headings in bold

■ values centred in cells.

3   Now use the **SUM** function to calculate the quarterly totals in cell E4 then copy the formula to cells E5 and E6 using **Edit-Fill-Down**.

Calculate the totals in row 9 next using **SUM** and **Edit-Fill-Right**.

4   Save the worksheet as **INS_SLS.XLS** (remember to select the correct drive).

5   We now wish to find the average sales for each type of insurance and place them in row 8.

Select cell B8 and enter the formula **=AVERAGE(B4:B6)**.

Click the tick box or press *Enter* and the three cells are averaged (1314).

Use **Edit-Fill-Right** to average the Life, Property and Total categories too.

6   Now centre the row 8 and 9 values in their cells.

Use the **Format-Cells-Number** command to remove the decimal places.

7   Next we will express the quarterly totals – cells B9–D9 – as fractions of the total sales – cell E9.

Select cell B10 and enter the formula **=B9/$E$9**

Click the tick box.

The quarterly total for motor insurance is shown as a decimal fraction of the overall quarterly total – the value 0.26294 is displayed in the cell.

8 **Explanation of the formula**

- The / sign represents division.

- **Absolute and relative references**. So far, all the cell references that you have been using are relative references. This means that the references of cells used in a formula are relative to the location of the cell where the formula is placed. In this way the cell references in formulae are automatically adjusted when cells are copied. However, this would not work for the percentages that we are calculating, as they must all be based upon one fixed cell – E9. We do not want this cell value to be adjusted when we use the **Fill-Right** command. The dollar signs in front of the column and row number make the cell reference into an absolute reference and prevent this happening.

You can convert a relative to an absolute reference by selecting the cell formula and pressing the *F4* function key. Continuing to press it gives combinations of absolute and relative references, known as mixed references.

9 **Percentages**. Now you will turn the fraction calculated in Step 7 into a percentage.

Make sure that cell B10 is still selected.

Open the **Format** menu and select **Cells** followed by the **Number** tab.

Click the **Percentage** option in the **Category** box.

Make sure that the **Decimal Places** box is set to 2 and click **OK**.

10 Motor insurance is now shown as 26.29% of total sales.

Use the **Edit-Fill-Right** command to show Life and Property as percentages too.

11 Finally, let us add a text box to the worksheet, explaining its function.

Click the **Text Box** tool on the Drawing Toolbar (see the toolbar key at the end of this unit) – the pointer changes to cross-hairs.

Locate the screen pointer on the top left-hand corner of cell B12.

Drag across and down to cell E14. The text box is now drawn.

Enter the following text: ***This worksheet shows a sales analysis of the three major insurance categories***. You will see that the text wraps automatically to the size of the box.

Remove an unwanted box by clicking the border to select it. Then select **Clear** from the **Edit** menu. Make sure that the border of the box is dotted rather than diagonal lines when you do this.

12 Compare your worksheet with Appendix 5.

13 Save and close the workbook.

Task 11: Further formatting of worksheets

Excel's **AutoFormat** feature allows you to format your worksheets automatically, offering 17 built-in formats to choose from. Excel will automatically detect which worksheet areas should be headings, data, totals etc. This allows you to format either a range of cells or a complete worksheet in attractive, standardised formats, thereby saving the time and effort of designing your own.

1 Open the worksheet **INS_SLS.XLS** if necessary.

   Select all the cells in the worksheet, i.e. cell range A1–E14.

2 Open the **Format** menu and select **AutoFormat**. A dialog box appears, showing a sample worksheet.

3 **Reviewing the formats**. Take some time to select each of the various formats listed in the **Table format** list; the sample worksheet changes to illustrate each format selected.

4 **Selecting a format**. Now select the **Classic 3** format and then **OK** . Your worksheet is converted to the format chosen, but you may not be happy with its appearance, e.g. the columns may be too wide.

5 **Undoing a format change**. Open the **Edit** menu and select **Undo AutoFormat** – your worksheet is restored to its previous format.

Edit-Undo will reverse up to 16 previous changes if you keep repeating the command. If this does not work, then select **Format-AutoFormat**, then scroll down the **Table format** list and select the **None** option followed by **OK** . You may find, however, that you have lost your original formatting, e.g. bold and centring.

If all else fails, then closing the worksheet without saving it will undo any disastrous mistakes – but you will also lose any other changes made since the worksheet was opened or saved.

6 **Selecting a sub-format**. Make sure that all the worksheet cells are still selected and open the **AutoFormat** menu again.

   Select the **Classic 3** format from the table and then click the **Options** button.

   Six **Formats to apply** are offered at the bottom of the dialog box; initially all options are selected. Try deselecting and reselecting all of them and notice their effects on the sample. When a format is deselected, such as **Border** or **Alignment**, the existing formats in the worksheet continue to apply.

7 Now deselect the **Font**, **Alignment** and **Width/Height** options, then click **OK** .

   The worksheet is reformatted in the **Classic 3** format, minus the options that we have deselected. Click the worksheet to remove the selection from the cells.

   Restore the worksheet to its original format – see Step 5.

8 **Indenting, rotating and aligning text in cells**. Select cells A4–A10.

Open the **Format** menu and select **Cells**. When the **Format Cells** dialog box is displayed click the **Alignment** tab.

■ **Indenting text**. Up to 15 indent steps are possible. Increase the indent steps to 2 and click **OK** – the text is indented.

■ **Rotating text**. Undo the indent using the **Edit** menu. Make sure that the cells are still selected; open the **Format Cells** dialog box again. This time select **10** in the **Degrees** box. Click **OK** and the text is rotated.

Undo the rotation using the **Edit** menu.

■ **Aligning text**. At the moment the text in the selected cells is aligned left.

Centre it horizontally and vertically using the dialog box.

 9 **Conditional formatting**. You can format only those cells whose values lie outside specified limits.

Select cell range B4–D6.

Open the **Format** menu and select the **Conditional Formatting** option – a dialog box appears. We wish to highlight those cells whose values fall between 1500 and 2000.

Complete the dialog box as shown in FIGURE 2.7.

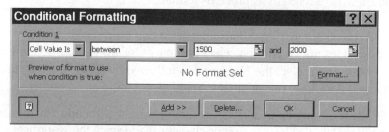

FIGURE 2.7

Click the **Format** button; when the **Format Cells** dialog box appears select the **Border** tab.

Click the **Outline** button followed by the **OK** button – you are returned to the **Conditional Formatting** dialog box. Click the **OK** button.

Deselect the cell range and you will see that the cells whose values fall between 1500 and 2000 have a border.

10 **Copying formatting**. The **Format Painter** allows us to copy formats quickly.

Format the label in cell A4, for example, to 12 point, bold, colour red.

Click the **Format Painter** button (on the Standard Toolbar, marked with a paintbrush – see the key at the end of this unit).

Then select another cell or range of cells that you wish to copy this format to, e.g. the column labels in cells A5 and A6. The format is copied to the A5 and A6 cells. Use Edit-Undo if it doesn't work correctly.

11 We could choose to save these changes using Save, but we won't bother in this instance. Close the workbook without saving.

Summary of commands and functions

 Menu commands show the menu name first, followed by the command to choose from the menu, e.g. **Edit-Clear** means open the **Edit** menu and select the **Clear** command.

Menu commands

Edit-Clear-All	Delete cell contents
Edit-Delete	Delete selected rows or columns
Edit-Delete Sheet	Delete selected worksheet
Edit-Fill-Down	Copy selected cells into selected lower cells
Edit-Fill-Right	Copy selected cells into selected right-hand columns
Edit-Undo	Undo previous operation
File-Close	Close current workbook
File-Exit	Exit Excel
File-New	Open new, blank workbook
File-Open	Retrieve an existing workbook
File-Page Setup	Amend page settings for printing
File-Print	Print worksheet
File-Save	Save current workbook
Format-AutoFormat	Apply built-in Excel format
Format-Cells-Border	Add cell borders
Format-Cells-Font	Bold, italic, character size and style
Format-Cells-Alignment	Align text blocks
Format-Cells-Number	Format numbers, percentages etc
Format-Conditional Formatting	Format cells meeting certain conditions
Format-Sheet-Rename	Rename Selected Sheet
Insert-Columns	Insert a blank column
Insert-Rows	Insert a blank row
Tools-Options	Do/do not display gridlines etc
View-Full Screen	Turn on/off full-screen mode
Window-Freeze Panes	Freeze row and column headings
Window-Unfreeze Panes	Unfreeze row and column headings

Functions

=AVERAGE()   Average range of cells

Standard Toolbar

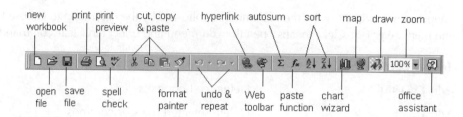

Formatting Toolbar

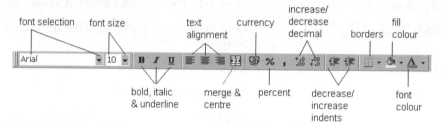

The Drawing Toolbar

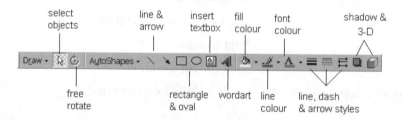

Creating charts

What you will learn in this unit

By the end of this unit you will be able to:

- add values to a chart
- add an arrow to a chart
- create a chart
- replot a chart
- move chart components
- alter a chart's size
- change a chart type
- use the ChartWizard
- change the colours on a chart
- create a column chart
- copy a chart
- change the fonts used in a chart
- format a chart
- insert a legend on a chart
- create a line chart
- move chart components
- name a chart
- chart non-adjacent cells
- use the Office Assistant
- change the patterns in a chart
- create a pie chart
- print a chart
- resize chart items
- add text to a chart
- add titles to a chart
- rearrange windows.

What you should know already

Before you start this unit, make sure that you can do the following:

Skill	Covered in
Use the basic features of Excel	Unit 1

What you need

No previously created worksheets are needed for this unit.

Introduction

In this unit we briefly review how to create charts; you are recommended to try these activities even if you are experienced in this area, as some of the commands, menus and dialog boxes have changed in Excel 97. Excel uses a special feature called the ChartWizard, which guides you through a series of simple steps and lets you create a wide variety of different chart types – line graphs, pie charts, bar charts etc, as well as many sub-types. You can either embed a chart in your worksheet or create it as a separate chart sheet. You will be looking mainly at the first approach and learning how to format charts for the best results.

Task 1: Creating some chart data

1 We need some worksheet data before we can produce charts. Create the simple worksheet shown in FIGURE 3.1. It shows the number of holidays sold by a travel company for various European countries. Format it as shown, i.e. column widths adjusted and headings and labels in bold.

	A	B	C	D	E	F
1	Sunfilled Holidays					
2			Holidays Sold - Europe			
3						
4		1st Quarter	2nd Quarter	3rd Quarter	4th Quarter	Total
5						
6	Italy	85	99	200	93	477
7	Spain	150	246	355	145	896
8	Portugal	120	180	300	123	723
9	Greece	168	277	320	162	927
10	France	70	120	250	110	550
11						
12	Total	593	922	1425	633	**3573**

FIGURE 3.1

2 Next, total the first column in cell B12, using a formula or the **AutoSum** button.

3 Copy this formula to the next three cells (C12–E12) using **Fill Right** or **AutoFill**.

4   Calculate the totals for cells F6 to F10 in a similar way.

As a check, calculate the grand total for all holidays – it should be 3573. If not, check your data and your formulae!

5   Now save the workbook as **EUROSLS**. If the Summary dialog box appears, enter some information, e.g. title and subject.

We can now use this worksheet to create a variety of charts.

Task 2: Creating a chart using the ChartWizard

The ChartWizard allows you to create simple charts using four steps. First select the cells you wish to use in the chart, then:

- Select the type of chart – bar, column, pie chart etc.

- Check or change the cells that you wish to chart.

- Specify the chart axis, titles, labels etc.

- Specify whether the chart will be embedded in the worksheet or in its own chart sheet.

Dialog boxes guide you through these steps. At each step you have the option of cancelling, getting help, going back a step, or going on to the next step.

First you will create a column chart of the first quarter's sales:

1   Select the cell range A6–B10 (i.e. 10 cells in all).

Open the **Insert** menu and select **Chart** (or click the ChartWizard button on the Standard Toolbar – see the key at the end of this unit).

Using the Office Assistant. When you call up the ChartWizard (and many other Excel dialog boxes) the Office Assistant dialog box may be displayed too. If not, click the Office Assistant button (marked with a '?') in the bottom left-hand corner of the ChartWizard. If nothing happens then it may be that the Office Assistant has not been installed on your computer.

Take the **Help with this feature** option. A further dialog box appears. If you wish, you can keep Office Assistant open to supplement the instructions that follow.

2   The first ChartWizard dialog box is displayed, with the title:

ChartWizard – Step 1 of 4 – Chart Type

Make sure that the Standard Types tab is selected.

Step 1 allows you to select the chart type. The default selected at the moment should be **Column** – check this.

Seven sub-types of the column chart are offered. Select each one in turn – an explanation of it is shown below the sub-types.

A button asks you to **Press and hold to view sample** . Do this and a preview of your worksheet data is charted.

Finally, reselect sub-type 1, the standard column chart.

Click the **Next** button to proceed to the second step of the ChartWizard:

ChartWizard – Step 2 of 4 – Chart Source

First make sure that the **Data Range** tab is selected.

Step 2 allows you to confirm or change the range of cells (A6–B10) that you wish to chart. Check them – notice that they are shown as absolute references. If they are incorrect then amend them or press the **Cancel** button and start again.

You can drag the dialog box to one side by the title bar in order to view the worksheet data better.

If the range is correct, click the **Next** button to go to the next step:

ChartWizard – Step 3 of 4 – Chart Options

Step 3 offers you the option to add titles, legend, data labels etc. Enter them as shown in FIGURE 3.2.

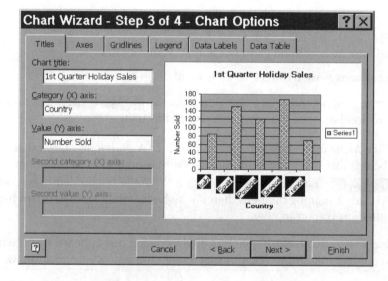

FIGURE 3.2

Click the **Legend** tab and deselect the option **Show legend**. The chart will not need one.

Click the **Next** button to move to the final step:

ChartWizard – Step 4 of 4 – Chart Location

Step 4 allows you either to embed the chart in the worksheet or to display it in its own chart window. Select the **As New Sheet** option.

Click the **Finish** button and the chart is displayed; it is given the default name **Chart1** – the name appears in the worksheet tabs.

Task 3: Resizing the chart

When a chart is first created its size is independent of the window size, with the result that the chart and the titles may be too small. The **View** menu offers two options to resize a chart.

1   First, maximise the chart window if necessary.

   Open the **View** window and select the option **Sized with Window**. The chart expands to fill the window space available.

2   Open the **View** menu and select **Full Screen**. The chart can be seen at maximum size.

3   Repeat Step 1 and the **Sized with Window** option is deselected – it is no longer 'ticked'. Now restore the window size and you will find that part of the chart may no longer be visible.

4   Open the **View** menu and select the **Zoom** option – a dialog box opens allowing you to specify a particular chart size, independent of window size (this option is unavailable while the **Sized with Window** option is selected).

   Try out various scales – the larger the scale, the more detail, but less of the chart will fit in the window.

   Finally try out the **Fit Selection** option on the **Zoom** dialog box. This fits the chart to the window size available.

5   Now open the **View** menu again. Deselect the **Full Screen** option and reselect the **Sized with Window** option.

6   **The Chart Toolbar**. At the moment the Chart Toolbar should be displayed. Normally it appears whenever a chart is displayed. Like other toolbars, the purpose of each button is displayed whenever the mouse pointer rests on it. As you will be using the ChartWizard and **AutoFormat** you can turn it off for these tasks. It can be turned on again using the **View-Toolbars** option.

Task 4: Changing the chart type using the ChartWizard

Although we have plotted the worksheet data as a column chart, we can convert it to another type of chart using the ChartWizard.

1   Make sure that **CHART1** and not the worksheet is the active document.

   Open the **Chart** menu and select **Chart Type**. A dialog box opens, offering you a choice of chart types – select **Pie** from the **Chart Type** menu. You are offered a choice of several pie chart formats. Format 1 is already selected.

2   Select **OK** – the chart is re-plotted as a pie chart. Pie charts are good for showing the relative contributions of various elements to the total 'pie'. This can be shown as a number or as a percentage. However, as there are now no X or Y

axes the coloured sections need a key or **legend** to explain them.

3   **Adding a legend**. Open the **Chart** menu and select **Chart Options**.

Click the **Legend** tab. Select **Show legend** and **Right** from the **Placement** box.

Click the **OK** button and the legend appears on the chart.

Open the **View** menu and check that the **Sized with Window** option is still selected.

Task 5: Moving between chart and worksheet

1   The pie chart **CHART1** and the worksheet **SHEET1** are two separate documents.

At the moment the chart overlays the worksheet – it is the 'active window'.

Click the sheet tab for **Sheet1** – it overlays the chart to become the active window.

 If the sheet tabs are not visible then maximise the workbook window.

2   Now you will make the two windows smaller so that you can see the chart and the worksheet alongside each other – see FIGURE 3.3.

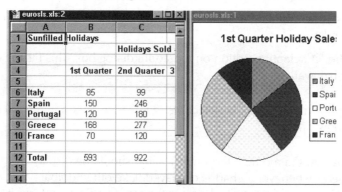

FIGURE 3.3

First make sure that the chart is the active window.

Use **New Window** from the **Window** menu to open a second window so that more than one workbook document can be seen at the same time.

Make sure that one window is showing the chart and the other the worksheet by following the next step.

3   **Arranging windows**. Windows offers several ways of viewing both windows at the same time.

Open the **Window** menu and select **Arrange**.

Experiment with the **Vertical** and the **Cascade** options.

Task 6: Replotting a chart

1   Now that the chart and the worksheet are both displayed side by side we can show the dynamic relationship between them.

Click the worksheet to activate it.

2 Select cell B7 and amend the number of Spanish holidays to **500.**

   Press *Enter*. The pie chart also changes to reflect this.

3 Open the **Edit** menu and select **Undo Typing**. The pie chart returns to its previous shape.

4 To close the extra window opened in the previous activity select the worksheet window and click on the **Close** button. Only one window is open now. Maximise it if necessary.

Task 7: Moving pie chart segments

1 Make sure that **CHART1** is the active sheet in the workbook.

   Activate the pie chart by clicking it once – square selection 'handles' appear.

2 Place the screen pointer on the segment denoting Portugal and click once – handles appear on the segment.

3 Hold down the left mouse button and drag the segment slightly away from the rest of the pie chart – this can be used for emphasis.

4 Press the *Esc* key to turn off the selection handles.

Use the **Edit-Undo** option to reverse any mistake you make.

If you accidentally double clicked on the pie you might have called up the **Format Data Point** dialog box. If so, cancel the dialog box and try again.

Task 8: Adding values to a chart

It can be difficult to judge the relative proportions of the pie chart segments unless the values are added. The **Chart Options** command allows us to add the actual values to pie segments (and other types of chart).

1 Open the **Chart** menu and select **Chart Options**. Select the **Data Labels** tab.

2 The dialog box offers a number of options – try each one in turn.

   Finally, select the option Show Percent and click **OK**.

3 If the percentages are too small then double click on one of them.

   The **Format Data Labels** dialog box appears. Click the **Font** tab and select a different font size, e.g. 9 or 10 points.

   Do the same for the legend box. Your pie chart will resemble FIGURE 3.4.

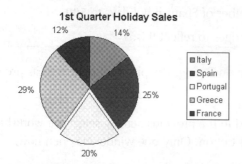

FIGURE 3.4

Task 9: Moving and resizing chart items

You may need to alter the size or layout of chart components, e.g. pie segments, title or legend. You can do this quite easily with the mouse – first click the item to select it, then use the appropriate menu or mouse operation. Any item in a chart can be selected in this way. You can also double click or right click a chart component as a shortcut to a menu or a dialog box.

 You will find that it takes a little practice to select the right item – particularly when they are close together. Persevere and remember these simple rules:

- An item is not selected unless it is enclosed in selection 'handles'.
- Click elsewhere or press the *Esc* key to remove selection handles.
- Undo an incorrect operation straight away using the **Edit-Undo** option.

1   First experiment and click the various parts of the chart in turn to select them – pie segments, segment labels, title and legend.

Now click on the legend box – it is surrounded by a selection rectangle upon which are a number of square 'selection handles'.

Drag a selection handle to make the legend slightly larger.

2   Click the outside edge of the pie chart until it is surrounded by a selection rectangle – this can be tricky. Make sure that the whole pie is selected not just the individual segments or labels – see FIGURE 3.5.

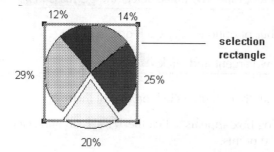

FIGURE 3.5

Now make the pie chart slightly larger by dragging the selection handle on the bottom right corner.

3 **Moving the title**. Click the title until it is surrounded by the selection rectangle.

Move the mouse pointer onto the edge of the rectangle and drag it up the window. (NB: the title cannot be resized by dragging – see the next task for formatting text.)

Next move the mouse pointer in front of the word 'Holiday' in the title and click – an insertion point is placed there.

Insert the word **European** – the title is amended.

Task 10: Formatting a chart

1 You are going to format the pie chart further to improve its appearance.

Make sure that the pie chart **CHART1** is still the active sheet.

2 **Changing text fonts and style**. First you will make the title more prominent.

Move the screen pointer onto the title and click once – it should be enclosed by a selection rectangle.

Open the Format menu and select Selected Chart Title – the Format dialog box appears.

Click the Font tab in the dialog box and alter the size to 12 point bold, then click OK .

The title will now change – press the *Esc* key to deselect it.

3 **Adding text and arrows**. The number of holidays sold for Portugal seems rather low for this quarter, so we'll add a comment to this segment. First check that the Drawing Toolbar is displayed at the bottom of the screen – if not, use the View-Toolbars command. Click the Arrow button.

■ The screen pointer changes to a cross; drag to draw the arrow as shown in FIGURE 3.6. If you make a mistake then make sure that the arrow is still selected and press the *Delete* key.

1st Quarter European Holiday Sales

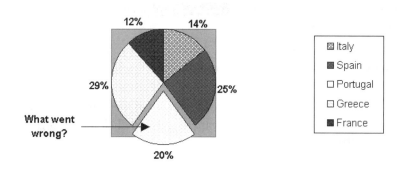

FIGURE 3.6

- Adding text to the arrow is simple: press the *Esc* key first if necessary to deselect the arrow, then click the Formula Bar at the top of the screen and type the comment **What went wrong?**.

- Click the tick box next to the Formula Bar. The comment now appears on the screen in a text box, enclosed by selection handles.

- Place the screen pointer on the selection rectangle itself but not on one of the handles and drag the box to move it next to the arrow.

- Now try resizing the box by dragging a selection handle. Then, assuming that the box is still selected, click the ▐ **Bold** ▐ button. If you wish to experiment with further styles or colours then use the **Format** menu as you did in Step 2. If you have made a serious mistake you can delete selected text with the *Delete* key and start again.

 Formatting all chart text. Click the edge of the chart window so that all of the chart is selected – small square 'handles' appear around it.

Open the **Format** menu and select **Selected Chart Area**. Any formatting options that you select will apply to all the chart elements.

4   **Independent activity**

Using the techniques you have just learned, format the percentage labels on the pie chart.

5   If you are happy with the changes – compare your chart with FIGURE 3.6 – then save them, if not use the **Edit-Undo** option.

Task 11: Printing a chart

1   Make sure that **CHART1** is the active sheet.

Open the **File** menu and select **Print** (you can also use the ▐ **Print** ▐ button on the Standard Toolbar).

 If the **Print** option is dimmed it is unavailable. Check that you have completed any operations – the tick box should not be displayed in the Formula Bar, for example.

2   A **Print** dialog box opens; click the ▐ **Print Preview** ▐ button to show the chart as it will appear on the printed page.

To see more detail either click the part of the image that you wish to enlarge or use the ▐ **Zoom** ▐ button at the top of the screen. Press the ▐ **Zoom** ▐ button again to restore the size.

If you wish to check the page setup or the printer setup then click the buttons at the top of the **Print Preview** window. If you are satisfied click the ▐ **Print** ▐ button; otherwise close the dialog box.

Task 12: Changing chart patterns and colours

If you are using a black and white printer you may find that the coloured segments of the pie chart lack contrast when printed, in which case you can use a pattern rather than a plain block of colour.

1   Make sure that **CHART1** is the active sheet. Click a segment of the pie chart (not the whole chart) – the selection handles appear.

2   Open the **Format** menu and select **Selected Data Point**.

3   A dialog box appears. Select the **Patterns** tab, which allows you to select:

Border Different edges for the segments

Area Different combinations of colour and pattern for the segments – black and white patterns are best for monochrome printers.

Select suitable combinations and click **OK** .

4   Save the changes to the pie chart.

Task 13: Creating line charts

1   Make sure that the workbook **EUROSLS** is open. Make sure that **SHEET1** is the active sheet.

2   Let's compare the sales for Italy and Spain for the four quarters.

Select cells A4–E7, a range of 20 cells.

3   Open the **Insert** menu and select **Chart**.

4   The **ChartWizard 'Step 1 of 4'** dialog box is displayed. Select **Line** from the **Chart type** box. Leave Chart sub-type 4 (the default) selected then click the **Next** button.

5   Make sure that the correct data range, i.e. *Sheet1!$A$4:$E$7*, is displayed in the **'Step 2 of 4'** dialog box, then click the **Next** button.

6   Click the **Next** button on the **'Step 3 of 4'** dialog box.

7   Select the **As new sheet** option on the **'Step 4 of 4'** dialog box and click the **Finish** button. The line chart appears with the default name **CHART2**.

8   Open the **View** menu and select the option **Sized with Window**. The line chart expands to fill the window – enlarge the window if necessary. It lacks titles because we did not use ChartWizard to add them; however we can do this at any stage, as in the next task.

Task 14: Adding titles and a legend to an existing chart

1   Make sure that the line chart created in the previous task is still the active document.

Open the **Chart** menu and select **Chart Options**.

2   Click the **Titles** tab on the **Chart Options** dialog box.

3   Enter *Sales for Italy and Spain* in the **Chart Title** box.

4   Add the title *Current Year* to the **Category (X) axis** box.

5   Similarly, in the **Value (Y) axis** box type the title *Holidays Sold*.

6   Now click the **Legend** tab to ensure that the **Show Legend** option is selected. Click **OK** .

Task 15: Repositioning titles and legend using the **Format** menu

You can drag titles and legends to new positions with the mouse, but the **Format** menu offers further options which we will try out now. (Remember that you can call up the menu directly by right clicking the chart component, or double click it to call up the dialog box.)

1   Click the title for the Y axis 'Holidays Sold' to select it.

Open the **Format** menu and select the option **Selected Axis Title**.

2   The **Format** dialog box opens; click the **Alignment** tab. You are offered various options. Make sure that horizontal and vertical text alignment are both set to **Center**. Change the text orientation to 0 degrees if necessary.

Use the **Font** tab to make the text larger then click **OK** .

3   The title 'Holidays Sold' is now displayed horizontally and more readably, but it may overlap the chart itself. You can select the title and then drag it and/or resize it if this is a problem. You can see in FIGURE 3.7 that it is also possible to split the title over two lines – see if you can work out how!

FIGURE 3.7

4 **Independent activities**

■ Using the above operations, adjust the font size, style or colour for:

– the X axis title

– the X and Y axes themselves

– the legend.

■ Use the **Chart Type** option on the **Chart** menu to try out other line chart types – return to sub-type 4 when you have finished.

■ Finally, print the line chart and compare it to FIGURE 3.7.

Task 16: Charting non-adjacent cell ranges

Sometimes you may wish to chart data from different parts of a worksheet. Using the *Ctrl* key you can select cell ranges that are not adjacent and base charts on them, e.g. those for Italy and France in our present workbook.

1 Make sure that **SHEET1** is the active sheet. Select the column headings A4–E4.

2 Now hold down the *Ctrl* key and select the four quarters' sales for Italy – cells A6–E6.

Repeat these operations for the row for France – cells A10–E10. The worksheet should resemble FIGURE 3.8.

	A	B	C	D	E	F
1	Sunfilled Holidays					
2			Holidays Sold - Europe			
3						
4		1st Quarter	2nd Quarter	3rd Quarter	4th Quarter	Total
5						
6	Italy	85	99	200	93	477
7	Spain	150	246	355	145	896
8	Portugal	120	180	300	123	723
9	Greece	168	277	320	162	927
10	France	70	120	250	110	550
11						
12	Total	593	922	1425	2940	3573

FIGURE 3.8

3 Now create another line chart on a new sheet, using the ChartWizard as before, and add a legend. Your chart should resemble FIGURE 3.9.

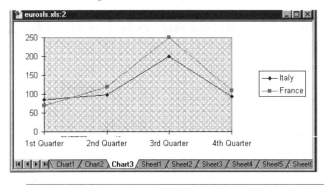

FIGURE 3.9

4   Add suitable titles to the chart and format the text – see the previous task.

This chart has the default name **CHART3** (or a later number if you have created other charts).

Task 17: Naming and copying charts

At the moment the workbook **EUROSLS.XLS** contains a worksheet with the default name **SHEET1**, plus three charts with the default names:

CHART1 – the pie chart created in Task 4

CHART2 – the line chart (Italy and Spain) created in Task 13

 CHART3 – the line chart (Italy and France) created in Task 16.

(Your documents may be numbered differently, depending on how many other sheets and charts you have created.)

You will now give them more meaningful names. A chart name, like a sheet name, can be up to 31 characters long. It can contain spaces, but the following special characters cannot be used: [,], /, \, ? and *.

1   Use the **Format-Sheet-Rename** command (or simply double click on the sheet name tab) to rename the sheets as follows:

Name the worksheet *Euro Hols Data*.

Name the pie chart *PIE1* and the line charts *LINE1* and *LINE2* respectively.

2   **Copying a chart sheet**. Click the name tab for **LINE2** to make it the active window.

Hold down the *Ctrl* key and then use the mouse pointer to drag the name tab along past the next name tab – the cursor changes to an icon marked with a + sign.

3   The place where the copy will be placed is marked with a small triangle.

First release the mouse button and then release the *Ctrl* key; the copy is made and the name tab is marked **Line2 (2)** .

 If you let go of the *Ctrl* key too soon then you may merely have moved **Line2** to a new position. In this case use the mouse to drag it back to its original position and try again.

4   Now use the **Format** menu as before to rename the copy **Line3** .

5   If you are not proceeding directly to the next unit then use the **File** menu to save and close your workbook.

Summary of commands

Menu commands show the menu name first, followed by the command to choose from the menu, e.g. **Edit-Clear** means open the **Edit** menu and select the **Clear** command.

Menu commands

Chart-Chart Options	Change title, legend, data labels etc
Chart-Chart Type	Change the chart type
Edit-Delete Sheet	Delete a chart or worksheet
Edit-Undo Entry	Reverse previous operation
Format-Autoformat	Select preformatted chart type
Format-Selected	Format selected chart element
Format-Sheet-Rename	Name a chart sheet
Insert-Chart	Create a new chart
View-Fit Selection	Chart fits window size available
View-Full Screen	Sheet increases to full screen size
View-Zoom	Specify a particular chart size
View-Sized with Window	Resize chart to window size
View-Toolbars	Show or hide a toolbar
Window-Arrange	Arrange layout of windows
Window-New Window	Open extra window

Standard Toolbar

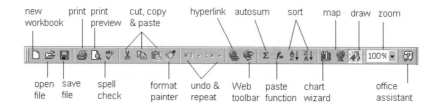

Formatting Toolbar

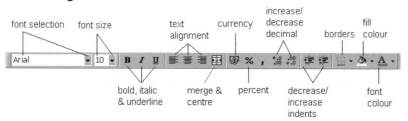

53

Further chart operations

What you will learn in this unit

By the end of this unit you will be able to:

- create a 3-D chart
- change the viewing angle of a 3-D chart
- format a 3-D chart
- create an area chart
- add arrows and shapes to charts
- alter chart axes
- remove and add chart values
- create custom charts
- create a data map
- enlarge a data map
- label a data map
- delete a chart
- create a doughnut chart
- create an embedded chart
- apply global formatting
- use goal seeking
- add trendlines.

What you should know already

Before you start this unit, make sure that you can do the following:

Skill	Covered in
Creating a worksheet	Units 1 and 2
Creating and formatting a chart	Unit 3

What you need

The workbooks **INS_SLS** created in Unit 2 and **EUROSLS** created in Unit 3.

Introduction

To round off your knowledge of charts you will be reviewing other chart types, especially three-dimensional charts and data maps. The third dimension offers extra opportunities to present the data and show the chart from a variety of angles. A data map allows you to plot geographically based data on maps.

Task 1: Rescaling a chart axis

On the line chart **LINE2** (and the copy **LINE3**) the values for Italy and France are very close at some points, making them difficult to read. This is because the scale is not the best one for the range of values on the chart. We can change this default scale.

1 Open the workbook **EUROSLS**. Make sure that **LINE3** is the active worksheet.

   Click the vertical axis to select it – selection handles should appear at both ends of the axis.

2 Open the Format menu and select Selected Axis; a dialog box appears.

   Select the **Scale** tab.

3 The axes and scales on charts are calculated automatically –the check marks in the Auto boxes show these default values.

   Type *50* in the Minimum box and click **OK** .

4 The chart is replotted to show the new range from 50 to 250, and the scale is also plotted in smaller divisions, making values easier to compare.

   Open the Edit menu and choose the Undo and Redo commands to review this.

5 Open the File menu and select Save to save the changes.

Task 2: Deleting a chart

Let's assume that you wish to use the rescaled chart **LINE3** and discard **LINE2**. You can delete this chart from the workbook.

1 Click the name tab for **LINE2** – check that it is now the active chart.

2 Open the Edit menu and select the Delete Sheet option.

3 A dialog box warns you that the sheet will be permanently deleted.

   Check that the correct sheet is selected then click **OK** . The sheet is now deleted – check that the name tab has disappeared.

(!) If you have deleted the wrong sheet there is still a last resort – exiting Excel without saving your work. Assuming that you save your work regularly then not too much work will be lost.

Task 3: Area charts

Area charts show both the amount of change over time and the sum of these changes. For example, in the case of European holidays we may be interested not only in the performance for each country, but in its individual contribution to the total holidays sold. In essence an area chart is a series of line charts stacked on top of each other with the areas between shaded in.

1   Make the worksheet **EURO HOLS DATA** the active window.

   Select cells A4–E10, i.e. all countries, all quarters.

2   Create a new chart as before using the ChartWizard, selecting Area as the chart type.

   There are a number to choose from. Select area chart sub-type 2.

3   When you get to Step 3 of the ChartWizard select the Data Labels tab.

   Select the Show Label option.

   At Step 4 of the ChartWizard select the As New Sheet option.

4   When you finish the ChartWizard use the View–Sized with Window option to enlarge the chart to the size of the window.

5   Using the Chart-Chart Options command add a suitable title to the chart – see FIGURE 4.1.

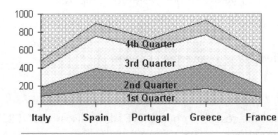

European Holiday Sales

FIGURE 4.1

6   **Formatting all chart text**. Click the edge of the chart window so that all of the chart is selected – small square 'handles' appear around it.

   Open the Format menu and select Selected Chart Area.

   Select the Font tab and change the fonts to 9 point bold.

7   Name the chart **AREA1**.

Task 4: Adding and removing chart values

You can remove a a range of values from a chart without needing to replot it; it is simply a matter of selecting that part of the chart and deleting it. Conversely, you can add a range of values to a chart simply by copying and pasting from the worksheet to the chart.

1 Make sure that **AREA1** is the active chart.

2 **Removing chart values**. Click once on the area for the third quarter (not on the name). It should now have a number of selection handles; the formula for the cell range is confirmed in the Formula Box at the top of the window. The formula looks more complex than it really is because for each cell in the range plotted – D4–D10 – Excel includes both the sheet name **EURO HOLS DATA** and the $ symbol, indicating an absolute reference.

(!) Make sure that you select the whole area, not just the area label; press the *Esc* key to deselect – or simply click the correct part of the chart. Double clicking calls up a dialog box – simply click the **Cancel** button.

3 Now press the *Delete* key and Quarter 3 is removed (the **Edit–Undo Clear** command will reverse this if you make a mistake).

4 **Adding values to a chart**. Click the name tab for the worksheet **EURO HOLS DATA** to make it the active window.

Select the cell range D4–D10, i.e. for the third quarter that we have just removed.

Open the **Edit** menu and select **Copy**.

5 Now make **AREA1** the active window again.

Open the **Edit** window and select **Paste**. The range of values for the third quarter is pasted back into the chart, but in an incorrect position.

6 **Changing the position of a data series**. Click the third quarter area of the chart again so that it is selected, i.e. enclosed in selection handles.

7 Open the **Format** menu and select the option **Selected Data Series**.

When the **Format Data Series** dialog box appears, click the **Series Order** tab.

The dialog box allows you to select the third quarter and move it to its correct position. Do this, then click **OK** . The third quarter is now restored to its correct position – compare it to FIGURE 4.1. You may need to resize the window.

Task 5: Reversing the chart axes

Study the chart **AREA1** carefully; it shows the five countries as the categories (along the X or category axis) and the holidays sold in each quarter as the values (along the Y or value axis). However, it could be equally useful if the axes were reversed, i.e. if each quarter formed the categories along the X axis and the number of holidays the values on the Y axis. When it plots a chart Excel assumes that you want fewer data series than categories, as this is easier to read. In the worksheet **EURO HOLS DATA**, five rows and four columns of data were charted (excluding cell labels), so the columns B–E became the values plotted and the rows 6–10 the categories. We can get reverse this by using the ChartWizard, either by creating a new chart or by modifying an existing one.

1 Make sure that **AREA1** is the active sheet.

2 Click the **ChartWizard** button on the Standard Toolbar – see the key at the end of this unit.

3 The **ChartWizard** dialog box appears.

Check that area chart sub-type 2 is still selected. Click the **Next** button.

4 ChartWizard – Step 2 is displayed next; make sure that the **Series** tab is selected.

Look at the **Category (X) axis** labels of the dialog box. At the moment the X axis is based on cells A6–A10 of the **EURO HOLS DATA** workbook, which contain the names of the countries.

The formula presently displayed, *='Euro Hols Data'!$A$6:$A$10*, reflects this:

!$A$6:$A$10 are the cells – the dollar signs indicate an absolute reference and are optional.

='Euro Hols Data'! is the name of the worksheet upon which the chart is based – the formula requires that it is enclosed in single quotes and that it is separated from the cell references by an exclamation mark.

5 Amend this reference to *='Euro Hols Data'!b4:e4* – see FIGURE 4.2.

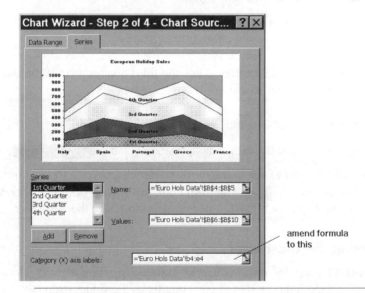

FIGURE 4.2

6 Click the **Data Range** tab now and enter the formula *='Euro Hols Data'!a4:e10* in the **Data range** box – see FIGURE 4.3. (The entire chart is based on the cell range A4–E10.)

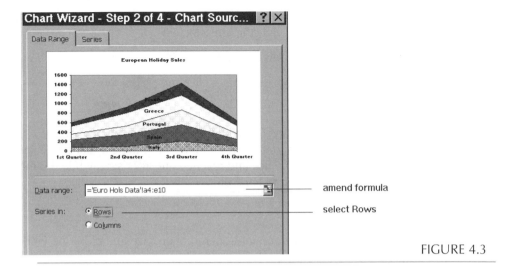

FIGURE 4.3

7 Click the **Rows** button and the chart axes are reversed.

Click the **Finish** button.

We can have, in effect, two views of the same data:

- **Data series in columns** – the countries are the categories and the values for the quarters are plotted on the value axis – see FIGURE 4.1.

- **Data series in rows** – the quarters are the categories and the values for the countries are plotted on the value axis. These techniques can be applied to other chart types.

8 **Independent activity**. Try reversing these changes, showing the data series in columns again – see FIGURE 4.1.

Task 6: Adding trendlines

1 First create a new worksheet **BOOKSLS** – see FIGURE 4.4.

	A	B	C	D	E
1		Book Sales - Current Year			
2					
3	Month	No. Sold	Revenue	Advertising	
4	Jan	850	2011	300	
5	Feb	1010	3155	425	
6	Mar	1175	3550	500	
7	Apr	1430	4536	750	
8	May	1710	5150	800	
9					

FIGURE 4.4

2 Make sure that cells **A3–D8** are selected and use the ChartWizard to create a standard column chart as a new sheet. This time, accept the default axis settings so that the months are the categories on the X axis.

 Open the **View** menu and select **Sized with Window**. Format the text labels as before if necessary (see Task 3, Step 6).

3   Move the screen pointer onto one of the bars representing advertising and click –
    all five bars representing advertising are selected.

    Open the **Chart** menu and select **Add Trendline**.

    The **Add Trendline** dialog box appears – click the **Type** tab.

    Select **Linear** and then the **Advertising** series, then click **OK**.

 A trendline is added to the chart. The trendline is useful for emphasising
    relationships between different data series – in this case the correlation between
    advertising, sales and revenue. Sales and revenue are still rising, while the money
    spent on advertising has started to level off.

4   Name the sheet **TREND1**.

    Experiment with the other trendlines offered, then save and close the workbook.

Task 7: Using goal seeking

Just as you can change the values in a chart by amending the underlying worksheet
data, you can also drag the data points in a chart and change the values on the
worksheet. If the changed values are derived from other values via worksheet
formulae then these will change too.

1   Open the workbook **EUROSLS** and make **EURO HOLS DATA** the active sheet.

2   Make sure that cells A12–F12, containing the overall totals, are selected and use
    the ChartWizard to create a standard column chart as a new sheet. Accept the
    default axis settings so that the months are the categories on the X axis.

 Open the **View** menu and select **Sized with Window**. Format the text labels as
    before if necessary (see Task 3, Step 6).

    Name the sheet **GOAL SEEK**.

3   Move the screen pointer onto the fifth (grand total) column and click once, then
    click again – the column should now be selected (enclosed in selection handles).
    Now move the pointer onto the top of the bar and the pointer should change to a
    double-headed arrow. An information box should also open.

4   Now drag the column upwards until its value equals 4000. A **Goal Seek** dialog
    box opens – see FIGURE 4.5 – and the worksheet is displayed.

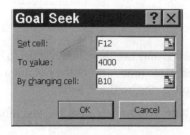

FIGURE 4.5

5   We can now modify any of the cells in the range B6–E10 to achieve the sales goal of 4000 holidays sold. Complete the dialog box as shown above and click **OK** . The value of cell B10 is changed to 497 – the number of French holidays sold to achieve the goal of 4000 in cell F12.

6   Click the **Cancel** button on the dialog box now; this restores the cells to their previous values.

Save and close the workbook.

7   **Notes on goal seeking**

The Goal Seek Status dialog box displays two extra buttons.

■ **Pause** allows you to pause during goal seeking.

■ **Step** allows you to continue one step at a time.

Goal seeking will only work if the cell whose value you set contains a value, not a formula. The cell whose value you set must be related by a formula to the cell whose target value you are changing.

You can also goal seek in a worksheet – see Unit 8, Task 1.

Task 8: Creating 3-D charts

If you are starting a new Excel session then you will need to open the workbook **BOOKSLS**. Make sure that **SHEET1** is the active sheet.

In this Task we will be building our first 3-D chart, based on the data in the **BOOKSLS** worksheet. Look at the 2D column chart in FIGURE 4.6.

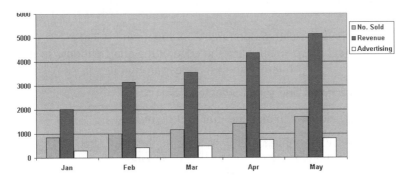

FIGURE 4.6

It shows the usual two-dimensional elements that we have charted so far: the X or horizontal axis shows the months as categories and the Y or vertical axis shows the values of the data points plotted – No. Sold, Revenue and Advertising.

Now compare it with the three-dimensional equivalent – FIGURE 4.7. Both charts are based on the same range of cell values – A3–D8 – but FIGURE 4.7 offers a third axis – the Z axis.

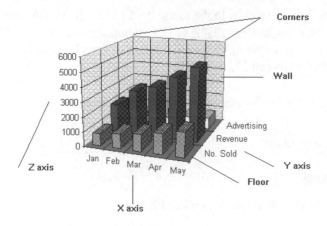

FIGURE 4.7

The X axis remains the category axis as before.

The Y axis (also called the depth or inward axis) now shows No. Sold, Revenue and Advertising as three data series.

The Z axis is now the value axis, showing the value of the data points.

The 3-D chart is plotted on a base floor against background walls. The 3-D chart can be rotated against this background giving you different views of the data.

 Some of Excel's 3-D charts, e.g. the 3-D pie and 3-D bar charts, simply use the third dimension to add depth to the 2-D version, but do not chart a third dimension.

1 Make sure that workbook **BOOKSLS** is open and that **SHEET1** is the active sheet.

2 Make sure that cells A3–D8 are selected and use the ChartWizard to select column chart sub-type 7 (3-D). Create it as a separate sheet.

3 When the 3-D chart is created, open the View menu and select Sized with Window. If the text is too small, click the edge of the chart window so that all the chart is selected – small square 'handles' appear around it.

Open the Format menu and select Selected Chart Area.

Select the **Font** tab and change the font to 9 point bold.

Your chart will now resemble FIGURE 4.7. Name the chart sheet **3-D COLUMN**, using the Format-Sheet-Rename command.

Task 9: Formatting a 3-D chart

The Insert and Format options offer the same range of options that we have already used for previous 2-D charts. Similarly, the **ChartWizard** button allows you to change the chart type and other parameters.

1 **Changing the order of columns**. At the moment the columns representing Advertising are hidden by taller columns. We will bring them to the front.

Click one of the Advertising columns – the whole series is selected.

Open the **Format** menu and select the Selected Data Series option.

2   A dialog box appears – click the **Series Order** tab.

Click Advertising in the Series Order box, followed by the **Move Up** button.

The Advertising columns move forward one column. Repeat until they move to the front of the chart, then click **OK**.

3   **Adding a chart title**. Open the **Chart** menu and select Chart Options.

Click the **Titles** tab.

Enter the title **Book Sales Analysis** and click **OK**.

You can change the position of the title by dragging with the mouse pointer.

4   **Altering text and columns**. The principle is exactly the same as for 2-D charts. It is a matter of:

■   clicking what you wish to modify, e.g. title, column, axis, gridlines – selection handles appear

■   opening the **Format** menu and selecting the first option, Selected..., and then making your choices using the dialog boxes provided.

Task 10: Changing the viewing angle of a 3-D chart

In a 3-D chart you can vary the angle at which you view the data. This allows you to emphasise different characteristics of the chart. You can do this either by direct chart editing – clicking the axis and dragging – or by using the **Format** menu. You will practise the second method, as it is more precise.

1   Make sure that the chart **3-D COLUMN** is still the active chart.

Open the **Chart** menu and select the option 3-D View.

2   The dialog box in FIGURE 4.8 appears.

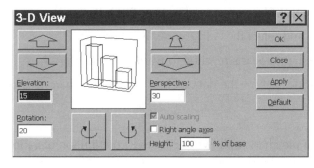

FIGURE 4.8

Move the mouse pointer onto the title bar of the dialog box and drag it to one side so that you can see the effects of the changes on the chart.

Read the following explanations carefully and follow the instructions:

 ■ **Elevation** is the height (in degrees) at which you view the columns; it can vary from 0 to 44 degrees in a column chart. Make a note of the present setting.

Click the up and down arrow buttons above the Elevation box and watch the angle of elevation change in the dialog box.

Click the **Apply** button and the changes are reflected in the column chart itself. Finally, return the Elevation box to its previous setting by pressing the **Default** button.

■ **Perspective** is the three-dimensional depth of the chart. The figure in the box (between 0 and 100) is the ratio of the size of the front of the chart to the back. Make a note of the present setting. Click the perspective arrow buttons above the Perspective box and watch the perspective change. Click the **Apply** button and the changes are reflected in the column chart itself. Finally, return the Perspective box to its Default setting.

■ **Rotation** rotates the chart about its vertical axis. Make a note of the present setting.

Click the rotation arrow buttons next to the Rotation box and watch the angle of rotation change. Click the **Apply** button and the changes are reflected in the column chart itself. Finally, return the Rotation box to its Default setting.

■ **Height % of base** alters the height of the chart relative to the base.

Amend the default figure to 50, then click the **Apply** button to see its effect.

Click the **Default** button to restore the original setting.

3 Finally, click the **Close** button to close the dialog box.

Task 11: Consolidation – check your progress

This activity gives you the chance to try out some additional techniques and briefly reviews some Excel charts and techniques that we have not yet covered.

1 Open the workbook **BOOKSLS** and open the sheet **TREND**.

■ Open the **Chart** menu and select the **Add Trendline** option.

Add a linear trendline that forecasts revenue forward for a month

■ Use **Chart-Chart Options** to show the data table on which the chart is based.

2 **Doughnut charts.**

 A **doughnut chart** is like a pie chart; it shows the relative contribution of various quantities to a total. However, unlike a pie chart it is not restricted to one data series.

Open the workbook **BOOKSLS** and highlight cell range A3–C6 in **SHEET1** – the columns showing revenue and number sold for January to March.

Using the ChartWizard create the doughnut chart shown in FIGURE 4.9. Name the chart **DOUGHNUT1**.

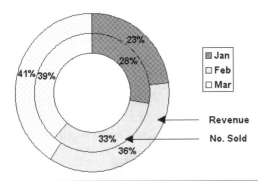

Sales and Revenue - Jan - May

FIGURE 4.9

3   **Adding arrows and shapes to a chart**. It is not clear that the outer ring on the chart represents revenue and the inner ring sales. Let's add notes to the chart to clarify this – see FIGURE 4.9.

If the Drawing Toolbar is not visible at the bottom of the screen open the View menu and select Toolbars.

Use the text box and the arrow tools to create the labels shown. You can delete a selected object by pressing the *Delete* key.

4   **Custom charts**. Step 1 of the ChartWizard offers a range of custom charts as a separate tabbed sheet **CUSTOM TYPES**. Open the ChartWizard and take time to review them. Many are just more showy versions of chart types that we have already used, e.g. **BLUE PIE** and **COLORED LINES**. Others offer monochrome versions of standard charts – useful if you don't have a colour printer. Some offer alternative ways of presenting data, e.g. Logarithmic or Lines on 2 Axes.

5   Save and close the workbook **BOOKSLS**.

Task 12: Embedded charts

So far you have created separate chart documents. Excel also allows you to create embedded charts which form part of the worksheet.

This is simply a matter of selecting the option at Step 4 of the ChartWizard. It is useful if you want to view or print a chart and worksheet on the same page.

1   Open the worksheet **INS_SLS**.

Maximise the worksheet window.

2   Highlight the cell range **A3–D6**.

3   Open the ChartWizard and create a standard bar chart. When you reach Step 4 leave the option As object in selected and press the Finish button.

4   The embedded chart is created; it can be moved or resized using the selection handles. The chart and the worksheet can be selected in turn by clicking.

 Notice that when one of the bars on the chart is selected Excel's Range Finder will outline the corresponding worksheet elements.

5   **Drag and drop** is a feature of all Excel's charts and worksheets; it allows you to select a cell range and drag it directly onto a chart to create a new data series. It is especially useful for an embedded chart. You can add the quarterly average figures to the chart in this way.

Select cell range A8–D8 on the worksheet.

Move the mouse pointer onto the edge of the selected range – see FIGURE 4.10.

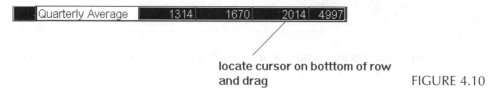

locate cursor on botttom of row
and drag   FIGURE 4.10

Now use the mouse to drag the cell range (represented by a dotted rectangle) onto the chart. The chart is redrawn to include a fourth data series.

Use the **Edit-Undo** command if you have made a mistake.

6   To format the embedded chart double click it; the dialog box will then be displayed and the chart can be formatted as if it were a separate document.

To view the embedded chart in its own window make sure that it is still selected. Then open the **View** menu and select **Chart Window**.

To view the chart as a separate sheet, open the ChartWizard again. When you reach Step 4 select the **As new sheet** option and then click the **Finish** button.

A chart can be deleted – select it and press the *Delete* key.

You can save or print the chart now as part of the worksheet.

Task 13: Displaying data on a map

If you have a worksheet that contains data on countries you can plot the data on a map. The map is an embedded chart and part of its associated worksheet. If Microsoft Data Map is not installed then you will need to do so using your setup disks or CD-ROM. Unless you have a fairly powerful PC you will find that it will take a long time to draw and redraw maps, especially if the workbook is stored on disk.

1   Open the workbook **EUROSLS**. Make sure that **EURO HOLS DATA** is the active worksheet.

2   Select cell range A6–B10 containing the holiday sales for five European countries for the first quarter.

3   Click the **Map** button on the Standard Toolbar (see key at the end of this unit). The button is marked with a globe. The cursor becomes cross-shaped; drag to select a fairly large area under the worksheet data, e.g. cell range B14–F25.

4   The toolbars change and a dialog box may appear, offering you a choice of maps. Select the **Europe Countries in Europe** option and click **OK**.

Eventually the map of Europe is plotted, showing the five countries (i.e. Italy, Spain, Portugal, Greece and France) in contrasting patterns. The map is enclosed in a selection rectangle and can be 'dragged' in the usual way to move or resize it – do this if necessary.

5   A map control dialog box is also shown – hide this for the moment using the **Show/Hide Map Control** button on the Map Toolbar at the top of the screen – see FIGURE 4.11.

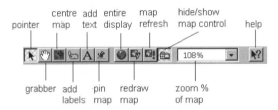

FIGURE 4.11

 If the Map Toolbar and the **Map** menu are not displayed this is probably because the worksheet rather than the embedded map is selected. Click on the map.

6   **Enlarging parts of the map**. Move the mouse pointer onto the Map Toolbar. A screen tip label explains the purpose of each button.

Use the **Zoom Percentage of Map** button to enlarge the map to about 250%.

Click the **Grabber** button on the Map Toolbar – the cursor becomes hand-shaped. Use this to drag Greece to the centre of the map, making sure that the other four countries are all fully visible.

7   **Labelling the countries**. Click on the **Map Labels** button – a dialog box appears. Select the option **Map Feature Names** and click **OK**.

As you move the mouse pointer over the map the countries are identified. Click the five countries France, Spain, Italy, Greece and Portugal in turn to label them.

Click the **Map Label** button again; this time select the **Values from – Column B** option from the dialog box and click **OK**.

Click the five countries again and they are labelled with the values from column B of the worksheet – the numbers of holidays sold.

The map should now resemble FIGURE 4.12. Its exact appearance will depend on your use of the **Zoom** and **Grabber** buttons in Step 6.

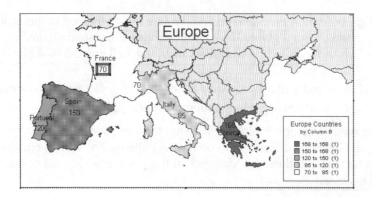

FIGURE 4.12

To format the text labels, right click them and select the **Format Font** option from the popup menu.

8 **Modifying the legend**. Double click the legend box. A dialog box appears.

Make sure that the **Legend Options** tab is selected.

Deselect the **Use Compact Format** option if necessary.

Amend the **Subtitle** box to **By Holiday Sales**. The dialog box should now resemble FIGURE 4.13.

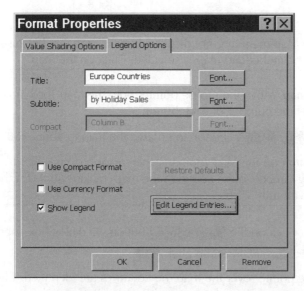

FIGURE 4.13

Click **OK** and the legend is modified. Move and resize it if necessary.

9 **Plotting multiple data ranges**. The present map shows a single data range – for the first quarter only. Delete it as follows.

Click the worksheet area to deselect the map, then click the map area once – selection boxes enclose it. Press the *Delete* key.

Now repeat Steps 2–7 to create a new map based on the first three quarters, cell range A6–D10.

When it appears, enlarge the map and reposition the countries as before.

Label each country by name but do not insert the values.

10 Make sure that the **Map Control** dialog box is displayed and drag it fully into view.

First drag any icons out of the white blank area of the dialog box – this will remove them.

Then, using FIGURE 4.14 as a guide, drag the pie chart button into the blank area of the dialog box, then drag down the buttons for columns B–D into the box too.

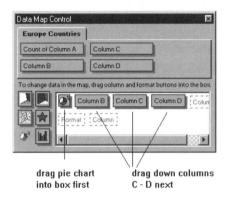

drag pie chart   drag down columns
into box first   C - D next   FIGURE 4.14

Pie charts should now appear on the map for each country.

Close the **Map Control** dialog box.

11 **Formatting the map**. Move the country names close to the pie charts, as shown in FIGURE 4.15.

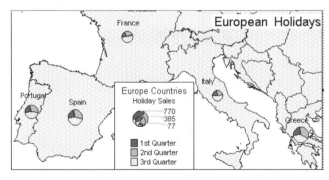

FIGURE 4.15

Double click the legend and complete the dialog box as before.

If you click the **Edit Legend Entries** button in the dialog box you can also amend the legend entries to 1st Quarter, 2nd Quarter etc.

Finally, double click the map title and amend it as in FIGURE 4.15.

Reposition the title and the legend so that the labels for each country are visible.

12 Close and save the workbook.

Summary of commands

Menu commands show the menu name first, followed by the command to choose from the menu, e.g. **Edit-Clear** means open the **Edit** menu and select the **Clear** command.

Menu commands

Chart-Chart Options	Change title, legend, data labels etc
Chart-Add Trendline	Add a trendline to selected chart data
Edit-Copy...Paste	Copy data from worksheet to chart
Edit-Delete Sheet	Delete a chart sheet
Chart-3-D View	Change viewing angle
Format-Selected...	Format selected chart element
Insert-Chart	Create a new chart
Insert-Chart-On This Sheet	Create an embedded chart
Insert-Titles	Insert chart or axis title
View-Sized With Window	Resize chart to window size

Standard Toolbar

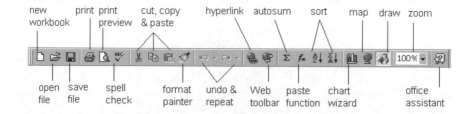

Formatting Toolbar

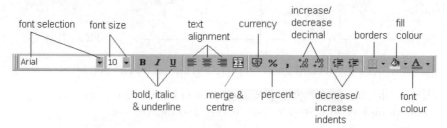

Creating and using a database

What you will learn in this unit

By the end of this unit you will be able to:

- use the * and ? operators
- use the **Advanced Filter** option
- use the **AutoComplete** feature
- create calculated fields
- use comparison operators
- define a criteria range
- use database functions
- use a data form
- create a data series
- define a database
- extract records from a database
- sort by key fields
- format numbers
- name cells
- use the Office Assistant
- use the **OR** operator
- create a PivotTable
- use search criteria
- sort data
- use statistical functions
- subtotal a database
- use wildcard operators.

What you should know already

Before you start this unit, make sure that you can do the following:

Skill	Covered in
Creating a simple worksheet	Unit 1

What you need

No previously created worksheets are required for this unit.

Introduction

In previous units you have covered worksheets and charts, the first two components of Excel. This unit covers the third component, databases. You will cover sorting and simple queries briefly, then proceed to advanced searches, database functions and PivotTables.

FIGURE 5.1 is an example of a simple database that records customer orders. We can use it to introduce certain key database terms.

	A	B	C	D	E
1	**Order No.**	**Order Date**	**Co.Ref**	**Co. Name**	**Value**
2	14000	10-Mar	1453	Wilson Garages	3200.00
3	14001	08-Mar	2413	Patel Industries	1466.00
4	14002	11-Mar	1453	Wilson Garages	98.76
5	14003	11-Mar	1289	Marsden Products	4456.00
6	14004	10-Mar	2413	Patel Industries	567.00
7	14005	11-Mar	955	Tilley Transport	1678.00
8	14006	10-Mar	2375	Patel Kitchens	55.54
9	14007	09-Mar	1453	Wilson Garages	2654.00
10	14008	12-Mar	2245	Goldfield Stables	123.85
11	14009	12-Mar	1289	Marsden Products	1652.54
12					

FIGURE 5.1

Record: There is an entry for each order. Each entry is called a record and takes up a row.

Field: Each record contains the same five fields or items of information – Order No., Order Date, Co. Ref, Co. Name and Value.

Each field takes up a column. The first row of the database contains the field names, while the other rows contain the actual data – the field values.

Database: At the moment our database consists of a range of 10 records.

Excel is primarily a spreadsheet and does not offer all the features of a special-purpose database management system such as Access or Paradox, but you can perform straightforward database tasks such as:

- finding individual records
- adding and deleting records

- editing existing records

- sorting records.

More complex tasks are also possible, such as sorting records into a different order, or extracting all records meeting a particular search criterion. However, the relational facilities of special-purpose databases, e.g. multi-table queries and reports, are not possible in Excel.

Database rules in Excel

Database size: A database can be as large as the entire worksheet, but cannot occupy more than one worksheet. A worksheet can hold several databases.

Fields and **field names**: A database can contain up to 256 fields.

The first row of the database must contain the field names.

Field names must consist of letters only, not numbers, blank cells etc.

Field names can be up to 256 characters long and must be unique.

Records: A database can contain up to 16,383 records. Every record must have the same fields, but fields can be left blank.

Do not enter extra blanks at the start of fields.

Capitalization: Excel ignores upper- or lower-case when searching or sorting the database, so you may use, for example, 'SMITH', 'smith' or 'Smith' to locate a record.

Task 1: Building the database

1   **Inserting the field names**. First open a new blank workbook, then enter the five field names shown in FIGURE 5.1 (cells **A1–E1**).

	A	B	C	D	E
1	Order No.	Order Date	Co.Ref	Co. Name	Value
2	14000	10-Mar	1453	Wilson Garages	3200.00
3	14001	08-Mar	2413	Patel Industries	1466.00
4	14002	11-Mar	1453	Wilson Garages	98.76
5	14003	11-Mar	1289	Marsden Products	4456.00
6	14004	10-Mar	2413	Patel Industries	567.00
7	14005	11-Mar	955	Tilley Transport	1678.00
8	14006	10-Mar	2375	Patel Kitchens	55.54
9	14007	09-Mar	1453	Wilson Garages	2654.00
10	14008	12-Mar	2245	Goldfield Stables	123.85
11	14009	12-Mar	1289	Marsden Products	1652.54
12					

FIGURE 5.1

Use the right arrow key to move across the columns.

Widen the columns where necessary, and centre and embolden the field names.

2   **Entering data using** AutoComplete. First complete columns C and D – the **Co. Ref** and **Co. Name** fields as shown in FIGURE 5.1. You may notice that when you enter a company name for the second time, e.g. **Wilson Garages**, Excel automatically completes the entry for you. Excel keeps a track of duplicated

entries and automatically finishes them for you after one or two letters have been entered. You can then stop typing and go on to the next cell entry.

As there are two companies starting with **Patel** you will need to type in the rest of the company name.

The AutoComplete feature can be set on or off. Open the **Tools** menu and select **Options**. A dialog box appears. Click the **Edit** tab and select the option **Enable AutoComplete for Cell Values**.

3 Next, enter the order values in column E, the **Value** field. Don't enter **.00** after a value if there are no pence; for example, in the case of cell E3 just enter the value 1466.

4 **Formatting the fields**. Format the ten **Value** fields (cell range E2–E11) to two decimal places, using the **Format-Cells-Number** command.

5 **Creating a data series**. The **Order no**. field is a numeric sequence – increasing by 1 for every new order record. We can use the **Fill Series** command when numbers or dates in adjacent cells increase (or decrease) by a constant factor.

   Enter the start value **14000** in cell A2, then select the whole range, A2–A11.

   Open the **Edit** menu and select the **Fill** option followed by the **Series** option.

   A dialog box appears. Make sure that the following options are selected, as shown in FIGURE 5.2.

FIGURE 5.2

   Series in: **Columns** – the data series will occupy a column.

   Type: **Linear** – the progression will be linear.

   Step value: **1** – the numbers will increase by 1 each time (for weekly dates you would step value 7).

6 Click the **OK** button and the column is filled with the order numbers 14000–14009.

You can create a data series based on dates and fractional numbers too.

7 **Entering the order date**. Excel allows dates to be entered in a variety of formats and in most cases will automatically assign the correct date format.

   Enter the first date field as **10mar** and press *Enter*.

Excel automatically converts it to the date format 10-Mar (if it doesn't then check what you have entered).

Enter the remaining field values in a similar way.

 Look at the status bar at the top of the screen as you do this. Irrespective of the date format in the cells, Excel displays dates in a numeric format, e.g. 10/3/97.

8   Finally, centre the field values for the **Order No.**, **Order Date** and **Co. Name** fields. The database should now resemble FIGURE 5.1.

9   Double click on the sheet tab and name the worksheet **ORDERS**.

Save the workbook as **DATABASE**.

You will see that it is assigned the usual worksheet extension **.XLS**.

Task 2: Sorting the database

A common business need is to present the same information in a variety of ways, e.g. in order number sequence (as at present) or in customer name sequence. Sorting involves rearranging the records in a new physical sequence, and speeds up the search time once a database gets over a certain size. We can sort the database in order of any field or fields.

Rules and hints for sorting

Sorting will work with any range of worksheet cells, not only databases.

Order of sorting: field values are sorted in the following order:

Numbers

Text

Logical values

Error values

Blanks

You can always undo an unsuccessful sort by selecting Undo Sort from the Edit menu, provided that you do so immediately.

 All the fields in the database, i.e. all columns, must be included in the sort, otherwise any fields omitted from the sort will remain in the same sequence and become attached to the wrong records.

1   Let's sort the customer orders into date sequence first.

Select cells A1–E11 – all fields, all records, including the field names in the header row.

Open the Data menu and select Sort. The Sort dialog box appears.

If necessary, locate the mouse pointer on the title bar and drag the dialog box down so that the database is visible.

2 Complete the dialog box as follows, using FIGURE 5.3 as a guide:

Sort by: At the moment the first field name, **Order No.**, is selected. Click the down arrow button on the **Sort by** box. A field list is displayed – select **Order Date**. Leave the ▐Ascending▐ button on (earliest dates first).

Then by: Ignore the next two boxes – we are only sorting by one field.

My list has: Leave **Header row** selected – the field names in row 1 will not be included in the sort.

The screen should now resemble FIGURE 5.3.

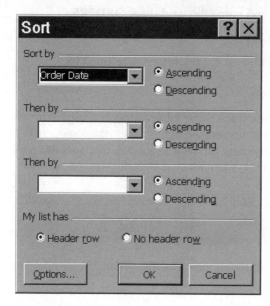

FIGURE 5.3

Click the ▐**OK**▐ button and the 10 records are sorted in a new sequence – date order.

 A sort can be changed either by selecting **Undo Sort** from the **Edit** menu or by another sort operation.

3 **Sorting by more than one key**. Let's sort the records in reverse date sequence within **Co. Name**. This means that all the records for, e.g. Wilson Garages, are grouped together, with the latest orders displayed first. This involves two 'keys', **Co. Name** as the primary key and **Order Date** as the secondary key.

Make sure that the entire database range is selected as before and issue the **Data-Sort** command.

Complete the **Sort** dialog box as follows:

- Ensure that **Co. Name** is selected in the first **Sort by** box.

- Now click the down arrow box next to the first **Then by** box. Select **Order Date** from the field list.

- Click the ▐**Descending**▐ button next to the first **Then by** box.

- Click the **OK** button.

- Click on the worksheet to remove the selection highlighting from the database. Check that the records are sorted in the correct order.

4 **Consolidation**. Try sorting the order records as follows:

- in descending order of value, i.e. largest orders first

- by **Co. Ref** in ascending date order – compare your result with Appendix 6.

Task 3: Creating new fields by calculation

We are going to add two new fields to the database.

- The *VAT* field, which will hold the 17.5% VAT to be added to the value of an order.

- The *Total* field, which will hold the VAT field added to the order value field. These new fields will both be calculated by formulae in the usual way.

1 Make sure that the workbook **DATABASES** is open and that the worksheet **ORDERS** is the active sheet.

Add the two new field names, *VAT* and *Total*, to cells F1 and G1.

Centre them in their cells.

2 VAT is 17.5% of **Value**; move to cell F2 and apply the formula *=E2*0.175*.

Remember to press *Enter*.

Now copy this formula to the rest of the VAT fields using the **Edit-Fill-Down** command.

3 Now calculate the first **Total** field by adding the **VAT** field to the **Value** field. Simply select cell G2 and click the **Sum** button on the Standard Toolbar.

4 Format the two new fields to 2 decimal places, using the **Format-Cells-Number** command (see Task 1, Step 4).

5 Calculated fields can be searched and sorted in the same way as any other fields. To try this, sort the database by the **Total** field (ascending order). Your database should now resemble FIGURE 5.4.

	A	B	C	D	E	F	G
1	Order No.	Order Date	Co.Ref	Co. Name	Value	VAT	Total
2	14006	10-Mar	2375	Patel Kitchens	55.54	9.72	65.26
3	14002	11-Mar	1453	Wilson Garages	98.76	17.28	116.04
4	14008	12-Mar	2245	Goldfield Stables	123.85	21.67	145.52
5	14004	10-Mar	2413	Patel Industries	567.00	99.23	666.23
6	14001	08-Mar	2413	Patel Industries	1466.00	256.55	1722.55
7	14009	12-Mar	1289	Marsden Products	1652.54	289.19	1941.73
8	14005	11-Mar	955	Tilley Transport	1678.00	293.65	1971.65
9	14007	09-Mar	1453	Wilson Garages	2654.00	464.45	3118.45
10	14000	10-Mar	1453	Wilson Garages	3200.00	560.00	3760.00
11	14003	11-Mar	1289	Marsden Products	4456.00	779.80	5235.80
12							

FIGURE 5.4

Task 4: Database maintenance using a data form

The data form is the simplest way of searching a database. Only one record can be displayed at a time. We will briefly review it.

1 Make sure that the **ORDERS** worksheet is the active sheet.

There is no need to select the whole database in order to search or maintain it; simply make sure one of the cells in the database is selected.

Select cell D2.

---

2 Open the Data menu and select the Form option. A data form is displayed. On the left-hand side of the form are shown the field names and field values for the first record. The form always shows the number of the current record displayed, Number 1 of 10.

---

3 Let's carry out some database searches using the **Criteria** button, which allows you to locate records by named criteria.

- Click the **Criteria** button. A blank record is displayed.

  Enter your first criterion, *Patel*, in the **Co. Name** field, then click the **Find Next** button.

  The first record matching this search criterion is displayed; press the **Find Next** button again to view any further matches. Click the **Find Prev** button to scroll back again. There are three records in all. Notice that both Patel companies are located – we would need to enter the complete company name to narrow the search further.

  A 'bleep' informs you when the last matching record is displayed.

- Press the **Criteria** button again. **Patel** is still displayed in the **Co. Name** field.

  Click the *Value* field and enter the second criterion: *<1000*

  Click the **Find Next** button.

  Two records match the combined criteria, i.e. company name = Patel and order value less than £1000.

  Click the **Criteria** button followed by the **Clear** button to remove the search criteria, then click the **Form** button to return to the data form.

---

4 **Editing data**. Using the data form find the record for order number 14005 and amend the **Co. Ref** to *965*

Press the **Close** button to exit from the data form.

The first five data fields can be edited, but the two calculated fields, **VAT** and **Total**, cannot be changed. Their data are produced by formulae which cannot be overwritten. This is why the data in these two fields are not enclosed in boxes.

Changes/deletions to a record made using a data form are saved permanently as soon as you move to another record, even though no specific **Save** command has been given.

 The   **Restore**   button will only undo the change providing you press it before you move to another record.

Task 5: Adding subtotals to a database

We can total up the values of the orders for each customer using the Subtotals command. This is much quicker and easier than using the *SUM* function.

We can also outline the database and just display the subtotals.

1   Make sure that the **ORDERS** worksheet is the active sheet.

Make sure that all the cells in the database are selected, i.e. cell range A1–G11.

 Use the Sort command to sort the database by **Co. Name** order – see Task 2.

2   Open the Data menu and select Subtotals. The whole database is selected and a dialog box opens. Complete the entries as follows, using FIGURE 5.5 as a guide.

FIGURE 5.5

At each change in: Select the Co. Name field from the list box – we want subtotals for each company.

Use function: Leave this as *SUM*, the default – we want to add the value of orders.

Add subtotal to: Make sure that Total is selected – this is the field value we want to add.

Finally, click the   **OK**   button.

3   Click the mouse to remove the highlighting. Your database should resemble FIGURE 5.6. After each customer a new row is inserted, holding the customer name and the value of their orders subtotalled.

At the end of the table a grand total for all orders is displayed – you may need to scroll down to see this.

outline and subtotal buttons

	B	C	D	E	F	G
1	Order Date	Co.Ref	Co. Name	Value	VAT	Total
2	12-Mar	2245	Goldfield Stables	123.85	21.67	145.52
3			**Goldfield Stables Total**			145.52
4	11-Mar	1289	Marsden Products	4456.00	779.80	5235.80
5	12-Mar	1289	Marsden Products	1652.54	289.19	1941.73
6			**Marsden Products Total**			7177.53
7	08-Mar	2413	Patel Industries	1466.00	256.55	1722.55
8	10-Mar	2413	Patel Industries	567.00	99.23	666.23
9			**Patel Industries Total**			2388.78
10	10-Mar	2375	Patel Kitchens	55.54	9.72	65.26
11			**Patel Kitchens Total**			65.26
12	11-Mar	965	Tilley Transport	1678.00	293.65	1971.65
13			**Tilley Transport Total**			1971.65
14	09-Mar	1453	Wilson Garages	2654.00	464.45	3118.45

FIGURE 5.6

4 **Outlining**. At the top left-hand corner of the screen are three small buttons, labelled 1, 2 and 3 – see FIGURE 5.6.

Click on button **2**. The records are hidden, and only the subtotals and grand total are displayed.

Click on button **1**. Only the grand total is displayed.

Click on button **3**. The records, subtotals and grand totals are all displayed.

Now experiment with the minus buttons displayed down the left side of the screen. You will find that you can hide individual groups of records so that only the subtotals are displayed. The button then displays a '+' sign.

Click the button again and the records are redisplayed.

5 **Removing subtotals**. Open the Data menu and select Subtotals. When the dialog box appears click the **Remove All** button. The database is now displayed without subtotals.

Task 6: More advanced searches

Excel offers an Advanced Filter option that allows you to search on more than two fields, and offers a wider range of operators than those offered by a data form.

1 We will conduct these searches using a new database that holds details of voluntary helpers who act as guides, gardeners, drivers etc at heritage sites in various areas – see FIGURE 5.7.

	A	B	C	D	E	F
1	SURNAME	FORENAME	AREA	JOB	AGE	AVAILABILITY
2	Berger	Richard	Winton	Driver	33	12-Jul
3	Murphy	Mike	Wimborne	Gardener	65	13-Jul
4	Wilson	John	Ringwood	Guide	34	20-Jul
5	Sutton	Tony	Winton	Driver	39	23-Jul
6	Sutton	Linda	Poole	Canteen	54	22-Jul
7	Smith	Louisa	Poole	Kitchen	50	26-Jul
8	Goldfield	Chris	Boscombe	Guide	34	30-Jul
9	Muir	Sue	Wimborne	Warden	43	30-Jul
10	Newsome	Jayne	Redhill	Warden	16	30-Jul
11	Burton	Judy	Mudeford	Kitchen	48	02-Aug
12	Pierce	Karen	Poole	Guide	20	02-Aug
13	Maycock	Ray	Wallisdown	Gardener	40	04-Aug
14	Povey	Malcolm	Downton	Driver	25	30-Aug
15	Greeves	John	Ringwood	Canteen	66	05-Aug

FIGURE 5.7

Open a new workbook and save it as **HELPERS**.

Create and format the worksheet as shown in FIGURE 5.7.

Make sure that the records are exactly as shown; it will be important in checking your search results.

2 **Defining the database**. The first step is to define and name the worksheet cells as a database.

Select all the cells A1–F15, i.e. the 14 records plus the field headings in row 1.

Open the **Insert** menu and select the option **Name** followed by the **Define** option.

A dialog box appears. Enter the name **DATABASE**.

The name **DATABASE** now identifies the first row of cells as field names.

Click the **OK** button. The database is now defined.

3 **Defining the search criteria**. Select all the six field names in row 1, i.e. cell range A1–F1.

Open the **Edit** menu and select **Copy**.

Select cell A17, then select **Paste** from the **Edit** menu – the cells are copied across row 17 as your search criteria.

Notes on defining search criteria.

■ These cells form your criteria range – the field names that you use as search criteria.

■ You don't have to use a **Copy** command to copy the field names from the database – you can type them if you wish.

■ You don't need to include all the field names in the criteria range, only those that you intend to use in your search.

■ The criteria range may be located at any convenient place on the worksheet – usually close to the database you are searching.

4 **Entering the search criteria**. The first row of cells (row 17) contains the field

81

names, while the next row of cells, row 18, is for you to enter your search criteria. You merely enter your criteria under the field that you want to search.

Let's select all the records for drivers first.

Enter the search term **Driver** in cell D18 underneath the field name *Job* – see FIGURE 5.8. (Don't worry about capital letters – the search is not case-sensitive.)

Remember to press _Enter_ or click the tick box after entering this search term.

16						
17	SURNAME	FORENAME	AREA	JOB	AGE	AVAILABILITY
18				driver		

FIGURE 5.8

5 **Using** Advanced Filter. Open the **Data** menu and select the **Filter** option followed by the **Advanced Filter** option.

The **Advanced Filter** dialog box is displayed – complete it as follows, using FIGURE 5.9 as a guide:

Action: **Filter the list, in-place**. Leave this option selected; the search will 'filter out' those records that do not match the search criterion **Driver** and will only show the matching ones.

List range: You must specify the range of cells for the database you are searching. Check that the cell references are the same as in FIGURE 5.9. Modify them if not. This can be done either by keying them in or by dragging the mouse across the cell range to select it.

Criteria range: This is the cell range holding your search criteria – see Step 4. Check that the cell references are the same as in FIGURE 5.9. Modify them if not.

Ensure that no other options are selected on the dialog box, then click **OK**.

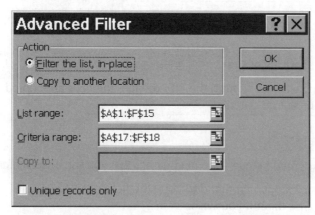

FIGURE 5.9

The three records for the drivers are selected. If not, repeat the above steps, checking the cell references very carefully.

6 Open the **Data** menu and select the **Filter** option followed by the **Show All**

option. This ends the search and displays the whole database again.

7 Now add a further search criterion, **Winton**, in cell C18 and press *Enter*.

Use the **Advanced Filter** option again; only two drivers match the second criterion; the other record is filtered out.

Open the **Data** menu and select **Filter** followed by **Show All**.

8 **Comparison operators**. The following six operators can be used in searching the database:

=   equal to (not needed on its own)

<   less than

>   greater than

<> not equal to

<= less than or equal to

>= greater than or equal to

9 Use them to make the following three searches:

■ All helpers living in Wimborne (no operator needed)

■ All helpers aged 50 or over

■ Poole helpers available before 25 July (enter a valid date first, then the < operator).

 Search tips

■ Erase previous search conditions using the *Delete* or *Backspace* keys.

■ Press *Enter* after entering the search criterion.

■ Use the **Data-Filter-Show All** command to show all the records before starting the next search.

If no records are selected check:

■ that the search criteria are correct

■ that the search criteria are entered under the correct field name

■ that the cell coordinates in the **Advanced Filter** dialog box are the same as in FIGURE 5.9.

10 **Wildcard searching**. The *** and *?* characters can be used as 'wildcards' to stand for one or more characters.

Try the following three searches:

■ Enter **ton* as a search condition in cell C18.

Records for both Winton and Downton are located.

The *** character can substitute for any combination of adjacent characters.

■ If you are unsure whether the forename 'Linda' is spelled with a 'y' or an 'i', the *?* character can be used to substitute for a single character.

Enter the search condition *L?nda* under the **FORENAME** field.

The record for Linda Sutton will be located.

■ Enter the search condition *Wi* under the **AREA** field. Records for both Wimborne and Winton are located, i.e. there is no need to use a wildcard character if you can supply the starting characters of the search criterion.

Restore all 15 records as before and remove any search criteria from row 18.

11 **AND vs. OR**. When we used more than one search criterion we implicitly used the AND condition; i.e. both conditions needed to be met for a record to be retrieved (e.g. Poole area AND available 25 July). We also need to search using the OR condition, e.g. Poole or Ringwood area, age under 20 or over 40. To do this involves entering the search criteria in different rows.

Let's retrieve records for areas Boscombe or Ringwood.

Enter **Boscombe** in the first cell below the **AREA** criterion – cell C18.

Enter **Ringwood** in the second cell below the **AREA** criterion – cell C19.

12 Next we need to amend the criteria range, as our criteria now occupy two rows.

Use the **Data-Filter-Advanced Filter** commands as before – the dialog box is displayed.

Select the **Criteria range** box and amend it to the references shown in FIGURE 5.10.

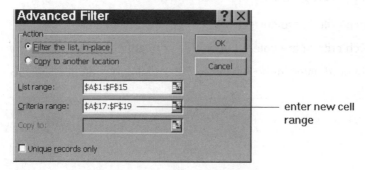

enter new cell range

FIGURE 5.10

Click **OK** – the three records that match either search condition are selected.

Restore all 15 records as before.

13 We can now make a more complex search – Guides for Ringwood or Wardens for Redhill. The logic is (guide AND Ringwood) OR (warden AND Redhill).

Enter the search criteria as shown in FIGURE 5.11.

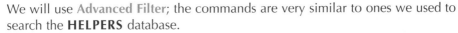

17	SURNAME	FORENAME	AREA	JOB	AGE	AVAILABILITY
18			Ringwood	guide		
19			Redhill	warden		

FIGURE 5.10

Run Advanced Filter and the two records that match both sets of criteria will be selected.

14 **Independent activities**. Try the following searches:

■ All helpers over 60 or under 21.

■ Any Guide available before 21 July or after 1 August (you will have to enter the job criterion twice – on both rows).

15 Save and close the workbook.

Task 7: Extracting records from the database

Once a database gets to a certain length, it can become unwieldy to use. In this situation we might find it useful to copy or extract selected records to another part of the worksheet and work with them separately. We will use the **ORDERS** database, created in Task 1, to practise this.

We will use Advanced Filter; the commands are very similar to ones we used to search the **HELPERS** database.

1 **Define the database**. Open the workbook **DATABASE** and then the worksheet **ORDERS**.

Select the whole database, including the field names (cells A1–G11).

Open the Insert menu and select Name followed by Define. The Name dialog box appears.

Enter the name **DATABASE** and click **OK** – the database is now defined.

The worksheet cells should be redefined as a database every time it is opened for use in case records have been added or deleted.

2 **Define the search criteria**. Select all the field names in row 1.

Open the Edit menu and select Copy.

Select cell A13, then select Paste from the Edit menu – the cells are copied across row 13.

3 **Enter the search criteria**. Let's extract all records totalling less than £1000.

Select cell G14, enter the criterion **<1000** and press *Enter*.

4 **Define the criterion and extract ranges**. Open the Data menu and select the Filter-Advanced Filter options. The Advanced Filter dialog box opens.

■ Click on the Copy to another location button.

■ Check the cell references in the **List range** box with FIGURE 5.12.

These cells define the database range. Amend them if necessary.

■ Select the Criteria range box and check the cell references shown against FIGURE 5.12. These cells define where we will enter our search criteria.

■ Select the Copy to box and check the cell references shown against FIGURE 5.12. These cells define where the records will be copied to.

Instead of typing the cell range into the range box click the Collapse dialog button next to the box – see FIGURE 5.12. The dialog box is shrunk; you can now select the cell range by dragging with the mouse. Click the Collapse button again and the dialog box is restored with the cell range inserted.

■ Finally, click the OK button.

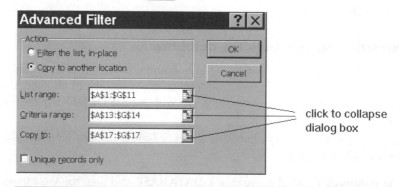

Advanced Filter

Action
○ Filter the list, in-place
● Copy to another location

List range: `$A$1:$G$11`
Criteria range: `$A$13:$G$14`
Copy to: `$A$17:$G$17`

☐ Unique records only

click to collapse dialog box

FIGURE 5.12

5 Four records matching the search criterion (Total < 1000) are extracted from the database and placed in row 17 below the field headings. You may need to scroll down to see them.

Any data in cells that are already in the extract range will be overwritten by the extracted data. They will be permanently lost, as you cannot undo an extract operation (unless you exit the worksheet without saving it). So either be careful where you place the extract range or limit it to a definite number of rows. This can be done by selecting a specific number of rows when you define the extract range.

6 **Independent activity**. Clear the search condition from cell G14 and the extracted records from row 18 and below.

Now extract all the records where the order date is on or before 10-Mar. Use the full date format in your search, e.g. 10/03/97. Five records should be extracted.

Remember to click on the **Copy to another location** button again – see Step 5 – the cell co-ordinates should remain unchanged.

7 **Consolidation**. Open the **HELPERS** worksheet and extract the following records:

■ all members aged 50 or over

■ all members aged 50 or over available on or after 26 July

■ the surname, area and job fields only for members from Poole (you will need to define a new extract range).

Task 8: Using database statistical functions

In addition to searching for records in the database, you can use functions to analyse the information it contains. A function is a built-in, predefined formula; you have already used the Excel functions **SUM** and **AVERAGE** in previous tasks. Excel provides special database functions, e.g. **DSUM, DAVERAGE, DMIN, DMAX**. Rather than operating on a whole range of cells, as the ordinary statistical functions **SUM, AVERAGE, MIN** and **MAX** do, they are used to select particular records on which to operate. For example, in the **ORDERS** database you can find not only the average order value, but the average order value for a particular customer, or since a certain date.

Taking **DSUM** as an example, database functions have the form:

DSUM(database,"field",criteria)

 database is the name of the database range that you have defined using the Name command – see Task 7.

field is the field whose values you wish to sum, e.g. **VAT**.

 criteria is the criteria range that you define using the Advanced Filter dialog box – see Task 6, Step 5.

 Paste Function replaces the Function Wizard.

You can either type the function yourself or use Paste Function to guide you through the steps. The latter is better if you don't use functions very often, as their syntax can be quite complex. A fuller list of database functions is given at the end of this unit.

1 Open the workbook **DATABASE** and select the worksheet **ORDERS** if necessary.

First we will check that the database and criteria ranges are correctly set.

Open the Insert menu and select Name-Define – the dialog box appears.

Click on the name **Database** and check in the Refers to box that the database range is set to **$A$1:$G$11**.

Click on the name **Criteria** and check in the Refers to box that the criteria range is set to **$A$13:$G$14**.

Reset these ranges if necessary and click **OK**.

On the left of the Formula Bar is a Name Box. Clicking the down arrow button on this box also allows you to review the names used in a workbook. When you define a name it is available to any sheet in the workbook, not just the sheet that contains the name.

2　Remove the extract range used in Task 7, i.e. the records from row 17 downwards.

3　Now let's designate a section of the worksheet for several database functions.

Starting in cell A16, enter the cell titles shown in FIGURE 5.13. Centre and embolden them. Format cells B17–E17 to show two decimal places.

	A	B	C	D	E	F	G
9	14007	09-Mar	1453	Wilson Garages	2654.00	464.45	3118.45
10	14008	12-Mar	2245	Goldfield Stables	123.85	21.67	145.52
11	14009	12-Mar	1289	Marsden Products	1652.54	289.19	1941.73
12							
13	Order No.	Order Date	Co.Ref	Co. Name	Value	VAT	Total
14							
15							
16	No of Orders	Avg. Value	Total Value	Total Vat	Min. Total		
17							

FIGURE 5.13

4　Using **Paste Function**. Let's use the **DSUM** function to total up the VAT that Wilson Garages have to pay on their orders.

First enter the search term **Wilson Garages** in cell D14.

Now select cell D17 – this is where the database function will be entered.

Click the **Paste Function** button – it is on the Standard Toolbar and marked 'fx'.

5　The **Paste Function** dialog box appears. If the Office Assistant is installed then this dialog box may be opened too. Close it for the moment.

Select **Database** from the **Function category** list.

Select **DSUM** from the **Function name** list.

Click the **OK** button.

6　A dialog box appears. Complete it as shown in FIGURE 5.14:

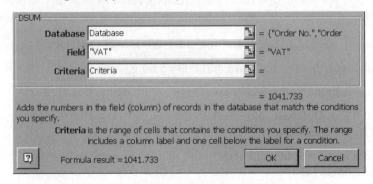

FIGURE 5.14

Enter **Database** in the **Database** box (this is the name of the database – see Step 1).

Enter *"Vat"* in the Field box (in double quotes) – this is the field to be summed.

Enter *Criteria* in the Criteria box – this is the name of the criteria range.

Click the **OK** button.

7   The total VAT on orders for Wilson Garages is placed in cell D17 (1041.73).

The formula *=DSUM(database,"VAT",criteria)* appears in the Formula Bar.

 Error messages. If you get an error message then check that each name is spelt correctly and the field name is entered in double quotes. You can edit it in the Formula Bar.

8   **Consolidation – Paste Function**. Select cell C17, then click the **Paste Function** button again. Use the *DSUM* function to calculate the total value of invoices (excluding VAT) for Wilson Garages in cell C17.

9   **Entering functions directly**. In cell A17 we will use the *DCOUNT* function to count the number of orders for Wilson Garages.

Select cell A17 then enter the formula *=DCOUNT(database,"total",criteria)*

 Error messages. If you get an error message then check that the field name is spelt correctly and entered in double quotes. You can edit it in the Formula Bar.

Check that you have placed the = sign, commas and brackets correctly.

Notice also that there are no spaces in the formula, and that you can use upper- or lower-case.

10 Activate cell B17 next and use the *DAVERAGE* function to calculate the average value of an order for Wilson Garages.

The formula is *=DAVERAGE(database,"value",criteria)*

11 **Using the Office Assistant**. Cell **E17** will use the *DMIN* function to find the order for Wilson Garages with the lowest total value. Select cell **E17**, then click the **Paste Function** button. The Office Assistant dialog box may be displayed too (the Office Assistant is displayed in many dialog boxes and allows you to request help in your own words). If not, click the **Office Assistant** button, marked with a '?', in the bottom left-hand corner of the Paste Function dialog box (if nothing happens then Office Assistant has not been installed).

Take the Help with this feature option.

12 A further dialog box appears. Enter a brief description e.g. 'find the minimum value in a database' and click the **Search** button. The Office Assistant should select one or two functions for you to choose. Successful Office Assistant searches depend on your skill in finding the appropriate search terms; you can

keep trying until you narrow down the search results to the ones that you want. For example, try substituting the word 'lowest' for 'minimum' in your description and Office Assistant doesn't perform as well. You can also just type in keywords rather than a complete sentence, e.g. 'database' and 'minimum'.

13 Select **DMIN** from the list offered, close Office Assistant and complete the Paste Function dialog box.

The resulting formula in cell E17 should be *=DMIN(database,"total",criteria)*

14 Using the Format menu, format the cells B17–E17 to two decimal places.

The cells containing the functions should now display the values shown in FIGURE 5.15.

A	B	C	D	E	F	G
14007	09-Mar	1453	Wilson Garages	2654.00	464.45	3118.45
14000	10-Mar	1453	Wilson Garages	3200.00	560.00	3760.00
Order No.	Order Date	Co.Ref	Co. Name	Value	VAT	Total
			Wilson Garages			
No of Orders	Avg Value	Total Value	Total VAT	Min.Total		
3	1984.25	5952.76	1041.73	116.04		

FIGURE 5.15

15 You have now created a number of database function formulae and can select different search criteria to retrieve particular records.

Clear the search condition **Wilson Garages** from cell D14.

Enter **2413** in cell C14 as a search criterion; the values in all the formulae cells change to reflect the totals for this company's orders.

Reading across row 17, two orders are counted, their average value is £1016.50, etc.

16 **Consolidation – search criteria**. Every time the search criteria in row 14 are changed the formulae immediately recalculate the results.

Enter the following search criteria, remembering to clear previous search conditions before you do:

■ Order numbers 14005 onwards.

■ Orders with VAT amounts less than £250.

 ■ Orders totalling less than £1000 or more than £5000 (you will need to reset the criteria range to use an 'OR' condition – see Task 6).

Task 9: Using PivotTables

A **PivotTable** allows you to rearrange the columns and rows of a database and summarise the data in new ways. It is quicker and easier than using formulae or queries.

1   If necessary, open the workbook **DATABASE** and make **ORDERS** the active worksheet.

2   You will create a PivotTable that analyses the total orders placed by each customer over time.

3   Open the Data menu and select PivotTable Report. Step 1 of the PivotTable Wizard is shown. Accept the default Microsoft Excel list or database and click the Next button.

4   Step 2 of the PivotTable Wizard is shown. It confirms that the whole range of cells in the database will be used. Click the Next button.

5   Step 3 of the PivotTable Wizard is shown. It allows you to drag the various fields to form the PivotTable. Using FIGURE 5.16 as your guide do the following:

■   Drag the *Co. Name* field into the ROW area – each company name will be a new heading.

■   Drag the *Order Date* field into the COLUMN area – each date will be a column heading.

■   Drag the *Value*, *VAT* and *Total* fields into the DATA area. They will form the summarised table data. Click the Next button.

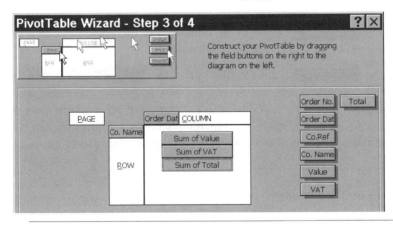

FIGURE 5.16

6 Step 4 of the PivotTable Wizard is shown. Click the ▌New Worksheet▐ button then the ▌Finish▐ button.

7 The PivotTable is created in a new worksheet; name it **PIVOTTABLE1**. It will resemble FIGURE 5.17 (first part only shown). If not, then reissue the **Data-PivotTable** command and check the steps.

To make the table more readable, format the numeric data in columns C to H to two decimal places and widen column A.

(If you get the error message *Enable Selection button on Select submenu... is not pressed in* then deselect the cells. Right click the worksheet and a menu appears. Choose **Select** followed by the **Enable Selection** option. Then try again.)

	A	B	C	D	E	F	G	H
1			Order Date					
2	Co. Name	Data	08-Mar	09-Mar	10-Mar	11-Mar	12-Mar	Grand Total
3	Goldfield Stables	Sum of Value					123.85	123.85
4		Sum of VAT					21.67	21.67
5		Sum of Total					145.52	145.52
6	Marsden Product	Sum of Value				4456.00	1652.54	6108.54
7		Sum of VAT				779.80	289.19	1068.99
8		Sum of Total				5235.80	1941.73	7177.53
9	Patel Industries	Sum of Value	1466.00		567.00			2033.00
10		Sum of VAT	256.55		99.23			355.78
11		Sum of Total	1722.55		666.23			2388.78

FIGURE 5.17

8 **Reorganising the PivotTable**. The labels ▌Co. Name▐ , ▌Data▐ and ▌Order Date▐ are shown in grey because they are buttons. Dragging them changes the order of the table data.

Try the following. The steps can be reversed if necessary using the **Edit-Undo** command.

- Drag the ▌Co. Name▐ button to the other side of the ▌Data▐ button – the table is reordered to present the data in a new way.

- Drag the ▌Co. Name▐ button to the right of the ▌Order Date▐ button.

9 **For information only**: In PivotTables you can carry out many of the tasks that you can in an ordinary worksheet, e.g. formatting, sorting, merging cell labels and calculated fields. There is also a special PivotTable Toolbar that offers many other features.

10 Close and save the workbook.

Summary of commands and functions

 Menu commands show the menu name first, followed by the command to choose from the menu, e.g. **Edit-Clear** means open the **Edit** menu and select the **Clear** command.

Menu Commands

Data-Filter-Advanced Filter	Search database using **Advanced Filter**
Data-Filter-Show All	Show all records in database
Data-Form	Use a data form
Data-PivotTable Report	Create a PivotTable from a database
Data-Sort	Sort selected cells
Data-Subtotals	Subtotal database/remove subtotals
Edit-Fill-Series	Create a data series
Edit-Undo Sort	Reverse a sort operation
Format-Cells	Format cells/cell contents
Insert-Name-Define	Define cell range as database
Tool-Options-AutoComplete	Turn **AutoComplete** on/off

Database functions

Database functions have the form:

[FUNCTION](database,"field",criteria)

'database' is the database range that you have defined.

'field' is the field name or cell reference in the database on which the function operates and must be enclosed in double quotes.

'criteria' is the criteria range that you have defined.

DAVERAGE	Average a numeric field
DCOUNT	Count number of records
DMAX	Find maximum
DMIN	Find minimum
DPRODUCT	Multiply
DSTDEV	Calculate standard deviation
DSUM	Add
DVAR	Calculate variance

Linking workbooks

What you will learn in this unit

By the end of this unit you will be able to:

- add comments
- link external ranges
- display file details
- create a folder
- add hyperlinks
- enter linking formulae
- display multiple workbooks
- open linked workbooks
- create templates
- arrange windows
- copy workbooks
- link workbooks
- search and locate workbooks
- create workspaces.

What you should know already

Before you start this unit, make sure that you can do the following:

Skill	Covered in
Creating a simple worksheet	Unit 1
Using formulae	Units 1 and 2

What you need

No previously created worksheets are required for this unit.

Introduction

This unit shows you how to link several workbooks together. Excel allows you to link workbooks together, so that you can share and exchange data between them. This has a number of advantages:

■ Although you could create several smaller worksheets within one large workbook, there are cases where separate workbooks are better. For example, it may also be more convenient for several workbooks to be created independently and combined and summarised later.

■ You can edit the linked workbooks as a group; changes made to one workbook will be reflected in the others.

■ Several linked workbooks can be open at once so that you can see the results of any changes.

A typical linking application is the departments or branches of a company. The same type of financial or numerical data is recorded for each, and they are combined into an overall summary.

You will create a set of simple profit forecasts for a group of three hotels – Greenlands, Whiteways and Blueskies – and combine them into an overall summary.

Task 1: Creating a template workbook

1   You will first create a master workbook, copy it and then customise it for each hotel.

Start Excel and open a new workbook.

2   Enter the data shown in FIGURE 6.1, using the following notes as a guide:

	A	B	C	D	E
1		Budget - First Quarter			
2					
3		Jan	Feb	Mar	Total
4	No. of Rooms				
5	No. of Days	31	28	31	
6	Occupancy Rate	0.7	0.6	0.65	
7	Ave.Rate per Room	40	40	40	
8	Total Room Revenue	0			
9	Estim. DOP - Rooms	0			
10	Estim Food Revenue	0			
11	Estim DOP - Food	0			
12					
13	Total Operating Profit	0			
14					

FIGURE 6.1

Row 4   ***No. of Rooms*** Leave this blank, as the number of rooms available will vary between hotels/months.

Row 5   The number of days in the month. Enter 31, 28 etc as shown.

Row 6   ***Occupancy Rate*** (not every available room is let). Enter as 0.7 (i.e. 70%) for Jan, 0.6 for Feb etc as shown.

Row 7 *Ave. Rate per Room* This is £40, the average charged per room per day, excluding food. Enter this for cells B5 to D5. Do not enter a £ sign.

Rows 4–7 Hold all the variables; the remaining rows are all based on formulae. Remember to begin every formula with an = sign.

Row 8 *Total Room Revenue* is the product of the first four cells, so enter the formula *=B4*B5*B6*B7* in cell B8. It will show a value of 0 at the moment until row 4 is completed.

Row 9 *Estimated DOP – Rooms* The direct operating profit or DOP is estimated as 40% of *Total Room Revenue* – cell B8. Enter the formula *=B8*0.4* in cell B9.

Row 10 The *Estimated Food Revenue* is 45% of the *Total Room Revenue*. Enter the formula *=B8*0.45* in cell B10.

Row 11 The *Estimated DOP – Food* is estimated as 45% of the *Estimated Food Revenue*. Enter the formula *=B10*0.45* in cell B11.

Row 13 *Total Operating Profit* is the operating profits for food and rooms added together, so enter the formula *=B9+B11* in cell B13.

Task 2: Filling right and formatting the worksheet

Now that we have created the data and formulae for January we need to copy them across to the other two months and to create the quarterly totals in column E.

After formatting the workbook will look like FIGURE 6.2 and will serve as a template for other workbooks.

	A	B	C	D	E	F
1			Budget - First Quarter			
2						
3		Jan	Feb	Mar	Total	
4	No. of Rooms					
5	No. of Days	31	28	31	90	
6	Occupancy Rate	0.70	0.60	0.65		
7	Ave. Rate per Room	40.00	40.00	40.00		
8	Total Room Revenue	0.00	0.00	0.00	0.00	
9	Estim. DOP - Rooms	0.00	0.00	0.00	0.00	
10	Estim Food Revenue	0.00	0.00	0.00	0.00	
11	Estim DOP - Food	0.00	0.00	0.00	0.00	
12						
13	Total Operating Profit	0.00	0.00	0.00	0.00	
14						

FIGURE 6.2

1 **Filling right**. Select the row of cells B8–D8.

Open the **Edit** menu and select **Fill** and then **Right**. The formula is copied into cells C8 and D8.

Now select the block of cells B9–D13 and repeat the fill right operation. Now all the formulae are copied for the three months.

2 We will create the totals in the *Total* column by adding across the three months.

Select cell E5 then click the **AutoSum** button (on the Standard Toolbar marked with the sigma (Σ) symbol.

Cells B5–D5 are outlined, and the correct formula *=SUM(B5:D5)* appears in the cell.

Enter the formula. The total days in the quarter (90) are displayed in cell E5.

3   Now repeat this **SUM** operation for cells E8–E11 (do not add the **Occupancy Rate** or the **Ave. Rate per Room** – these cannot sensibly be summed).

Finally do the same for cell E4. You may find that AutoSum identifies an incorrect cell range and have to correct the formula.

4   As a check that your formulae are correct, enter the figure *100* in cell B4.

Your **Total Operating Profit** should be 52,297. If not, you will need to check the formula and the data entered. Erase this entry once you have checked it.

5   Format the worksheet as shown in FIGURE 6.2.

6   We will save the workbook as a template, which will serve as a pattern for future workbooks, and create a folder to store them.

 These instructions assume that you are saving your work to a floppy disk. If not, then substitute the appropriate drive.

7   Open the **File** menu and select **Save As**. A dialog box appears. Use FIGURE 6.3 as a guide to completing it.

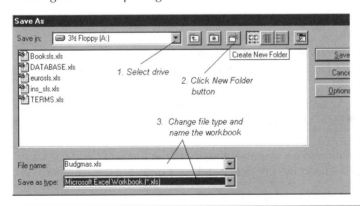

FIGURE 6.3

8   Move the mouse pointer onto the **Create New Folder** button – an identifying screen tip box will open. Click the button and a dialog box appears.

Name the new folder **HOTELS** and click **OK** . The **HOTELS** folder appears in the list of workbook files.

9   Click the down arrow on the **Save as type** box and select **Template (*.xlt)**.

Now enter the name **BUDGMAS** in the **File name** box.

10 Click the down arrow on the **Save in** box and select the drive 3¹/₂ **Floppy (A:)**.

Double click on the folder icon **Hotels** – it now appears in the **Save in** box.

11 Finally, click the **Save** button – the workbook **BUDGMAS** is saved in a template file (special extension **.XLT**) in the **HOTELS** folder. The template cannot be accidentally changed; when you amend it you are forced to save the amended version as a new file.

Task 3: Copying workbooks

You now have an empty template which can be copied to create workbooks for the three hotels.

The three hotels are called Greenlands, Whiteways and Blueskies, so the workbooks will be named **GREEN**, **WHITE** and **BLUE**. To do this we need to create three copies of the workbook, plus extra copy to hold the summary figures. There are two ways to do this: you can either use the **Save As** command to save the workbook **BUDGMAS** under different names, or you can copy and paste the cells from **BUDGMAS** into a new empty workbook. I assume that you are familiar with these techniques; the following brief notes are for guidance.

1   Open the **File** menu and select **Save As** (not **Save**) – a dialog box appears.

The **File name** box contains the current name **BUDGMAS.XLT**. Enter the new name **GREEN** and check that the folder name **Hotels** appears in the **Save in** box.

Click the down arrow on the **Save as file type** box and select **Microsoft Excel Workbook**.

Click the **Save** button.

The original template workbook **BUDGMAS** is copied under the new name **GREEN** and then closed, leaving the **GREEN** workbook displayed.

2   Now repeat this operation to create three more workbooks in the same folder – **WHITE.XLS**, **BLUE.XLS** and **SUMMARY1.XLS**.

3   **SUMMARY1** will hold an overall summary of the totals of the three other workbooks, so we need the title and cell labels only, not the data and formulae; i.e. cell ranges:

A1–E3   the titles and heading

A4–A13   the row labels

Make sure that **SUMMARY1** is the active workbook and delete the cell range B4–E13 containing the data and formulae.

We now have four copies of the original template workbook **BUDGMAS**: they are **GREEN**, **WHITE** and **BLUE** for the three hotels and **SUMMARY1**.

4   Save and close all the workbooks that remain open, using the **File-Close** option.

Task 4: Locating workbook files on disk

Folders are a useful unit of organisation; however, it is easy to forget which folder the files are stored in. The folder structure can also get quite complex, with many levels of files and subfolders within other folders. Fortunately, Excel provides a powerful search facility to locate files.

These instructions assume that you have created the workbooks mentioned in previous units and are saving your work to a floppy disk; if not, then substitute an appropriate drive or workbook.

1   Make sure that Excel is running, but close any open workbooks. If you have been saving your workbooks to a floppy disk then make sure the disk is in the disk drive.

Open the **File** menu and select **Open**. The **Open** dialog box is displayed – see FIGURE 6.4.

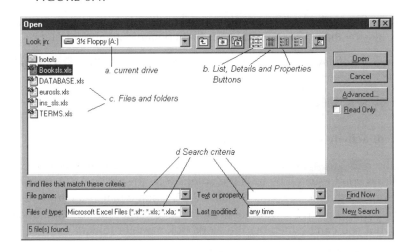

FIGURE 6.4

- The current drive and/or folder is shown in the **Look in** box – change it to 3¹/₂ **Floppy (A:)** if necessary.

- Various buttons are displayed on the right of the dialog box.

- The folders and/or workbook files on the current drive are displayed.

- The search criteria are displayed at the bottom of the dialog box.

You can search by name, contents, file type and date.

2   **More details on a file**. First click the **List** button, then select any file from the list and click the **Details** button. Full file details are given – its size, type, and date of creation or last modification.

Try this for a few other files.

3   **File properties**. Click the **Properties** button – the name of the file's creator is also given. Finally, click the **List** button.

4 **Opening a folder**. Double click the **HOTELS** folder. It opens, becoming the current folder. The five workbooks that you created in the last activity are shown – **BLUE**, **BUDGMAS**, **GREEN**, **SUMMARY1** and **WHITE**.

Click the down arrow on the **Look in** box and reselect the drive again, e.g. 3¹/₂ **Floppy (A:)**. The **Hotels** folder is closed and the files on the main drive are redisplayed.

5 **Searching by name**. Let's locate all the files with the letters 'sls' in their names.

Enter *sls* in the **File name** box and click the **Find Now** button. Three workbooks are located – **BOOKSLS**, **EUROSLS** and **INS_SLS** – and could be opened if so desired (this search will only work if they are located in the current folder).

Click the **New Search** button to redisplay the other files.

6 **Searching by file contents**. If you can't remember the file name then you can search for files by their contents, e.g. ones that contain data about holidays.

Enter the word *holiday* in the **Text or property** box and click the **Find Now** button. One workbook is located – **EUROSLS**.

Click the **New Search** button to redisplay the other files.

7 **Independent activity** – advanced searching

■ Click the **Advanced** button and a new **Advanced Find** dialog box opens; this allows you to search by multiple criteria, e.g. to specify AND and OR conditions for the file contents or name. Let's assume that you can remember generally that you have a workbook with an analysis of profits from food or rooms, but you can't remember the workbook name or folder.

■ Using FIGURE 6.5 as a guide, complete the dialog box; remember to enter the drive that you want to search in the **Look in** box, to search subfolders, and to combine the terms 'food' and 'room' with an 'OR' condition.

You will need to use the **Add to List** button to enter each search condition.

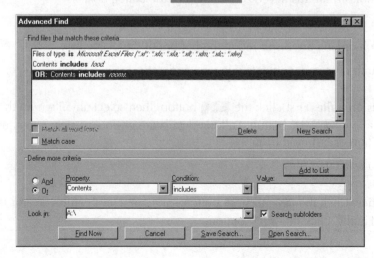

FIGURE 6.5

■ Click the **Find Now** button and the five workbooks in the **HOTELS** folder are located – **BLUE**, **BUDGMAS**, **GREEN**, **SUMMARY1** and **WHITE** (plus the **TERMS** workbook if it is located on this disk).

This advanced search could be saved and run again on a future occasion if required.

Click the **New Search** button to redisplay the other files.

 8 **The FAVORITES folder (optional)**. Excel provides two folders as an additional way of keeping track of folders. The **FAVORITES** folder provides a shortcut or link to any folder that you need to find quickly. This is most appropriate when you have a large number of folders and subfolders on a hard drive. If this is your situation then try the following.

■ List the workbooks that you have already created.

■ From the list click one, but do not open it, e.g. **BOOKSLS**.

Now click on the **Add to Favorites** button – this is next to the **List** button – see FIGURE 6.4.

Now click the **Look in Favorites** button – the **BOOKSLS** workbook is listed in the **FAVORITES** folder and can be opened from there.

 9 **The MY DOCUMENTS folder** (for information only). The **MY DOCUMENTS** folder is provided for you to store current work. It is stored in the main or root folder on the hard drive. The first time that you use the Open or Save As commands in an Excel session it is offered as the default folder. If you share your PC with others this folder can soon get very full if it is used indiscriminately.

10 Cancel the Open dialog box and then exit from Excel.

Task 5: Opening and displaying multiple workbooks

1 **Opening multiple workbooks**. We need to open the four workbooks **GREEN**, **WHITE**, **BLUE** and **SUMMARY1**. As Excel lists the four last documents used, the workbooks are probably listed at the bottom of the File menu. Open each one in turn. If a workbook is not listed at the bottom of the File menu then use the File-Open option.

2 **Handling multiple workbooks**. There are several ways of arranging the four workbook windows on screen using the Window-Arrange menu.

Open the Window menu – notice that all the open workbooks are listed. Take the Tiled option.

The workbooks are arranged side by side on the screen – see FIGURE 6.6.

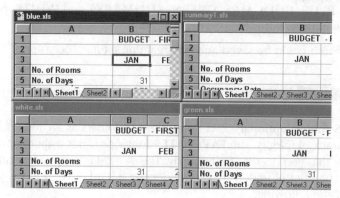

FIGURE 6.6

It doesn't matter if your workbooks are in a different order from that shown in FIGURE 6.6. Click on each workbook in turn – each one that you click on becomes the active workbook.

3 Now activate each workbook in turn and enter the number of rooms for each hotel in row 4 as follows:

	Jan	Feb	Mar
GREEN	55	48	55
WHITE	72	66	75
BLUE	92	88	95

Task 6: Linking workbooks with formulae

1 We can now use the workbook **SUMMARY1** to link the workbooks using external references. We want to create a formula that adds together the contents of, for example, cell B4 for the three hotels and places them in cell B4 in the summary workbook.

Click cell B4 in the **SUMMARY1** workbook; this activates both the worksheet and the cell.

2 Type the formula *=WHITE.XLS!B4+BLUE.XLS!B4+GREEN.XLS!B4* in this cell.

This linking formula contains external references to three different workbooks. (Each external reference must consist of the full name of the external workbook, plus the cell reference, both separated by an exclamation mark. If more than one sheet in a workbook is used then the sheet name should be included as well.)

Click the tick box in the Formula Bar and the number of rooms for January at the three hotels is placed in cell B4 in workbook **SUMMARY1**. The total should be 219 – if not, check the data you have entered – see Task 5 – or the cell references in the formula above.

An error message indicates that the formula is wrongly typed. If the formula is correct then Excel will add brackets around the three external cell references and include the sheet names.

3 **Copying linking formulae**. Maximise the **SUMMARY1** workbook if necessary.

Select cells B4–D4, then use Edit-Fill-Right to copy the formula to cells C4 and D4. The linking formulae, with their external references, are copied to the two other cells.

Now select the cell range B4–B11 and select the Edit-Fill-Down options.

Next select the cell range B5–D11 and select the Edit-Fill-Right options.

Now select cell range B6–D7 and press the *Delete* key to clear their contents.

(Rows 6 and 7 – the **Occupancy Rate** and **Ave. Rate per room** cannot meaningfully be summed and should be left blank.)

The **SUMMARY1** workbook should now resemble FIGURE 6.7 – check the totals.

	A	B	C	D	E
1		BUDGET - FIRST QUARTER			
2					
3		JAN	FEB	MAR	TOTAL
4	No. of Rooms	219	202	225	
5	No. of Days	93	84	93	
6	Occupancy Rate				
7	Av Rate per Room				
8	Total Room Revenue	190092	135744	181350	
9	Estim DOP - Rooms	76036.8	54297.6	72540	
10	Estim Food Revenue	85541.4	61084.8	81607.5	
11	Estim DOP- Food	38493.63	27488.16	36723.38	
12					
13	Total Operating Profit				
14					

FIGURE 6.7

4 Format the cells to include commas, using the Format-Cells command or the comma button; the columns may need to be widened to accommodate this new number format. (A row of hash symbols – ##### – indicates a cell that is too narrow.)

5 **Independent activity**. Create the totals in row 13 and column E using the Edit-Fill command.

Check your totals with FIGURE 6.8. (Remember that row 13 is the sum of rows 9 and 11.)

	A	B	C	D	E
1			Budget - First Quarter		
2					
3		Jan	Feb	Mar	Total
4	No. of Rooms	219.00	202.00	225.00	646.00
5	No. of Days	93.00	84.00	93.00	270.00
6	Occupancy Rate				-
7	Ave. Rate per Room				-
8	Total Room Revenue	190,092.00	135,744.00	181,350.00	507,186.00
9	Estim. DOP - Rooms	76,036.80	54,297.60	72,540.00	202,874.40
10	Estim Food Revenue	85,541.40	61,084.80	81,607.50	228,233.70
11	Estim DOP - Food	38,493.63	27,488.16	36,723.38	102,705.17
12					
13	Total Operating Profit	114,530.43	81,785.76	109,263.38	305,579.57
14					

FIGURE 6.8

6   Use the **Window-Arrange** command to view the four workbooks in a tiled display again.

Changes made to any three of the supporting workbooks – **WHITE**, **GREEN** or **BLUE** – will be reflected in the summary or dependent workbook **SUMMARY1**.

Try the two following 'what if?' experiments:

■   At the moment the group's *Total Operating Profit* for January is £114,530.43. The target is £120,000.

Amend the *Ave. Rate per Room* for January (B7) to 42 for each of the three workbooks in turn.

Now activate the **SUMMARY1** workbook and look at cell B13 – the target is now achieved.

■   The occupancy rate for March for Greenways Hotel drops to 60% (amend cell D6 on the **GREEN** workbook to *0.6*) – will the quarter's total operating profit still exceed £305,000 for the three hotels?

Now look at cell E13 in the **SUMMARY1** workbook – the target is still achieved.

Task 7: Saving linked workbooks as a workspace

Linked workbooks need to be saved in the correct sequence, otherwise the links between them may be lost. The dependent workbook **SUMMARY1** must be closed and saved last – after the three supporting workbooks, **WHITE**, **GREEN** and **BLUE**. If you close the dependent workbook first there is a danger that any external formula may be lost. To make it easier, all four linked workbooks can be saved and opened again under one group name, called a *workspace* in Excel. As well as making it easier to save and retrieve, a workspace will also preserve the arrangement of the workbooks on screen so that you can continue where you left off last time.

1   Return to the tiled layout for the four workbooks.

2   Open the **File** menu and choose **Save Workspace**. A menu box appears, offering you the default name **RESUME.XLW**.

Type the workspace name *Group Profits* and check the drive – I assume that you will want to save it to floppy disk, so make sure that the **Drives** box shows that the correct folder name, **Hotels**, is selected. Click the `Save` button.

The four workbooks are saved under the workspace name **GROUP PROFITS** – the extension **.XLW** is automatically added. If the workbooks have changed you will be prompted to save each one – do so.

It will take some time to save all four workbook files to a floppy disk under the workspace name **GROUP PROFITS**, as all the links must be saved too.

3   Now exit Excel, saving the workbooks if prompted to do so.

4   Start Excel again. It is not necessary for all the linked workbooks to be open for the links to operate.

Open the **File** menu – at the bottom of the menu the workspace file **Group Profits** is listed, but so are the individual workbooks as well – they can still be opened as separate files.

To make this point open one of the supporting workbooks, **WHITE.XLS**.

Amend the *Occupancy Rate* for February to *0.66*

Save and close the workbook.

5   Now open the **SUMMARY1** workbook; a message appears, asking you if you wish to update links to another workbook. Click the **Yes** button and observe the totals for February.

They are updated to reflect the changes made in the supporting workbook, **WHITE.XLS**.

6   Save and close the workbook **SUMMARY1.XLS**.

Task 8: Linking external ranges

In the previous activities we linked workbooks using formulae with external references – references to cells in other workbooks.

Another way of achieving the same result is to use the **Paste Link** command. This ensures that when the original workbook changes the copy changes also. To demonstrate this we will copy some of the totals from the **SUMMARY1** workbook to a new workbook, **SUMMARY2**.

1   Open the workbook **SUMMARY1** again. Enlarge it if necessary so that all the cells are visible. If a message appears, asking you if you wish to update links to another document, click the **Yes** button.

2   Open the **File** menu and select **New**.

Double click the workbook icon. A new blank workbook is displayed.

Open the **File** menu and select **Save As**.

When the **Save As** dialog box appears, type the workbook name **SUMMARY2** and check the **Save in** box – ensure that you are saving it in the **HOTELS** folder along with the other related workbooks.

3   Click **Save** – the workbook is now saved as **SUMMARY2**.

4   Now open the **Window** menu and select **Arrange** followed by **Cascade**.

The edges of both workbooks are visible. Click the edge of **SUMMARY1** so that it is on top.

We are going to copy rows 9, 11 and 13, which hold the summaries of the operating profits for the quarter.

5   Select the row of cells A9–E9.

Open the **Edit** menu and select **Copy**.

Now click the workbook **SUMMARY2** to select it (or use the **Window** menu).

Select cell A3.

Open the **Edit** menu and select **Paste Special** – a dialog box appears – click the
Paste Link button. The four cells are copied from **SUMMARY1** to
SUMMARY2 – note the linking formula in the Formula Bar at the top of the
worksheet.

6   Now repeat the above **Paste Link** operations twice more to copy rows 11 and 13
    from the **SUMMARY1** workbook to rows 4 and 5 respectively of the
    SUMMARY2 workbook.

7   Now, using FIGURE 6.9 as your guide, format the **SUMMARY2** workbook.

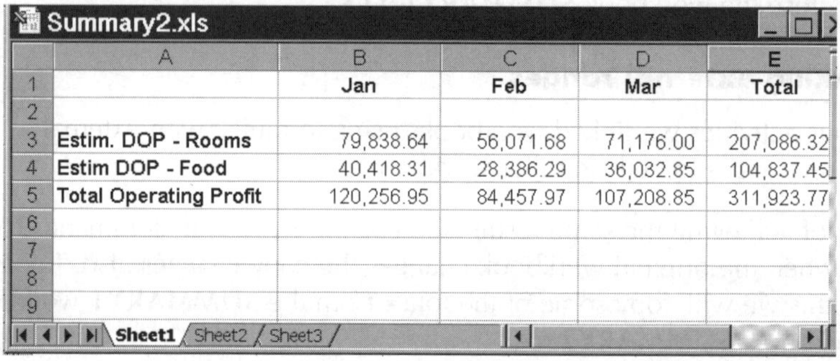

Summary2.xls				
A	B	C	D	E
1	Jan	Feb	Mar	Total
2				
3 Estim. DOP - Rooms	79,838.64	56,071.68	71,176.00	207,086.32
4 Estim DOP - Food	40,418.31	28,386.29	36,032.85	104,837.45
5 Total Operating Profit	120,256.95	84,457.97	107,208.85	311,923.77
6				
7				
8				
9				

Sheet1 / Sheet2 / Sheet3 /

FIGURE 6.9

8   Now save and close the two workbooks **SUMMARY1** and **SUMMARY2**.

9   Let's test the links now; open the workbook **GREEN.XLS** and amend the number
    of rooms for March to 80.

    Save and close the workbook.

10 Now open the workbook **SUMMARY1**. A message appears, asking you if you
    wish to update links to another document. Click the **Yes** button and note down
    the grand total in cell E13. The figure is updated to reflect the changes you have
    just made to the supporting workbook, **GREEN.XLS**.

11 Now open the workbook **SUMMARY2** and note the grand total in cell E13 – it
    has automatically changed to reflect the updates that have taken place in
    SUMMARY1.

Task 9: Adding comments and hyperlinks

Once the worksheet relationships start to become complex it is a good idea to add
comments to as reminders to yourself (or co-workers). You are already familiar
with hyperlinks in the Help text. Clicking on coloured text or an icon will
automatically 'jump' you to another location in Help. They can also be used in Excel
to link you to another cell (either in the same or another workbook) or to a different

type of document entirely. You can also link to another file or files on a network, including the Internet. In this activity we will link cells in two workbooks.

1   **Adding comments to a workbook**. Make **SUMMARY2** the active workbook.

Open the File menu and select Properties. Make sure that the Summary tab is selected. The Summary dialog box allows you to add a title, subject and brief summary of the workbook. Do this. If you select Save preview picture then you will be able to preview the file before opening it using the Open dialog box. This facility is useful for large files that take a long time to load.

2   **Adding comments to cells**. Activate the **SUMMARY1** workbook and select cell B13.

Right click the cell and a popup menu appears. Select the Insert Comment option.

Add a suitable comment in the box, e.g. *Based on operating profits for rooms and food at the Greenlands, Whiteways and Blue Skies Hotels*.

Click the cell to deselect the comment box.

To hide the comment open the View menu and select Comments. The mark in the cell corner indicates a hidden comment that can be viewed whenever the mouse pointer rests on the cell (to delete a comment right click the cell and choose Delete from the popup menu).

3   **Creating hyperlinks**. Select cell A13 of the **SUMMARY1** workbook.

Open the Insert menu and select Hyperlink. A dialog box appears – see FIGURE 6.10.

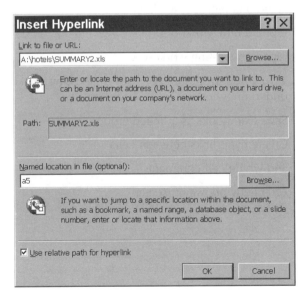

FIGURE 6.10

We wish to link row 13 in **SUMMARY1** with its equivalent row in the **SUMMARY2** workbook, row 5. This will allow us to go quickly from one to the other. Using FIGURE 6.10 as a guide, proceed as follows:

- Click the **Browse** button next to the **Link to file or URL** box.

The **Link to File** dialog box opens. Select the workbook **SUMMARY2** from the list and click **OK** .

Now type the cell reference A5 in the **Named location in file** box. Click **OK** .

4 The text in cell A13 of **SUMMARY1** is now coloured blue, indicating a hyperlink.

Click the cell and you are taken to the equivalent row in the **SUMMARY2** workbook.

Create a hyperlink in cell A5 to return you to the starting cell.

5 Save and close both workbooks.

Summary of commands

Menu commands show the menu name first, followed by the command to choose from the menu, e.g. **Edit-Clear** means open the **Edit** menu and select the **Clear** command.

Menu Commands

Edit-Fill-Right/Down	Copy selected cells to selected right-hand/lower columns
Edit-Paste Special-Paste Link	Link copied cells in two workbooks
File-Properties-Summary	Add comment to a workbook
File-New	Open a new workbook
File-Open	Open an existing workbook
File-Save As	Save a new workbook, or copy an existing workbook under a new name
File-Save Workspace	Save workbooks as a linked group
Insert-Hyperlink	Create hyperlinks between cells
View-Comments	Show/hide cell comments
Window-Arrange	Arrange windows on screen

Using tables

What you will learn in this unit

By the end of this unit you will be able to:

- create data series
- create lookup tables
- name cells
- create one-input tables
- use the **PMT** function
- create two-input tables.

What you should know already

Before you start this unit, make sure that you can do the following.

Skill	Covered in
Creating a simple worksheet	Unit 1
Using formulae	Units 1 and 2

What you need

No previously created worksheets are required for this unit.

Introduction

Excel allows you to build data tables of various types. You will be experimenting with two types.

- **Input tables** can be created to hold data based on variables and formulae held in the worksheet, e.g. FIGURE 7.1 shows a table of mortgage repayments based on different interest rates.

- **Lookup tables** work the other way round; the table is already created and you use a formula to look up values in it. FIGURE 7.8 shows a table to look up the commission payable on orders of different values.

Task 1: One-input tables

You have seen in previous tasks how you can perform 'what if?' analysis by substituting different values in formulae. If you want to test a range of values it is quicker to hold them in a data table rather than change them one by one.

1 We will set up a one-input table first, which sets up a range of values for one variable – the mortgage interest rate.

Open a new workbook and create the worksheet shown in FIGURE 7.1 as follows:

	A	B	C
1		Mortgage Repayments Schedule	
2			
3	Interest Rate:	8%	
4	Repayment Term:	240.00	(Enter term in months)
5	Amount Borrowed:	50000.00	
6			
7	Possible	Repayment per month	
8	Interest Rates		
9	7.00%		
10	7.25%		
11	7.50%		
12	7.75%		
13	8.00%		
14	8.25%		
15	8.50%		
16	8.75%		
17	9.00%		

FIGURE 7.1

Widen the columns and centre and embolden the title and cell labels as shown.

Use a data series to produce the range of percentages in column A as follows.

Begin by entering **7.00%** in cell A9 – the percentage sign must be entered.

2 Open the **Edit** menu and select **Fill** followed by **Series**.

The **Fill** dialog box is displayed. Enter the values as follows, using FIGURE 7.2 as a guide.

Click **Columns** in the **Series** in box.

Enter the step value of 0.25% in the **Step value** box.

Enter the stop value of 9.00% in the Stop value box.

Finally, click **OK** .

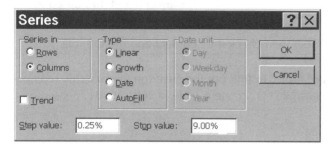

FIGURE 7.2

3 Enter the interest rate as **8%** in cell B3 – the percentage sign must be entered.

Enter the repayment term as **240** in cell B4 (240 months = 20 years).

Enter the amount borrowed as **50000** in cell B5.

Centre these three values in their cells and format cells B4 and B5 to number format **0.00**, using the **Format-Cells-Number** command.

Select cell B8 and open the **Format** menu. Select the **Cells** option followed by the **Border** tab to outline the cell. This will emphasise where the result is to appear. The worksheet should now resemble FIGURE 7.1.

Save the workbook as **MORTGAGE**.

4 **Naming cells**. Instead of referring to cells by their row and column references, we can name them and use their names in formulae and functions. Names can be shorter and easier to remember than cell references.

Select cell **B3**, then open the **Insert** menu and select **Name** followed by **Define**. A dialog box appears with a default name already inserted.

Simply overtype with the name **RATE**, then click **OK** .

Similarly, give cell B4 the name **TERM**, and give cell B5 the name **AMOUNT**

We will use these cell names in the formula that follows.

 The Name box to the left of the Formula Bar keeps track of all the names used in the workbook (a name can be used by any sheet in the workbook). If you wish you can enter cell names in a formula by selecting them from the name box.

5 **Setting up the *PMT* formula**. We will use the **PMT** function to calculate the monthly repayments.

The Help facility will tell you more about this function; it is used to calculate payments made at regular intervals at fixed interest rates, such as mortgages.

The syntax is **=PMT(interest,term,principal)**, where **interest** is the interest rate, **term** is the repayment term and **principal** is the amount borrowed.

Select cell B8 and enter the formula **=PMT(rate/12,term,-amount)**

111

RATE is divided by 12 as we want the monthly repayment and the minus sign will convert the amount to a positive rather than a negative number.

The monthly repayment of 418.22 is now displayed in cell B8, based on the values entered in cells B3 to B5.

 If your formula is not correct then check the cell data and the formula.

6 **Creating the one-input table**. To find out the effect on the monthly repayments if the interest rate changes, we can create a table in cells A9–B17, based on the interest rates.

Select cell range A8–B17.

Open the **Data** menu and select the **Table** option; a dialog box appears.

Select the **Column input cell** box and enter the cell reference B3. Click **OK**.

You have defined the cell range A8–B17 as an input table and cell B3 as the cell where data will be entered – the varying interest rate.

7 The repayment figure is shown in cell B8 as before. However, different monthly repayments, based on different rates of interest, are now shown in cells B9–B17, and can be compared with cell B8.

Format the table entries to two decimal places, using the **Format-Cells-Number** command.

Compare your table with FIGURE 7.3.

	A	B	C
1		Mortgage Repayments Schedule	
2			
3	Interest Rate:	8.00%	
4	Repayment Term:	240	(Enter term in months)
5	Amount Borrowed:	50000.00	
6			
7	Possible	Repayment per month	
8	Interest Rates	418.22	
9	7.00%	387.65	
10	7.25%	395.19	
11	7.50%	402.80	
12	7.75%	410.47	
13	8.00%	418.22	
14	8.25%	426.03	
15	8.50%	433.91	
16	8.75%	441.86	
17	9.00%	449.86	

FIGURE 7.3

8 **Consolidation**. Amend the interest rate in cell B3 to **9%**, and the amount borrowed in cell B5 to **70000**.

The new repayment is shown in cell B8 – 629.81 per month. The other repayments in cells B9–B17 are also recalculated.

■ At what interest rate would you start to pay more than £600 per month?

9 **Adding further formulae to the one-input table**.

You can create another table on the same worksheet, showing the effect of changing interest rates on another variable – the total cost of the loan. This is the monthly repayment multiplied by the term of the loan – see FIGURE 7.4.

Put the title *Total Repaid* in cell C7.

Enter the formula *=B8*TERM* in cell C8. Format to two decimal places and insert commas.

Now select the cell range A8–C17 (the new table range).

Open the Data menu and select the Table option – a dialog box is displayed.

Select the Column input cell box and enter the cell reference B3. Click **OK** .

You have created a second table in column C, showing the total amount repaid over the period of the loan.

10 Format the table values C8–C17 to two decimal places and insert commas.

Select Cells followed by the Border option to outline cell C8. This will emphasise where the result is to appear. The worksheet will now resemble FIGURE 7.4.

	A	B	C
1		Mortgage Repayments Schedule	
2			
3	Interest Rate:	9.00%	
4	Repayment Term:	240	(Enter term in months)
5	Amount Borrowed:	70000.00	
6			
7	Possible	Repayment per month	Total Repaid
8	Interest Rates	£629.81	151,153.96
9	7.00%	542.71	130,250.22
10	7.25%	553.26	132,783.17
11	7.50%	563.92	135,339.66
12	7.75%	574.66	137,919.36
13	8.00%	585.51	140,521.93
14	8.25%	596.45	143,147.03
15	8.50%	607.48	145,794.30
16	8.75%	618.60	148,463.40
17	9.00%	629.81	151,153.96

FIGURE 7.4

11 **Consolidation**. Alter the interest rate to 8.5%, the term to 360, and the amount borrowed to 65,000.

- What is the total amount repaid?

- What is the monthly repayment?

12 Save and close the workbook.

Task 2: Two-input tables

The one-input data table used in the previous task is one-dimensional; it can only show table values based on one input variable – the interest rate. Although we built a second table to show the total amount repaid, it was still based on this same variable.

In this task we will use a two-input table to calculate salespersons' monthly commissions. It uses a two-dimensional table or matrix; one variable – monthly sales – is in column B, the other, the commission rate, is in row 5. We will create a table that will use both variables to calculate commission, e.g. £50,000 sales at 5% commission rate.

1 Start a new workbook and enter the information shown in FIGURE 7.5. Format it as shown.

	A	B	C	D	E	F
1		Monthly Commission Table				
2						
3			Commission Rates			
4						
5			5%	6%	7%	8%
6		50000				
7		60000				
8	Monthly Sales	70000				
9		80000				
10		90000				
11						

FIGURE 7.5

  If you wish, use the **Edit-Fill-Series** command to create the percentages in row 5 and the sales figures in column B (see Task 1).
Arrows may be selected from the Drawing Toolbar at the bottom of the window.

2 The commission earned is the commission rate multiplied by the monthly sales. The formula must be entered where the row and column variables intersect in cell B5.

Select cell B5 and enter the formula *=B3*B4*

You may wonder why cells B3 and B4 have been chosen. In fact you won't be entering any values in these cells. This is because in this example the two-input table provides the full range of values we are interested in (unlike the previous example of the one-input table). However, the table needs to use two cells when it calculates its values. We have nominated B3 and B4, but any empty cells outside the table could be used.

3 Now select the cells that the table will fill, i.e. cell range B5–F10.

Open the **Data** menu and select **Table** – the **Table** dialog box appears.

Enter B3 in the **Row input cell** box and B4 in the **Column input cell** box – see FIGURE 7.6.

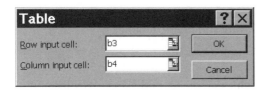

FIGURE 7.6

Click **OK**.

The commission table is calculated, equivalent to 25 separate calculations – see FIGURE 7.7. This makes the table a valuable tool.

Save the workbook as **COMMISSION.XLS**.

	A	B	C	D	E	F
1		Monthly Commission Table				
2						
3			Commission Rates			
4						
5		0	5%	6%	7%	8%
6		50000	2500	3000	3500	4000
7		60000	3000	3600	4200	4800
8	Monthly Sales	70000	3500	4200	4900	5600
9		80000	4000	4800	5600	6400
10		90000	4500	5400	6300	7200
11						
12	Enter No of Months:					

FIGURE 7.7

4   **Consolidation**. We will adapt the table so that we can calculate the commission for a number of months.

Enter the label in cell A12 – see FIGURE 7.7.

Now format cell B12 with a border as shown.

Amend the table formula in cell B5 to include cell B12 in its product, i.e.
=B3*B4*B12

Notice that when you amend a formula coloured borders identify the constituent cells.

Now enter **6** in cell B12 – the table is recalculated, showing the commission earned for 6 months at various rates of commission.

5   Save and close the workbook.

More information on tables

To move or delete a table
Select the whole table and then select **Cut** or **Clear** from the **Edit** menu (or press the *Delete* key).

To modify a table
Select the whole table and choose the **Table** command from the **Data** menu.

To extend the range of a table
Enter the extra values then proceed as for modifying a table.

Task 3: Lookup tables

The table values in the previous activities are generated using variables and a formula. The user inputs a number of variables, e.g. mortgage amount or term, and then the Table command builds a table based around one or more of them. A lookup table involves the reverse procedure; the table is already created and you look up a value in it. Lookup tables can be used to hold various types of fixed information that can be 'looked up' from another part of the worksheet, e.g. rates of pay, credit ratings or addresses.

Look at FIGURE 7.8.

	A	B	C	D	E	F	G
1				Order Discount Look-up			
2							
3	Cash Order						
4	Order Value:						
5	Discount						
6	Net Value			Order Value	Cash	Credit	
7				0	5%	0%	
8	Credit Order			500	10%	5%	
9	Order Value:			1000	15%	10%	
10	Discount			5000	20%	15%	
11	Net Value			10000	25%	20%	
12							

FIGURE 7.8

In columns D–F is a table to look up customer discounts, based on the order value – from £0 to £10,000 – and the type of order (cash or credit). As the discount rates in the table do not follow any obvious numerical sequence, using a formula to generate them would be difficult.

You can use two lookup functions to get data from a table, **HLOOKUP** and **VLOOKUP**:

HLOOKUP is used if the lookup values are arranged horizontally in a row.

The syntax is **=HLOOKUP(x,range,index)**

VLOOKUP is used if the lookup values are arranged vertically in a column, as they are in the table shown above (the more usual arrangement).

The syntax is **=VLOOKUP(x,range,index)**

- **x** is the value that you want to look up; it can be entered as text, a number, or a cell reference.

- **range** is the range of cells forming the table.

- **index** tells you which column or row to look in.

Applying this to FIGURE 7.8:

- *x* is cell B4, where the value of the order will be entered

- *range* is the cell range D7–F11 holding the lookup table

- *index* is columns E and F, where the lookup values are held.

 For the **LOOKUP** function to work the first column of the lookup table must consist of entries that are used to look up items of data in immediately adjacent columns. These entries must be unique and in ascending order.

1   Open a new workbook. Create the data as shown in FIGURE 7.8 and enter an order value of **600** in cell B4.

2   In cell B5 enter the formula *=VLOOKUP(B4,D7:F11,2)* Enter it in lower-case – if it is correct it is converted to upper-case.

The formula means 'look up the value in cell B4, from the table in cell range D7 to F11, in the second column of the table'. The lookup function searches the first column of compare values – column D – until it reaches a number equal to or higher than 600 (cell D9). It then goes back a row if it is higher (to cell D8), then goes to the second column (E) and looks up the discount of 10% (in cell E8). For this reason the values in the first column of the lookup table – column D – must be in ascending sequence.

3   The discount is displayed as **0.1**. Use the **Format-Cells** command followed by the **Number** tab. From the dialog box select **Percentage** from the category list, then select **0** from the **Decimal places** box and click **OK**.

The discount is now displayed as 10% in cell B5.

4   The formula to calculate the net value of the order (i.e. order value minus discount) can now be entered in cell B6.

Enter the formula *=B4-(B4*B5)* in this cell. The order value minus discount is shown in cell B6 – the value should be 540.

Try entering some other order values in cell B4 to test this.

5   **Consolidation**. Now repeat these steps and enter another *VLOOKUP* formula in cell B10 to calculate the discount on credit orders.

 You will need to modify the cell references, i.e. the cell reference for the lookup value (B9) and the column number (3) where the lookup values are held.

Enter a credit order value of 10,000 in cell B9. Check that the discount is 20% and the net order value is 8,000.

6   Save the workbook as **DISCOUNT** and close it.

Summary of commands and functions

 Menu commands show the menu name first, followed by the command to choose from the menu, e.g. **Edit-Clear** means open the **Edit** menu and select the **Clear** command.

Menu Commands

Data-Table	Create a table from selected cells
Edit-Fill-Series	Create a data series
Format-Cells-Border	Add cell border
Format-Cells-Number	Format numeric data in cells
Insert-Name-Define	Name cell/cell range

Functions

Functions require you to supply information for their operations. These are called arguments, e.g. **SUM(range)** requires the argument cell range to be added. Arguments must be enclosed in brackets.

Optional arguments are shown in the lists that follow in square brackets – [ ]. These brackets are for your guidance only and should *not* be typed.

Function arguments are separated by commas. The commas *must* be typed.

HLOOKUP(x,range,index)

– look up a value in a table where the values are displayed horizontally.

VLOOKUP(x,range,index)

– look up values in a table where the values are displayed vertically.

- *x* is the value that you want to look up; it can be entered as text, a number or a cell reference.
- *range* is the range of cells forming the table.
- *index* tells you which column or row to look in.

PMT(interest,term,principal,[,fv,type])

– gives the repayments required for a loan amount (principal) based on the interest rate and the term. Options are to enter future value and whether payment is made at the end of the period (*type=0*, the default) or at the beginning (*type=1*).

Excel analysis tools

What you will learn in this unit

By the end of this unit you will be able to:

- use the Goal Seek function
- use the Report Manager
- use the Scenario Manager
- print scenarios
- use the Solver.

What you should know already

Before you start this unit, make sure that you can do the following:

Skill	Covered in
Creating a simple worksheet	Unit 1
Using formulae	Units 1 and 2

What you need

To complete this unit you will need:

- The workbooks **BLUE** created in Unit 6 and **TERMS** created in Unit 1.

Introduction

In the previous unit you used input and lookup tables to compare values for one or more variables. In the next few tasks you will look at the special-purpose analysis tools Goal Seek and Solver. These two tools also automate the process of repeated 'what if?' trials.

First open the Tools menu and check that you have Goal Seek and Solver listed as options. If not then select the Add-Ins option on the Tools menu. If they are listed then you can open them now. If not then they will need to be installed, using a set of Excel or Office 97 disks/CD-ROM.

Task 1: Goal Seek

The 'what if?' abilities of Excel allow us to try out alternative values for a given situation. The first and simplest is Goal Seek; often you want to know what value a variable needs to be for a formula to equal a particular value. Goal Seek keeps changing the value of the variable until the formula achieves the target value.

1   Open the workbook **BLUE.XLS**. It is in the folder **HOTELS**. You will recall from Unit 6 that it calculates the quarterly operating profit for Blueskies Hotel.

We want to find out what occupancy rate for February would achieve a total operating profit of £40,000 for this month. We could keep amending the occupancy rate cell (C6) and observe the effects, or create a table, but Goal Seek is easier.

2   Open the Tools menu and select Goal Seek – a dialog box appears.

If necessary, move the box so that you can see column C – see FIGURE 8.1. Alternatively you can use the Collapse button, located next to the data entry boxes on the dialog box, to reduce its size.

	A	B	C	D	E	F	
1			Budget - First Quarter				
2							
3		Jan	Feb	Goal Seek		?✕	
4	No. of Rooms	92	88	Set cell:	C13		
5	No. of Days	31	28				
6	Occupancy Rate	0.70	0.60	To value:	40000		
7	Ave. Rate per Room	42.00	40.00	By changing cell:	C6		
8	Total Room Revenue	83848.80	59136.00				
9	Estim. DOP - Rooms	33539.52	23654.40	OK	Cancel		
10	Estim Food Revenue	37731.96	26611.20				
11	Estim DOP - Food	16979.38	11975.04	15505.43	44459.85	Collapse Box	
12							
13	Total Operating Profit	50518.90	35629.44	46133.43	132281.77		
14							

FIGURE 8.1

3   Complete the box as shown in FIGURE 8.1, i.e.:

Set cell: *C13*

To value: *40000*

By changing cell: *C6*

Make a note of the present value of cell C6 and click   **OK** .

A further Goal Seek Status dialog box appears reporting the solution. The value of cell C6 is changed to *0.67* – the occupancy rate needed to reach the £40,000 goal.

4   Click the   **Cancel**   button now; this restores the previous value for cell C6 and all the dependent cells.

If you click   **OK**   by accident then select Undo from the Edit menu.

5   Now try the following **Goal Seek**: what average rate per room for January would achieve a total room revenue of £100,000?

6   **Consolidation (optional)**. Open the workbook **TERMS.XLS** created in Unit 1 and make **SPRING TERM** the active sheet. Scroll to week 9.

How large a bank loan would you need in week 9 to achieve a closing balance of £150 in week 9?

7   Close the workbooks **BLUE** and **TERMS** without saving any changes.

8   Notes on **Goal Seek**

The **Goal Seek Status** dialog box displays two extra buttons:

- **Pause** – allows you to pause during goal seeking

- **Step** – allows you to continue one step at a time.

Goal seeking will only work if the cell whose value you set contains a value, not a formula. The cell whose value you set must be related by a formula to the cell whose target value you are changing.

You can also goal seek by dragging data points in charts – see Unit 4, Task 7.

Task 2: Solver

The **Goal Seek** tool used in the previous activity can substitute various values for a variable in a formula. It cannot determine what the 'best' ones are for your purpose.

Solver, as its name suggests, can solve certain types of problem. It will juggle with multiple values for variables and find the combination producing the optimum or target result, e.g. it can determine the most profitable mix of products, schedule staff to minimise the wages bill, or allocate working capital to its most profitable use.

Solver allows you to specify up to 200 variables; it also allows you to put constraints on variables by specifying the limits that they can take (e.g. minimum and maximum values for a machine's output or for a working week).

Solver is Excel's most powerful analysis tool and uses complex mathematical methods to solve equations and arrive at its optimum or target values. It tries out various input values for the formulae and observes not only the corresponding outputs, but also their rate of change. Each trial is known as an iteration. The results of a previous iteration are analysed and used to work out the next set of trial inputs. **Solver** converges on the optimum or target value by repeated iterations. This method can be much quicker than **Goal Seek**, tables or manual calculations, especially if you are working with multiple variables and constraints.

However, **Solver** poses certain problems for the user.

- There is a limited range of problems that can or need to be solved in this way.

- For complex problems there may be more than one solution; Solver may provide the best given the range of values that you have specified, but it may not be the best overall. You may need to run Solver more than once with different ranges of values.

- To use Solver effectively, then, you must thoroughly understand the nature of the problem that you are trying to solve, otherwise Solver will either fail to work altogether or give you misleading results.

We will first set up a typical Solver problem – see FIGURE 8.2.

	A	B	C	D	E	F	G	H	I	J
1		Staff Scheduling - New Branch								
2					Mon	Tue	Wed	Thu	Fri	Sat
3	Rota	Rest Days	Employees							
4			per Rota							
5	1	Mon, Tue	0		0	0	1	1	1	1
6	2	Tue, Wed	0		1	0	0	1	1	1
7	3	Wed, Thu	0		1	1	0	0	1	1
8	4	Thu, Fri	0		1	1	1	0	0	1
9	5	Fri, Sat	0		1	1	1	1	0	0
10										
11		Staff Allocated per Day:			0	0	0	0	0	0
12										
13		Staff Needed per Day:			14	14	16	17	20	22
14										
15		Av. Pay per Day (£)	30							
16		Wages Bill per Week:	0							

FIGURE 8.2

Your company wishes to open a new branch and needs to work out the optimum staff allocation throughout the working week of Monday to Saturday. The numbers of staff needed each day are already known and are shown in row 13; more staff are needed towards the weekend as the branch gets busier.

Each staff member must get two consecutive rest days; these are staggered to produce five different rotas, which are entered in columns A and B. So staff on rota 1 get Monday and Tuesday off, staff on rota 2 get Tuesday and Wednesday off etc. In columns E to J this is represented as a 0 for a rest day and 1 for a working day.

You need to:

- calculate how many staff need to be on each rota (cells C5–C9)

- ensure that the staff allocated each day (cells E11–J11) cover the number of staff needed (cells E13–J13).

A problem will be that to achieve full staffing levels on busy days we may need to employ more staff then we need on other days.

1 First, let's build the basic worksheet; start a new workbook and create the title and cell labels. Format them as shown in FIGURE 8.2, then enter the figures shown.

Format cell ranges C5–C9 and E11–J11 as whole numbers, i.e. no decimal places (all staff are full time, so no fractional amounts are allowed).

2 Apply the following formulae:

- Cell C10 is the sum of cells C5–C9 (this gives the total days worked by all staff). Format to a whole number.

- Cell C16 is the product of cells C10 and C15 (i.e. the weekly wages bill is the total days worked multiplied by the average rate per day).

- To calculate the number of staff working on each day you need to multiply column C – the number of staff working the rota – by column E – which indicates whether that rota is working on that day. Hence for Monday cell C5 is multiplied by cell E5 for rota 1, then added to C6 multiplied by E6 for rota 2, etc.

Enter the following formula to calculate staff working on Monday in cell E11:

=($C5*E5)+($C6*E6)+($C7*E7)+($C8*E8)+($C9*E9)

Use the Edit-Fill-Right command to copy this formula to cells F11–J11.

The $ sign in the formula ensures that column C is an absolute reference and is copied unchanged into any new formulae. Absolute references are explained in Unit 2, Task 10. Column E is a relative reference and gets adjusted to F, G, H etc when the formula is copied to rows F, G, H, I and J (this combination of fixed and relative references is called a mixed reference or address).

3 Save the workbook as **SCHEDULE**.

4 Open the Tools menu and select Solver. If Solver does not start then it will need to be installed, using a set of Excel 97 or Office 97 disks/CD-ROM.

The Solver Parameters dialog box appears – FIGURE 8.3 shows the completed parameters.

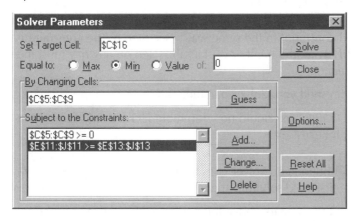

FIGURE 8.3

We wish to minimise the wages bill; complete the first part of the dialog box as follows, using FIGURE 8.3 as a guide. (Solver converts the cell references to absolute references.)

Set Target Cell: Enter *C16*

Equal To buttons: Make sure that Min is selected and the Value of box is set to 0.

5 Click the By Changing Cells box and enter *C5:C9* (we want to vary the cells containing the number of employees per rota to minimise the wages bill).

6   We must apply two constraints now:

■   the number of staff per day must be >0 (i.e. not a negative number), and

■   the number of staff allocated on any day must meet or exceed the demand.

Click the **Add** button and a new dialog box appears – **Add Constraint**.

Add the following constraints using FIGURE 8.4 as a guide.

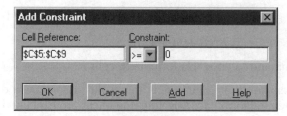

FIGURE 8.4

Insert the cell references *C5:C9* in the **Cell Reference** box.

Change the relationship to **>=** in the middle box.

Finally click the **Constraint** box and insert 0.

Click **OK** and you are returned to the **Solver Parameters** dialog box. The constraint is shown: *$C$5:$C$9>=0* (**Solver** converts the cell references to absolute references).

If you have made an error then click either the **Change** button to edit it or the **Delete** button and start again.

7   Add the second constraint in the same way – see Step 6. The constraint is *E11:J11>=E13:J13* (i.e. the number of staff allocated on any day must meet or exceed the demand).

You have now finished your **Solver** parameters.

The completed dialog box should now resemble FIGURE 8.3. Cancel the **Add Constraint** box if necessary.

8   Click the **Solve** button and **Solver** goes through a complex series of iterations until it finds the first valid solution. The worksheet figures are modified to show it.

A **Results** dialog box appears; move this aside so that you can see the solution. Solver has worked out:

■   how many staff need to be on each rota (cells C5–C9) in order to ensure...

■   ...that the staff allocated (cells E11–J11) cover...

■   ...the numbers of staff needed (cells C13–J13).

You will notice that for one day – Monday – you are overstaffed by three people.

9 The **Solver Results** dialog box offers you the option of keeping the **Solver** solution or restoring the original values.

Click the **Restore Original Values** button then click **OK**.

10 **Consolidation**. Call up **Solver** again and add a third constraint – that the staff allocated for Monday should not exceed those needed. The constraint is therefore that *E11<=14*.

Enter this and run **Solver** again – you will notice that the overstaffing has merely been transferred to another part of the week. Given the staffing needs at this branch and the rota system there is no way round this.

11 **Solver reports**. If the **Solver Results** dialog box is still on the screen you may wish to generate a **Solver** report at this stage.

Click the **Answer** option in the **Reports** box then click **OK**.

The report is generated and stored as a separate worksheet – Answer Report 1 – in the workbook. Change to this worksheet. It summarises all the solver input data:

■ the value of the target cell C16

■ the values reached for the adjustable cells C5:C9

■ how well the constraint were met:

Binding means that the cell value equals the constraint value

Not Binding means that the constraint was met but the values were not equal

Not Satisfied means that the constraint value was not reached.

12 Save the workbook and close it – the report and the latest set of **Solver** settings are saved too.

Task 3: Consolidation of Goal Seek and Solver

To reinforce the previous activities we will use **Goal Seek** and **Solver** on a new example. FIGURE 8.5 shows the profits that a company makes from three products A, B and C.

	A	B	C	D	E
1					
2		No of	Profit	Profit	
3		Units	per Unit		
4					
5	Product A	100	46	4600	
6	Product B	100	53	5300	
7	Product C	100	69	6900	
8	Totals	300		16800	

FIGURE 8.5

1 Open a new workbook and create the simple worksheet shown in FIGURE 8.5.

Format all the numbers to whole numbers.

Total columns B and D down, and multiply the values in rows 5 to 7 across to calculate the profit figures shown in column D.

Save the workbook as **PROFITS**.

 2 **Goal Seek** (refer to Task 1 for guidance if necessary).

Find out how many of product B we need to make to raise total profits from £16,800 to £20,000.

 Appendix 7 shows the correct entries for the Goal Seek dialog box.

Click the Cancel button on the dialog box so as not to save the Goal Seek variables.

3 **Solver**. We wish to make a profit of £20,000 for the three products subject to the following three constraints, which are based on production capacity and customer demand:

- The maximum number we can make of Product A is 50.

- We must make at least 40 each of Products B and C.

- Overall production can rise to a maximum of 350.

Enter these constraints into Solver and run it.

 Refer back to Task 2 if necessary – Appendix 8 shows the correct Solver parameters to enter.

4 When the Solver Results dialog box is displayed, click the Save Scenario button.

Save the scenario as **PROFIT1**, then click OK.

You are returned to the Solver Results dialog box.

Click the Restore Original Values option then click OK.

5 We will now change the above constraints and save the Solver results as a second scenario. Repeat Steps 3 and 4, changing the first constraint – the maximum number we can make of product A is raised to 60.

Save the second scenario as **PROFIT2** and restore the original values.

6 Now save the workbook – the most recent Solver settings are saved too.

7 Carry straight on with the next task.

Task 4: Using Scenario Manager

Scenario Manager allows you to save different combinations of variables as named scenarios and run and print them later. In the previous task you saved Solver values as scenarios, but you can equally well use Scenario Manager with Goal Seek or manually generated variables. Scenario Manager will let you store as many different scenarios as you wish; you can then view them, change them and print reports showing alternative scenarios.

1   **Running different scenarios**

Open the Tools menu and select Scenarios. A dialog box appears; move it to one side so that you can see the values.

Select the **PROFIT1** scenario and click the **Show** button.

The first Solver solution is applied to the worksheet and the cell values change.

Select the **PROFIT2** scenario and click the **Show** button – the second Solver solution is applied.

Close the Scenario Manager dialog box – the values remain assigned to the cells.

2   **Printing scenarios**

■   Open the View menu and select Report Manager.

The Report Manager dialog box appears – click the **Add** button.

■   The Add Report dialog box appears – see FIGURE 8.6.

Enter the Report Name as *PROFITS*.

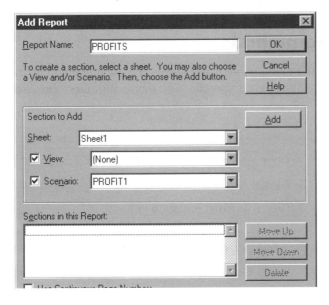

FIGURE 8.6

■   Move the screen pointer to the Section to Add section.

Click the down arrow on the Scenario box.

Select the scenario **PROFIT1**.

Click the **Add** button.

- Click the down arrow on the Scenario box again.

  Select the scenario **PROFIT2**.

  Click the Add button again.

- Two scenarios are added to the report – click the OK button.

The Report Manager dialog box appears now – check that your printer is turned on and connected.

3   Click the Print button and the report will print; it contains the printout of both versions of the worksheet, showing the two different sets of values generated by Solver in the previous activity.

4   **Printing using Report Manager (information only)**. Report Manager is useful when you have many different scenarios set up, perhaps for different sheets in your workbook, and wish to print a copy of each. Because Report Manager allows you to print them all at once it can save a lot of time. It is an add-in program, so you will need to check that it is an option on the View menu. If not then it will need to be installed, using a set of Excel 97 or Office 97 disks/CD-ROM.

5   Save the workbook and close it.

Summary of commands

 Menu commands show the menu name first, followed by the command to choose from the menu, e.g. Edit-Clear means open the Edit menu and select the Clear command.

Menu Commands

Edit-Fill-Right	Copy selected cells into right-hand columns
Format-Cells-Number	Format numeric values
Insert-Name-Define	Create a name, e.g. for a cell
Tools-Goal Seek	Change values of selected cell(s) so that the formula achieves a specified target value
Tools-Add-Ins	Install Goal Seek or Solver
Tools-Scenarios	Run Scenario Manager
Tools-Solver	Use Solver
View-Report Manager	Create a printed report

Using Excel functions

What you will learn in this unit

By the end of this unit you will be able to:

- use **AutoFill**
- calculate averages
- display the current date
- perform date calculations
- use forecasting
- use function help
- use the Office Assistant
- use **Paste Function**
- use functions
- find future values
- use the *IF* function
- find a maximum value
- find a minimum value
- calculate the standard deviation
- find straight line depreciation
- use trend analysis.

What you should know already

Before you start this unit, make sure that you can do the following:

Skill	Covered in
Creating a simple worksheet	Unit 1
Using formulae	Units 1 and 2

What you need

To complete this unit you will need:

- The workbook **BOOKSLS** created in Unit 4.

Introduction

It is beyond the scope of these units to deal with all of the Excel functions; many, such as trigonometric and engineering functions, have little general business application. To use others, such as financial functions, you need some specialist background in the subject to understand the significance of the results. You have already used some functions, such as the simpler maths functions in Unit 1 and the database functions in Unit 5. The first task reviews the various types of functions. In Task 2 you will use some widely used functions in worksheets. Other useful functions are listed at the end of this unit.

Task 1: Review of Excel functions

Notes on using functions

- Functions are ready-made formulae that perform useful calculations.

- They produce their results in the cells in which they are entered.

- Every function must start with the = sign.

- Functions can be entered in lower- or upper-case. It is a good idea to type functions in lower-case – if Excel converts it to upper-case then you know that it is typed correctly.

- Normally a function contains no spaces.

- Functions can form part of a formula – or another function.

- Functions require you to supply information for their operations, called *arguments*; e.g. **SUM(range)** requires the *cell range* argument to be added.

- Arguments are enclosed in round brackets – ( ) these *must* be typed. Optional arguments are shown in the lists that follow in square brackets: [ ]. These brackets are for your guidance only and should *not* be typed.

- Two or more arguments are separated by commas. The commas *must* be typed.

- You can either type the function yourself or use **Paste Function**, which lets you choose the function from a list and paste it into a cell.

1 **Types of function**. Open a new workbook.

   Open the Insert menu and select the Function option (or use the **Paste Function** button on the Standard Toolbar, marked 'fx').

The Paste Function dialog box appears, listing 11 categories of functions – see FIGURE 9.1. If the Office Assistant dialog box opens then read the note in Step 3 below – you may decide to use it as supplementary guidance in this activity.

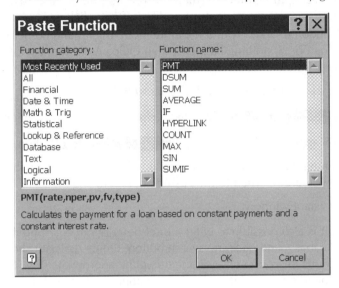

FIGURE 9.1

Click the first Function category – Most Recently Used.

In the right-hand box – Function name – are some of the functions you have used so far. Click each function in turn – the syntax of the function and a brief explanation are given at the bottom of the dialog box.

Click the second function category – All. All the functions are listed alphabetically in the right-hand box.

2   Now carry on reviewing the other function categories in the same way:

■ **Financial** functions are used in the next task.

■ **Date & Time** functions are used in the next task.

■ **Math & Trig** (mathematical and trigonometric) functions calculate square roots, cosines etc as well as the simpler functions such as *SUM*.

■ **Statistical** functions, such as average and standard deviation, are used in the next task.

■ **Lookup & Reference** functions were used in Unit 7 for lookup tables.

■ **Database** functions carry out operations on database records only, e.g. summing or averaging selected records – see Unit 5, Task 8. Some are listed in the next section.

■ **Text** functions manipulate strings of text, e.g. finding the length or converting to upper-case. A few are listed at the end of this unit.

■ **Logical** functions test for the truth of certain conditions. The *IF* function is used in the next task.

- **Information** functions test and report on cell references and contents, e.g. blanks or errors; a few are listed at the end of this unit.

3 **Help on functions – using the Office Assistant**. When you start **Paste Function** the **Office Assistant** dialog box may be displayed too. If not, click the **Office Assistant** button (marked with a '?') in the bottom left-hand corner of the **Paste Function** dialog box. If nothing happens, then Office Assistant has not been installed – go to Step 4.

   - Click the **Financial** function category, then select **FV**.

   - Click on the **Office Assistant** and take the **Help with this feature** option.

   A further dialog box appears; click the **Help on selected function** button.

   - Help text explaining the FV (future value) function is displayed. Close the Help window – you are returned to the **Paste Function** dialog box.

   Close the Office Assistant window.

In the Office Assistant it is also possible to enter a brief description, e.g. 'find the minimum value in a database' and click the search button. Office Assistant should select one or two functions for you to choose, including the appropriate one, **DMIN**. Successful searches depend on your skill in finding the appropriate search terms; you can keep trying until you narrow down the search results to the ones that you want. For example, try substituting the word 'lowest' for 'minimum' in your description and Office Assistant does not perform as well. You can also just type in keywords rather than a complete sentence, e.g. 'database' and 'minimum'.

4 Click the **Cancel** button on the **Paste Function** dialog box. You are returned to the blank worksheet.

Task 2: Using Excel functions

In the previous activity we reviewed the major categories of functions. We shall try some of them out now, bearing in mind that these only represent a fraction of those available. Below are listed some of the functions that we will be using.

- **Date and time functions**

Date and time functions display dates and times, or can calculate the time elapsed between two dates or times; e.g. the function **NOW( )** displays the current date and time – see Step 2.

- **Financial functions**

Financial functions calculate such things as investments, repayments and depreciation. It is essential that the term of the investment, repayment etc is in the same time units as the interest rate; e.g. if you are investing £5000 over six months at an annual interest rate of 10%, then the interest rate must be converted to a monthly rate too.

FV(interest,payments,amount[pv,type])

Gives the future value of an investment, based on a fixed interest rate, the number of payments and the amount of the payment. The payments are assumed to be equal throughout. Options are to enter present value (**pv**) and whether payment is made at the end of the period (**type=0**, the default) or at the beginning (**type=1**).

NPV(interest,range)

Gives the net present value of an investment based on a fixed interest rate and series of cash flows within a given range.

PMT(interest,term,principal,[,fv,type])

Gives the repayments required for a loan amount (principal) based on the interest rate and the term. Options are to enter future value and whether payment is made at the end of the period (**type=0**, the default) or at the beginning (**type=1**).

 We have already used **PMT( )** in Unit 7, Task 1.

SLN(cost,salvage,life)

Calculates the depreciation of an asset using the straight-line method, based on the initial cost, its salvage value at the end of its life and the time period over which it is depreciated.

■ **Statistical functions and database functions**

AVERAGE(range)

– gives the average value of a range of cells.

MIN(range)

– gives the minimum value in a range of cells.

MAX(range)

– gives the maximum value of a range of cells.

STDEV(range)

– gives the standard deviation of a range of cells – how much they vary from the average.

 DAVERAGE, DMIN, DMAX, DSTDEV and **DSUM** are special database functions; they work in the same way as their statistical equivalents, but can be used with search criteria – see Unit 5, Task 8.

 Excel 97 also offers the functions **AVERAGEA, MINA, MAXA** and **STDEVA**. These work the in the same way as the normal functions **AVERAGE, MIN, MAX** and **STDEV** but include in their calculations cells that contain text and the logical values true and false.

■ Logical functions

IF(condition,true result,false result)

Tests a condition to see whether it is true or false, then takes one action for a true result and another for a false result (see Step 7).

AND(condition1,condition2,...)

Tests for all conditions being true and returns a logical True value if they are.

OR(condition1,condition2,...)

Tests for at least one condition being true and returns a logical True value if so.

1 We will now use some of these functions in the following worksheet (FIGURE 9.2).

	A	B	C	D	E	F
1	Share Analysis					
2						
3	Date	Alpha	Beta	Gamma	Changes	Share
4		Tours	Tours	Tours	in Value	Performance
5	01-Sep	19.44	50.88	123.54		
6	02-Sep	19.44	51.32	122.88		
7	03-Sep	20.65	51.36	124.55		
8	04-Sep	20.30	52.01	125.56		
9	05-Sep	19.25	52.64	125.95		
10	08-Sep	21.00	53.24	125.54		
11	09-Sep	21.35	54.25	124.54		
12	10-Sep	21.47	55.34	123.87		
13	11-Sep	20.83	55.00	127.28		
14	12-Sep	20.50	53.89	124.55		
15						
16	Hi Val					
17	Lo Val					
18	Av Val					
19	St Dev					
20						

FIGURE 9.2

This monitors the performance of the shares of three travel companies over a two-week period (weekends excluded).

2 **Displaying the current date**. Open a new workbook. Select cell E1 and enter the formula *=NOW( )*.

If a row of hash symbols (###) appears, widen the column.

Format it to date format if necessary using the **Format-Cells-Number** command.

Enter the rest of the worksheet data. Format the cell range B5–D19 to two decimal places.

3 Rows 16–18 will contain respectively the maximum, minimum and average value of the shares over the two weeks. Row 19 will show the standard deviation – the extent to which share prices have fluctuated from the average.

In cell B16 enter the function *=MAX(B5:B14)*

In cell B17 enter the function *=MIN(B5:B14)*

4 Similarly, apply the **AVERAGE** function to cell B18 and apply the **STDEV** function to cell B19.

5 Use **Edit-Fill-Right** to copy these functions to columns C and D.

6 Finally, columns E and F are used to calculate how the three sets of shares have changed in value over the two weeks.

Add the share values for the three companies for 1-Sep, i.e. add cell range B5–D5 and place the result in cell E5.

Similarly, add the cell range for 12-Sep, B14–D14 and place the value in E14. The combined value of the shares has grown between the two dates. Your worksheet will now resemble FIGURE 9.3.

	A	B	C	D	E	F
1		Share Analysis			27-Dec-96	
2						
3	Date	Alpha	Beta	Gamma	Changes	Share
4		Tours	Tours	Tours	in Value	Performance
5	1-Sep	19.44	50.88	123.54	193.85	
6	2-Sep	19.44	51.32	122.88		
7	3-Sep	20.65	51.36	124.55		
8	4-Sep	20.30	52.01	125.56		
9	5-Sep	19.25	52.64	125.95		
10	8-Sep	21.00	53.24	125.54		
11	9-Sep	21.35	54.25	124.54		
12	10-Sep	21.47	55.34	123.87		
13	11-Sep	20.83	55.00	127.28		
14	12-Sep	20.50	53.89	124.55	198.94	
15						
16	Hi Val	21.47	55.34	127.28		
17	Lo Val	19.25	50.88	122.88		
18	Av Val	20.42	52.99	124.83		
19	St Dev	0.81	1.60	1.29		

FIGURE 9.3

7   We will now monitor whether the shares have shown an overall increase or decrease. We will use the logical function **IF( )** so that if the share values increase then a 'share increase' message is displayed; if not, a 'share decrease' message is displayed.

Activate cell F14 and enter the formula:

=IF(E14>E5,"share increase","share decrease")

Test the function by amending the value of cell B14 to **14.50**.

The message in cell F14 will change to 'share decrease' as the **IF** condition becomes false. Use the **Edit-Undo** command to restore the original cell value.

The **IF** function does allow us to test for a third possibility - that the share value remains the same. To do this we would have to create an Excel procedure using Visual Basic. An example of such a procedure is given in Unit 15, Task 2, Step 4.

8   **Date calculations**. Dates can be added, subtracted and used in calculations. To make this point we will calculate the time in days between the opening and closing dates.

In cell G14 enter the label **Time in Days**.

In cell H14 enter the formula **=A14-A5**

The result is 11 – the number of days. You may need to format the cell to a whole number – see Step 2.

9   Save the workbook as **SHARES.XLS** and close it.

10 **Consolidation**. Now open a new blank workbook and try out the following financial functions:

■ **Future value**: You are going to save £1000 a year at 10% interest for five years.

Enter the following in a blank cell: *=FV(10%,5,-1000)*

The result is the value of your investment after five years – £6,105.10.

■ **Straight line depreciation**: You have bought a PC for £1000 and estimate that in four years it will be worth £300. We will use **Paste Function**.

First select a blank cell in the worksheet.

Open the **Insert** menu and select **Function** – the **Paste Function** dialog box appears.

Select **Financial** from the **Function category** box and **SLN** from the **Function name** box – you may have to scroll down to find it.

Click the **OK** button – the second **Paste Function** dialog box appears.

Enter the arguments as shown in FIGURE 9.4. Notice that as each box is selected **Paste Function** explains what you need to enter. It also tells you what the formula result will be.

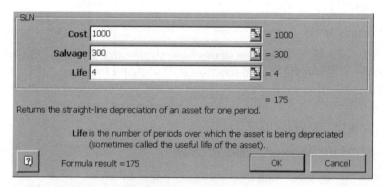

FIGURE 9.4

Finally click the **OK** button on the dialog box. The result is the annual amount of depreciation – £175.00.

11 Close the workbook without saving.

Task 3: Forecast and Trend functions

The statistical functions **FORECAST** and **TREND** allow you to predict future results based on past data. They are valuable tools in predicting many business trends, including share prices, sales figures and stockholding needs.

1   Open the workbook **BOOKSLS** and make **SHEET1** the active sheet. It records book sales and revenue for January to May. We will forecast June sales using the **FORECAST** function. First, however, we must convert the months in column A to numbers in order for the function to work – see FIGURE 9.5.

	A	B	C	D	E	F
1		Book Sales · Current Year				
2						
3	Month	No. Sold	Revenue	Advertising	as % of Revenue	
4	1	850	2011	300	15%	
5	2	1010	3155	425	13%	
6	3	1175	3550	500	14%	
7	4	1430	4356	750	17%	
8	5	1710	5150	800	16%	
9						
10						

FIGURE 9.5

Type **6** in cell A9.

Now select cell B9.

2 Open the **Insert** menu and select **Function** (or use the **Paste Function** button on the Standard Toolbar, marked 'fx') – the **Paste Function** dialog box appears.

Select **Statistical** from the **Function category** box and **FORECAST** from the **Function name** box.

Click the **OK** button – the second **Paste Function** dialog box appears.

Enter the arguments as shown in FIGURE 9.6. Notice that as each box is selected **Paste Function** explains what you need to enter.

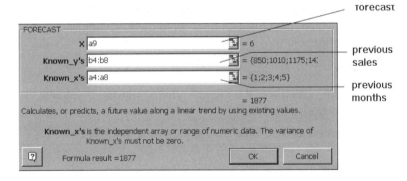

FIGURE 9.6

Finally, click the **OK** button on the dialog box. The result shows that the sales forecast is 1877 for month 6 – based on a linear trend.

3 Next we will find out how fast the cost of advertising will continue to rise, using the **TREND** function. We can use **AutoFill** to calculate it quickly.

Select cell range D4–D8.

Move the mouse pointer onto the **AutoFill** handle – the small square in the bottom right-hand corner of the selected cell range.

Hold down the right mouse button and drag down a few cells – see FIGURE 9.7 – notice that the linear trend figures are shown for each cell as you do this.

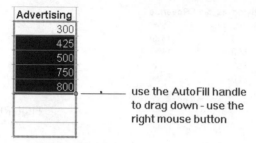

use the AutoFill handle to drag down - use the right mouse button

FIGURE 9.7

Release the mouse button and a menu appears – select either **Linear Trend** or **Growth Trend** and the trend for advertising expenditure is calculated. Use **Edit-Undo** to undo the trend calculation if necessary.

You can also project figures by adding a trendline to a column chart. This is simply a matter of clicking the first column, opening the **Insert** menu and selecting the **Trendline** option.

4   Save and close the workbook.

Task 4: Independent activity

Use the **Paste Function** dialog box (and the Office Assistant button too if necessary) to find out which functions can be used in the following situations. The answers are given in Appendix 9.

1   **Financial functions.**

   (a)   Which function calculates the interest rate for a given investment amount for a given period?

   (b)   Which function calculates the interest rate on a loan?

2   **Math & Trig functions.**

   (a)   Which function rounds a number up or down?

   (b)   Which function subtotals a list?

3   **Statistical functions.**

   (a)   Which function counts blank cells?

   (b)   Which function calculates normal distribution?

4   **Text functions.**

   (a)   Which function replaces a text string with another?

   (b)   Which function removes spaces from a text string?

   (c)   Which function converts text to upper- or lower-case?

5 **Information functions**.

(a) Which function tests for the type of data in a cell?

(b) Which function tests for a cell being blank or containing an error message?

Some additional functions (for others see Task 1)

Functions require you to supply information for their operations. These are called arguments – e.g. **SUM(range)** requires the argument cell range, to be added. Arguments must be enclosed in brackets.

Optional arguments are shown in the list that follows in square brackets – [ ]. These brackets are for your guidance only and should not be typed.

Function arguments are separated by commas. The commas must be typed.

Information functions

COLUMNS(range) Counts the number of columns in a specified range

ISBLANK(value), **ISNUMBER(value)**, **ISTEXT(value)**. **IS** functions check the type of value in a cell and report TRUE or FALSE accordingly, depending on whether the cell is blank, text etc.

Text functions

EXACT(string1,string2) Compares two text strings. Reports TRUE if they are the same or FALSE if they differ.

LEN(string) Counts the number of characters in a text string.

Protecting and checking workbooks

What you will learn in this unit

By the end of this unit you will be able to:

- use the Auditing Toolbar
- highlight changes
- trace errors
- view formulae
- apply passwords
- protect cells
- protect worksheets
- protect workbooks
- validate data entry
- audit a worksheet.

What you should know already

Before you start this unit, make sure that you can do the following:

Skill	Covered in
Creating a simple worksheet	Unit 1
Using formulae	Units 1 and 2

What you need

To complete this unit you will need:

- The workbooks **BUDGMAS**, **GREEN**, **WHITE**, **BLUE**, **SUMMARY1** and **SUMMARY2**, created in Unit 6.

- The workbook **DATABASE** created in Unit 5.

If these are not available then any workbooks containing formulae will do.

Task 1: Protecting worksheets and workbooks

Excel offers various levels of protection. You can protect a worksheet or a workbook from being opened; this is vital if the whole document is confidential. You can also protect a workbook or a worksheet from being changed; this is important if it contains sensitive data or formulae which must not be deleted, amended or overwritten. Similar protection is available for individual ranges of cells, as well as for charts and macro sheets.

1 **Protecting a workbook**. Open the workbook **SUMMARY2** (in the folder **HOTELS**). It contains profit forecasts that we might want to keep confidential.

If a message appears saying, 'The workbook you opened contains automatic links...' then click the **Yes** button.

Open the File menu and select Save As.

When the dialog box appears click the **Options** button. Various types of security are offered. Make the following entries:

Always create backup: Leave this option blank. Clicking it will create a backup copy of the old version of your workbook every time that you save it.

Password to open: Enter **JMUIR** as the password. The password will be invisible on the screen, hidden by a row of asterisks. Entering a password in this box prevents the document from being opened unless the password is entered first. A password may be up to 15 characters long – numbers, letters, spaces or symbols.

Warning: If you forget the password you cannot open the workbook; you must also remember to match the case – upper or lower – that you use.

Password to modify: Enter the password **JMUIR** again. Entering a password in this box prevents you from opening, saving or making any changes to the document unless you know the password. If you do not know it the changed document must be saved as a new document under a new name. This is useful for protecting documents from being overwritten.

Read-only recommended: Leave this box blank – selecting this box will prompt (but not compel) users to open the worksheet as read-only. This alerts users if a document should not be changed unless necessary.

Finally click **OK**. You will be prompted to re-enter both passwords to confirm them.

Now click **Save** in the main **Save As** dialog box. You will be asked if you wish to replace the original **SUMMARY2** workbook – click the **Yes** button.

2   Now close the **SUMMARY2** workbook and then open it again. Enter the password *JMUIR* when prompted to do so.

Now change the heading in cell E1 from **Total** to **Totals** – you can do this as the write protection password lets you do so.

To remove or change the passwords you must first open the workbook as we have just done, then use the File-Save As-Options command to remove or change them. These levels of protection are not available for individual worksheets – only for the whole workbook.

3   Save and close the workbook.

4   **Protecting a worksheet**. Open the workspace file **GROUP PROFITS**, which is in the folder **HOTELS**. If a message appears saying, 'The workbook you opened contains automatic links...' then click the **Yes** button.

The worksheet **SUMMARY1** uses external reference formulae in order to extract data from its three supporting worksheets, **BLUE**, **GREEN** and **WHITE**. Once established the formulae should be protected from any amendment.

Click on **SUMMARY1** to activate it. If necessary, use the **Window-Arrange** command to restore the tiled display.

Open the **Format** menu and select the **Cells** option – the **Format Cells** dialog box appears. There are six sub-menus, each selected by clicking a tab.

Click the **Protection** tab and make sure that the **Locked** option is selected (do not select the second **Hidden** option – this hides the formulae).

Finally, click **OK** to return to the workbook **SUMMARY1**.

5   **Activating sheet protection**. Open the **Tools** menu then select **Protection** followed by **Protect Sheet**.

Check that the **Contents** option is selected – this ensures that none of the cells can be altered (the other two options, **Objects** and **Scenarios**, do not apply to **SUMMARY1** and can be deselected if you wish).

We won't bother with a password in this instance. Click the **OK** option to return to the workbook.

Now try to edit any cell in the **SUMMARY1** workbook – a message box informs you that the cell is locked. (To unprotect a worksheet select **Tools-Protection** followed by **Unprotect Sheet**.)

6   **Protecting cells**. Sometimes we do not need to protect the whole workbook or worksheet, only individual cells.

Activate the workbook **BLUE.XLS** and click the **Maximize** button.

Cells B4–D7 contain numeric data that need to remain amendable. The data in the remaining rows are all based on formulae that need protecting from alteration (this is standard practice, as a complex model may be destroyed by accidentally keying data into formulae cells).

First select cells B4–D7 – the range of cells to be unprotected.

Open the **Format** menu and select the **Cells** option – the **Format Cells** dialog box appears.

Click the **Protection** tab and click the **Locked** option box to deselect it.

Finally click **OK** to return to the workbook **BLUE**.

7   Now repeat the **Tools-Protection-Protect Sheet** command as in Step 5 to protect the whole worksheet.

Check that cells B4–D7 are unprotected by attempting to alter them. You will find that it is possible. Experiment if you wish, but restore the original values.

Now try to amend a cell containing a formula – a message informs you that the cell is locked.

Finally, restore the worksheet to its previous size.

8   **Consolidation**. Repeat Steps 5–7 to protect the workbooks **GREEN.XLS** and **WHITE.XLS** in a similar way.

Restore the worksheets to their previous size.

9   **Protecting a workbook**. Steps 1 and 2 protected a workbook from being either opened or changed. A lower level of protection is also possible, allowing you to prevent new worksheets being added or existing ones being moved.

Activate the workbook **WHITE**.

Open the **Tools** menu and select **Protection** followed by **Protect Workbook**.

The **Protect Workbook** dialog box appears – complete it as follows.

Do not enter a password.

Make sure the **Structure** box is selected – this prevents the sheets in the workbook being moved, hidden or renamed.

Make sure that the **Windows** box is selected – this prevents changes to the whole workbook – windows cannot be moved or resized.

Finally click **OK** to return to the workbook **WHITE**.

10 Now open the **Edit** menu – you will see that the **Delete Sheet** and **Move** or **Copy Sheet** options are unavailable.

Now open the **Insert** menu – the **Worksheet** option is also unavailable.

Notice also that the **Minimize** and **Maximize** buttons and other window sizing or closing features are hidden on the window for the **WHITE** workbook.

11 Finally open the **Tools** menu and select **Protection** followed by **Unprotect Workbook**. The workbook is now unprotected. However, the individual worksheet – **SHEET1** in the workbook **WHITE** – still retains its protection – see Step 8.

12 Finally, save and close all the workbooks.

Task 2: Checking your worksheet

The worksheets that you have created have been fairly small, occupying no more than a couple of screens. As worksheets get larger and more complex there is a danger of design and data entry errors creeping in which can invalidate the whole model. These are surprisingly common in business. Excel has a number of tools to help you check your worksheet, some of which we have already used, e.g.:

 Naming cells: naming cells and groups of cells makes them easier to refer to and makes the worksheet more readable – see Unit 7, Task 1.

 Worksheet protection: prevents crucial data and formulae being overwritten or deleted – see Task 1.

 View document: the **Print Preview** option allows you to get an overview of the whole document – see Unit 2, Task 2.

In this task we will use the Excel auditing facilities, which allow you to trace formulae relationships in order to trace errors.

 1 **Using the Auditing Toolbar**. Open the workbook **BUDGMAS**, which is in the **HOTELS** folder. This is the template model for all three hotels in the group – see Unit 6. (If you use another workbook then you will have to change the cell references.)

Open the **Tools** menu and select **Auditing** followed by the **Show Auditing Toolbar** option.

The Auditing Toolbar appears – see FIGURE 10.1. It can be dragged to a new position if necessary.

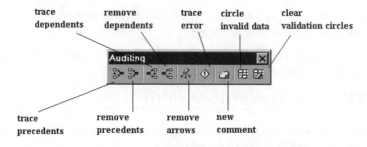

FIGURE 10.1

2 Select cell D13, then click the **Trace Precedents** button. Arrows make clear the cells on which the formula in cell D13 is built.

Select cell E13 and click the ▌Trace Precedents▐ button again.

Finally, click the ▌Remove all Arrows▐ button.

3 Now use the ▌Trace Dependents▐ button to find the dependents for cells B6 and B8. Arrows will show the chain of cells which directly and indirectly depend on these buttons.

 Click the ▌Remove Dependents▐ button to remove the last arrow.

4 **Tracing errors**. Select cell B5 and enter the letter **A**. Immediately the worksheet shows a series of value errors – obviously an arithmetic formula cannot use non-numeric data, i.e. a letter.

Select cell E13 and then the ▌Trace Error▐ button – the source of the error is shown.

Restore the value of cell B5 to *31* again to remove the errors.

5 Remove all the arrows and click the ▌Close▐ box on the Auditing Toolbar.

6 **Viewing formulae**. Let's check which cells contain formulae.

Open the Tools menu and select Options.

A dialog box appears – make sure that the ▌View▐ tab is selected.

Click the ▌Formulae▐ button in the Window Options section followed by ▌OK▐. All the formulae are displayed in the worksheet cells and can be checked and/or printed.

Repeat this operation to deselect the formula option and restore the worksheet to its usual appearance.

 7 **Highlighting changes**. You can keep track of any changes to a workbook that you or other users may have made. As this feature is primarily designed to record changes made by users sharing workbooks on a network you must also turn on two other features – workbook sharing and change history – even though your PC may be standalone.

Shared workbooks cannot use all the Excel commands and features and you should consult Excel Help before using it.

8 Open the Tools menu and select Track Changes followed by Highlight Changes.

9 A dialog box appears. Make sure the Track changes while editing box is selected, select the Highlight changes on screen option, and then click ▌OK▐.

10 If prompted, save the workbook.

11 Make a few changes to the worksheet – the cells are outlined. When the mouse pointer is positioned over the cell a comment box details the change.

When you print a worksheet that has changes highlighted, the highlighting also appears on the printed page. To disable change highlighting, repeat Steps 8 and 9 and deselect the **Track changes while editing** option. This will also remove it from shared use.

12 Close the **BUDGMAS** workbook without saving it.

 ## Task 3: Validating workbook data

We have seen how workbooks and worksheets can be protected and audited to an extent, but it is also vital to check that data entered into worksheets is initially correct.

When computerised information systems are designed much effort is devoted to data validation – it is essential to control what users are allowed to input, otherwise careless or inexperienced users could wreak havoc. FIGURE 10.2 shows a summary of customer orders; there are various types of check we could carry out when a new order is added.

	A	B	C	D	E
1	Order No.	Order Date	Co.Ref	Co. Name	Value
2	14000	10-Mar	1453	Wilson Garages	3200.00
3	14001	08-Mar	2413	Patel Industries	1466.00
4	14002	11-Mar	1453	Wilson Garages	98.76
5	14003	11-Mar	1289	Marsden Products	4456.00
6	14004	10-Mar	2413	Patel Industries	567.00
7	14005	11-Mar	955	Tilley Transport	1678.00
8	14006	10-Mar	2375	Patel Kitchens	55.54
9	14007	09-Mar	1453	Wilson Garages	2654.00
10	14008	12-Mar	2245	Goldfield Stables	123.85
11	14009	12-Mar	1289	Marsden Products	1652.54
12					

FIGURE 10.2

Mandatory entry: All details must be entered; none can be left blank.

Range/limit checks: You might, for example, wish to place upper or lower limits on an order value.

Format check: You might wish to check that, for example, an order number or company reference contains a set number of characters or is all numeric.

Restrict any entries to those on a list, e.g. customer names.

1 Open the workbook **DATABASE** and make sure that **ORDERS** is the active sheet – see FIGURE 10.2.

Select the first blank cell beneath the present list of orders, cell A12.

2 When a new order number is entered we want it to be a five-digit whole number in the range 14000 to 14999.

Open the **Data** menu and select **Validation**. Click the **Settings** tab if necessary.

Now, using FIGURE 10.3 as a guide, make the following entries:

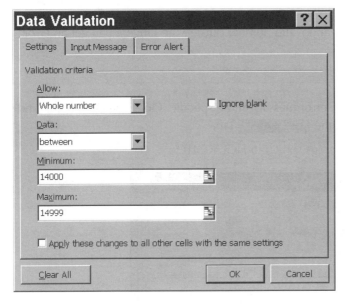

FIGURE 10.3

In the **Allow** box select **Whole number**.

In the **Data** box select **between**.

Enter the **Minimum** and **Maximum** quantities as shown.

Click the **Ignore blank** box to deselect it.

3   We can now add instructions to guide the user in entering the data. Click the
    Input Message tab.

    Complete it as shown in FIGURE 10.4.

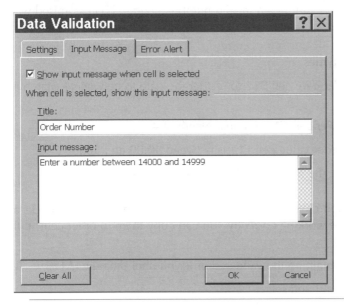

FIGURE 10.4

4 Click the **OK** button to return to the worksheet. When the cell A12 is selected an instruction box appears.

Now try entering an invalid number outside the range – you get an error message.

Cancel the entry.

5 We can make the error message more specific. Open the **Data** menu and select **Validation**. Click the **Error Alert** tab.

Now make the entries shown in FIGURE 10.5.

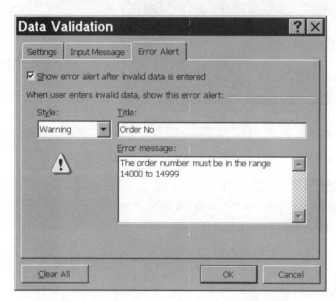

FIGURE 10.5

Click **OK** and try entering an invalid number again – the customised warning message appears.

6 **Independent activities**

Validate the ***Order date*** cell B12 to restrict the date to between 1 March and 31 March.

Validate the ***Co. Ref*** cell C12 to a text length of 4.

Ensure that the order value cell E12 is between 50.00 and 5000.

In each case click the **Ignore blank** box to deselect it.

7 **Copying validation checks.** Once you are sure that the validation checks and any user messages are working correctly you can copy them to other cells in the worksheet.

Select the cell containing the validated order number data, i.e. A12.

Open the **Edit** menu and select **Copy**.

Select the other order number cells, i.e. cell range A2–A11.

Open the **Edit** menu again and select **Paste Special**.

A dialog box appears. Click the **Validation** button followed by **OK**.

Test that the validation has been applied to other cells in the column.

8 **Identifying cells containing invalid data**. Open the **Tools** menu and select **Auditing** followed by **Show Auditing Toolbar**.

The **Auditing Toolbar** appears – see FIGURE 10.1.

Click the **Circle Invalid Data** button. Various cells should be circled – these are cells that are blank. You will recall that the **Ignore blank** box has been deselected, so blank cells are not allowed.

9 Click the **Clear Validation Circles** button on the Auditing Toolbar, then close the Auditing Toolbar.

10 **Restricting entries to those on a list**. We might, for example, wish to ensure that customer names are spelled correctly by making the user choose them from an approved list. Normally the list would be in a separate range of cells, but to make the point we can use the present customer names.

Select cell D12. Open the **Data** menu and select **Validation**. Click the **Settings** tab if necessary.

In the **Allow** box select **List**.

In the **Source** box enter the cell range containing the present customer names, *=D2:D11*

Deselect the **Ignore blank** box and click **OK**. The cell now has a down arrow that can be used to select from the present list of customers. If we were using a proper customer list there would be no repeated entries in the list.

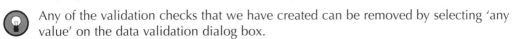 Any of the validation checks that we have created can be removed by selecting 'any value' on the data validation dialog box.

 If you want to enforce a numeric entry but not specify a range then it is best to specify a number not equal to 0.

11 Save and close the workbook.

Summary of commands

 Menu commands show the menu name first, followed by the command to choose from the menu, e.g. **Edit-Clear** means open the **Edit** menu and select the **Clear** command.

Menu Commands

Data–Validation	Validate data entered into cells
Edit-Copy/Edit-Paste Special	Copy cell validation to other cells
Edit-Delete Sheet	Delete worksheet from workbook
File-Save As-Options	Use various security options
Format-Cells-Protection	Protect selected cells
Insert-Worksheet	Insert worksheet into workbook
Tools-Auditing-Show Auditing Toolbar	Display the Auditing Toolbar
Tools-Options-View	Display formulae in worksheet
Tools-Protection-Protect Sheet	Protect/Remove protection from worksheet
Tools-Protection-Protect Workbook	Protect workbook
Tools-Protection-Unprotect Workbook	Remove protection from workbook
Tools-Track Changes-Highlight Changes	Highlight any changes made to a workbook
View-Toolbars-Auditing	Display Auditing Toolbar

Using macros

What you will learn in this unit

By the end of this unit you will be able to:

- assign a macro to a button
- create a button
- delete a button
- modify a button
- add a Custom Toolbar button
- delete a Custom Toolbar button
- assign a macro to a toolbar button
- run a macro automatically
- delete a macro
- disable a macro
- name a macro
- record a macro
- run a macro
- stop recording a macro
- view the macro sheet
- hide the macro sheet.

What you should know already

Before you start this unit, make sure that you can do the following:

Skill	Covered in
Creating a simple worksheet	Unit 1
Using formulae	Units 1 and 2

What you need

To complete this unit you will need:

- The workbook **INS_SLS** created in Unit 2.
- The workbook **DATABASE** created in Unit 5.
- The workbook **MORTGAGE** created in Unit 7, Task 1.
- The workbook **DISCOUNT** created in Unit 7, Task 3.

Introduction

This unit introduces the last main element of Excel – macros. A macro lets you save commands in a special macro sheet. The commands can then be run automatically whenever one needs to use them. Nearly any series of keystrokes, menu choices and mouse movements can be stored in a macro and used again when required.

There are several advantages to using macros.

Saving time. Issuing the same series of commands repeatedly is time-consuming. A macro provides a shortcut.

Reducing error. Long sequences of commands, mouse movements, and menu choices can be error-prone. A macro achieves a consistent, correct result.

Controlling user input. In a commercial situation users of varying skill and knowledge may be using the same worksheet model. The designer of the model wants to prevent users destroying data, amending formulae or modifying assumptions.

Macros allow the designer to place limits on what users of worksheets can do. For example, they can disable certain menu choices; add user instructions, error messages, custom menus and dialog boxes; and, at their most complex, design a complete custom-built system.

Excel 97 uses the Visual Basic programming language, an 'object-oriented' programming language specially developed for Windows applications.

In this unit we shall be starting with some simple Visual Basic (VB) macros which automate simple tasks. In later units we shall be building a complete user application using Visual Basic macros.

Tips and rules for macros

■ A macro is stored on a special module sheet.

■ Many macros can be stored on one module sheet.

■ Macros store commands using the Visual Basic (VB) programming language.

■ Macros can control worksheets, charts and databases.

■ Every macro is saved and run under a different name. The macro name can be up to 255 characters long, must begin with a letter, and can consist of letters, numbers, full stops or underscores.

■ Spaces are not allowed in macro names, so underscores or full stops are often used instead.

■ Macro names are not case-sensitive.

■ A macro can be run in several ways. It can be assigned to a special button or menu choice, or it can be assigned a to shortcut key – a single letter. Pressing down the *Ctrl* key and keying this letter will run the macro. The letter that you assign to a macro is case-sensitive; e.g. holding down the *Ctrl* key and pressing *e* would run a particular macro; pressing *Ctrl* and *E* would not. This gives you a potential 52 shortcut key combinations. However, many are already used by Excel as keyboard shortcuts, e.g. *Ctrl/S* to save. Assigning the same key to a macro will override the keyboard shortcut while the workbook that contains the macro is open. If you use keyboard shortcuts it is best not to use these letters.

Task 1: Creating a simple macro

You can create a simple macro by using the macro recorder. Actions such as menu choices, mouse movements and keystrokes are then recorded and can be 'played back' when required. Our first macro will automate the simple task of adding the date and time to a worksheet. Instead of entering the **NOW( )** function every time, you can use a shortcut by, say, pressing the *Ctrl* key and the letter *e*.

1 **Recording a macro**. Open the workbook **DISCOUNT.XLS**.

If you don't have this workbook then any workbook containing worksheet data will do, although you may need to adjust some of the cell references.

Select cell A1.

Open the Tools menu and choose Macro followed by Record New Macro.

The **Record Macro** dialog box appears; use FIGURE 11.1.as a guide to completing it.

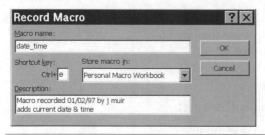

FIGURE 11.1

2   Enter the name *date_time* in the **Macro name** box.

Enter the letter *e* in the **Ctrl+** box (letters a–d are already used as Excel keyboard commands).

3   Now click the down arrow on the **Store macro in** box. Select the option **Personal Macro Workbook**.

 There are three ways to store macros.

■   The Personal Macro Workbook is opened automatically whenever you start Excel, and can be used to store and run commonly used macros.

■   The **This Workbook** option stores macros on a module sheet associated with the workbook. This restricts using the macro to one workbook.

■   **New Workbook** stores the macros in a new workbook. If you use this option then you have to open the workbook containing the macro sheet whenever you want to run the macro.

4   Select the **Description** box. This always contains the creation date plus the name of the author or organisation. Add the description *Adds current date & time*.

Click the **OK** button. A 'Recording' message appears at the bottom of the screen and a single Stop Recording toolbar is displayed with a **Stop Macro** button on it.

5   **Recording the macro**. We are now ready to record the macro steps. All your actions are being recorded now, so don't issue any superfluous commands.

Enter the function *=NOW()* in cell A1, then click the 'tick' button in the Formula Bar.

Open the **Format** menu and select **Cells** followed by the **Number** tab.

Select the **Date** category, followed by a date and time format that shows both the date and the time. Click **OK**.

The date appears, correctly formatted, in cell A1 of the **DISCOUNT** workbook.

Click the **Stop Recording** button. The 'Recording' message at the bottom of the screen is no longer displayed.

You have now recorded your first macro, date_time, which automates entering the date and time. Let's see how this has been recorded.

If the column displays a row of '####' symbols then the column needs to be widened to display the date.

6   **Viewing the macro sheet**. Whenever you first open Excel the personal macro workbook is opened but remains hidden.

Open the **Window** menu and select **Unhide**. A dialog box appears.

Select **PERSONAL.XLS** then **OK**. The macro workbook appears on the screen.

Open the **Tools** menu and select **Macro** followed by **Macros**. A dialog box appears that lists all the macros; at present there is only one – date_time.

Click the **Edit** button and the **MODULE1** sheet appears, which contains the macro. It is in fact a very simple Visual Basic (VB) program, consisting of introductory comments, plus a single subroutine called *date_time( )*. This subroutine contains two VB commands:

ActiveCell.FormulaR1C1 = "NOW()"

Selection.NumberFormat = "d/m/yy h.mm am/pm"

The date format may be different from the one you chose. If the date format is incorrect you can edit it directly on the macro sheet.

Click the **Close** button at the top of the window to return to the workbook.

Open the **Window** menu again and select **Hide** – the macro workbook is hidden again and the **DISCOUNT** workbook is displayed.

7   **Troubleshooting – if your recording fails...**

The Excel Macro Recorder will record all your commands and keystrokes – right or wrong. If you make a mistake while recording a simple macro then it is best to stop recording, open the **Tools** menu and select **Macro** followed by **Macros**.

Click the **Delete** button. If the macro is stored in the **PERSONAL** workbook it must be unhidden (see Step 6).

8   **Running the macro using the shortcut key**

Make sure that cell A1 is still selected.

Hold down the _Ctrl_ key and press the *e* key.

The hourglass symbol will confirm that the macro is running – the time will be updated.

Unhide the macro workbook again and save and close it, using **Close** on the **File** menu.

Now try running the macro again (_Ctrl/e_). Nothing will happen. Once the special macro workbook has been closed during an Excel session it will need to be opened before any macros can be run from it.

Now open the macro workbook **PERSONAL** using **File-Open** – it should be located in the **XLSTART** folder, which is in the **OFFICE** subfolder of the main **EXCEL** folder.

 Macro viruses. A dialog box will appear warning you of macro viruses and giving you three options. Click the ▐ **Tell me more** ▐ button. You will see that a macro virus becomes active once the workbook associated with the infected macro is opened. From then on, every workbook you open and save can be infected automatically with the macro virus. If other users on a network open infected workbooks, the macro virus can be passed on to their computers too. Also note that Excel 97 doesn't actually scan your disks for macro viruses – it merely displays a warning message whenever you try to open a workbook that uses macros. So to detect and remove viruses you would still need to have antivirus software installed.

The three options are:

Enable Macros: Open the workbook with the macros enabled – this is acceptable if the worksheet must use macros in order to work correctly and it comes from a reliable source. If you do not expect the workbook to contain macros, or you aren't certain about the reliability of its source, you might want to click the second option.

Disable Macros: Open the workbook with macros disabled – this is a safe option if you cannot rely on the source, e.g. the workbook is from an unfamiliar Internet site. However, not only will you be unable to use essential macros, but other features will not work, e.g. custom functions, event handlers and ActiveX controls. You can still view, edit and save the macros.

Do not Open: Cancels the opening of the workbook.

If the virus message does not appear, open the **Tools** menu and select **Options**.

When the dialog box appears select the ▐ **General** ▐ tab and check that the **Macro Virus Protection** option is selected.

9   Click the ▐ **Enable Macros** ▐ button and hide the **PERSONAL** workbook as before.

10 Leave the **DISCOUNT** workbook open and open the workbook **MORTGAGE**.

 If you don't have this workbook then any workbook containing worksheet data will do, although you may need to adjust some of the cell references.

Use the shortcut keys *Ctrl/e* again to add the date to cell **A1** (the special menu option 'Add date and time' can be used from any worksheet).

You may need to widen the column for the date and time to display properly.

Close the **MORTGAGE** workbook, leaving the **DISCOUNT** workbook open.

11 **Running a macro by name**. Open the **Tools** menu and select **Macro** followed by **Macros**.

Select the macro **date_time** and click **Run** . The macro will run again, updating the date and time in cell A1.

12 **Recap – the steps in recording a macro**

- Activate the worksheet that the macro will control.

- Open the **Tools** menu and select the **Macro-Record New Macro** options.

- Complete the dialog box, i.e. name the macro and allocate the shortcut letter.

- Record the actions in the macro.

- Click the **Stop Macro** button.

Task 2: Assigning a macro to a button

In the first activity you ran a macro in two ways – assigning it to a shortcut key (*Ctrl/e*) and running it from the macro menu. A third way is to assign a macro to a button. Clicking the button will run the macro, without needing to remember key strokes or menu choices. The button can either be part of the worksheet or placed on a toolbar.

We will create a new macro **print_mortgage** that will automate the printing of part of a worksheet.

1 Open the workbook **MORTGAGE** if necessary.

 If you don't have this workbook then any workbook containing worksheet data will do, although you may need to adjust some of the cell references.

We will create a print macro that prints the mortgage interest table held in cells A7–C17.

2 Open the **View** menu and select **Toolbars**.

Select **Forms** from the Toolbars list.

The **Forms** Toolbar is displayed. Click the **Button** tool – see FIGURE 11.2.

FIGURE 11.2

The screen pointer changes to cross-hairs.

3 **Creating the button**. Drag the screen pointer so that the box covers cells E2 and E3.

Release the mouse button and the button is drawn with the default name Button1 . We can reposition it later if necessary.

4 **Assigning a macro to the button**. The Assign Macro dialog box opens automatically. Close the Forms Toolbar.

Click the Record button. The Record Macro dialog box appears.

Complete the dialog box as follows:

Enter the macro name as ***print_mortgage***.

Leave the Shortcut key box blank – this macro will be run from a button.

Select This Workbook from the Store macro in box (the cells to be printed will only apply to this workbook, so there is no point in storing the macro in the PERSONAL macro workbook).

Complete the Description box, e.g. ***Prints the mortgage table***.

Click OK – the macro is now assigned to the button and you are ready to start recording.

5 **Recording the macro**. Make sure that your printer is turned on and connected.

Open the File menu and select Page Setup.

Click the Sheet tab.

Enter the cell references ***A7:C17*** in the Print Area box.

Click OK .

Open the File menu and select Print; choose one copy and whatever other settings you wish.

Click OK .

Printing will now take place; when it is finished click the Stop Recording button.

You have now created a print macro on a new macro sheet.

 Troubleshooting: see Step 11.

6 **Labelling the button**. To change the size and colour of the button, or the text that appears on it, you must first select it.

Hold down the _Ctrl_ key and click the button – selection handles appear round the button.

First erase the default name by clicking on the button again and deleting the text. Then open the Format menu and select Control – a dialog box appears.

Choose **8** from the Size box.

Click the down arrow button on the **Color** box and select a colour for the text.

Click **OK**.

The button should still be selected; type the label on the button ***Click to Print***.

Click elsewhere on the worksheet to deselect the button.

7 **Moving or sizing the button**. Hold down the *Ctrl* key and click the button – selection handles appear.

Release the *Ctrl* key and drag one of the selection handles – the screen pointer will change to a double-headed arrow.

To move the button make sure that it is still selected and place the screen pointer on the edge of the button – not on a selection handle – and drag. The button can now be moved. (Don't move the button within the print area or the button outline will be printed along with the worksheet.)

Finally press the *Esc* key to deselect the button and remove the selection handles.

8 **Running the macro**. If you are happy with the appearance of your button then try running it.

Move the screen pointer on top of the button – the screen pointer becomes hand-shaped.

Click once and the worksheet should print as before.

9 **Viewing the macro**. The macro has been recorded on a module sheet in the **MORTGAGE** workbook.

Open the **Tools** menu and select **Macro** followed by **Macros**. A dialog box appears; select the **print_mortgage** macro.

Click the **Edit** button and the **MODULE1** sheet appears. Maximise it – it contains the macro in VB code. It is quite lengthy, as all the standard page setup settings are listed.

Click the **Close** button at the top of the window to return to the worksheet.

10 Save and close the **MORTGAGE** workbook.

 Troubleshooting – information only. If a simple recorded macro doesn't work then it is usually easiest to delete it and re-record it (in future activities you will learn how to debug and edit macros).

■ **Deleting a button**. If you have made a mess of your button, or no longer need it, then you can delete it.

Select the button as before (*Ctrl/click*), then press the *Delete* key.

■ **Deleting a macro**. If the macro doesn't work correctly then open the **Tools** menu and select **Macro** followed by **Macros**. Select the macro name and then click on **Delete**.

■ **Assigning a new macro**. Right click the button and select Assign Macro from the pop-up menu that appears. Enter the new name and click the Record button.

Task 3: Consolidation

An unavoidable limitation of the print_mortgage macro that we have just created is that it only applies to one specific worksheet in the workbook **MORTGAGE.XLS**. This is because it sets a print area that is unlikely to apply to any other worksheet, so each worksheet needs its own print macro.

1 Open the workbook **HELPERS**.

 If you don't have this workbook then any workbook containing worksheet data will do.

Now, using the operations in Tasks 1 and 2 as a guide, add a new macro to print the **SHEET1** worksheet.

Call the macro *print_helpers* and assign a shortcut key to it.

2 Create and assign a print button for this worksheet too.

3 Save and close the workbook.

Task 4: Assigning a macro to a toolbar

A fourth method of running a macro is to attach a macro to a button on a toolbar. The macro can either take over the function of an existing button or you can create a custom toolbar button. We will try the second method to add a button that will format a worksheet.

1 Open the workbook **INS_SLS**. If the virus warning dialog box appears click the Enable Macros button. If necessary, drag aside the embedded chart to show the worksheet data. We are going to select a button, add it to the formatting toolbar, assign a macro to it and then record the macro.

 If you don't have this workbook then any workbook containing worksheet data will do, although you may need to adjust some of the cell references.

2 **Choosing a custom button**. Open the Tools menu and select Customize.

A dialog box appears. Click the Commands tab.

Select Macros from the Categories list – you may need to scroll down to see it.

Drag the custom button from the dialog box to a position next to the Bold button on the Formatting Toolbar at the top of the window – see FIGURE 11.3.

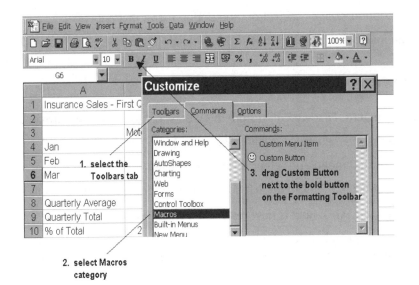

2. **select Macros category**

FIGURE 11.3

Do not close the dialog box.

3 **Changing the custom button**. Right click the custom button on the toolbar (not in the dialog box).

Select the option Change Button Image from the popup menu that appears.

Select a suitable icon – the custom button on the toolbar changes.

Now close the dialog box.

4 **Recording the macro**. Open the Tools menu and select Macro followed by Record New Macro. A dialog box appears.

Type in the macro name *format_worksheet*.

Leave the Shortcut key entry blank.

Make sure that the This Workbook option is selected in the Store macro in section (the formatting macro will only apply to this worksheet).

Click the OK button. From now on your actions are being recorded.

5 Select the worksheet cells holding the data, i.e. cell range **A1–E10**.

Open the Format menu and select AutoFormat.

Select the format Colorful 2 from the AutoFormat box.

Click OK .

Click the Stop Macro button.

6 **Assigning the macro**. Open the Tools menu and select Customize. A dialog box appears.

Right click the custom button on the toolbar.

Select the option **Assign Macro** from the popup menu that appears.

Select the macro **format_worksheet** from the dialog box that appears and click **OK**.

Close the **Customize** dialog box.

7 **Testing the macro**. First we will restore the worksheet to its normal format.

Make sure that the cell range is still selected.

Open the **Format** menu and select **AutoFormat** again.

Select the format **None** from the list box – you may have to scroll down to see it.

Click **OK** – the worksheet is now restored to its previous format.

Now click the special custom button that you have created on the Formatting Toolbar – the macro reformats the worksheet to the format previously recorded.

8 **Viewing the macro**. The macro has been recorded on a module sheet in the **INS_SLS** workbook. Open the **Tools** menu and select **Macro** followed by **Macros**. A dialog box appears; select the **format_worksheet** macro.

Click the **Edit** button – the Module sheet appears displaying the macro in VB code.

Click the **Close** button at the top of the window to return to the worksheet.

 9 **Troubleshooting – information only**. If a simple recorded macro doesn't work then it is usually easiest to delete it and re-record it (in future activities we will be learning how to debug and edit macros).

■ **Deleting a custom toolbar button**. Open the **Tools** menu and select **Customize**.

A dialog box appears. Click the **Command** tab.

Select **Macros** from the **Categories** list – you may need to scroll down to see it.

Drag the custom button from the toolbar back to the dialog box.

■ **Deleting a macro**. If the macro doesn't work correctly then open the **Tools** menu and select **Macro** followed by **Macros**. Select the macro name then use the **Delete** button.

10 Close the workbook **INS_SLS**. If you don't wish to keep the formatting or the macro then don't save it.

Task 5: Running a macro automatically

In the previous activity you created a button that had a macro assigned to it. Clicking the button calls the macro, which in turn formats the worksheet. It is also possible to run the macro automatically every time the workbook is opened, i.e. the worksheet is formatted whenever the workbook is opened.

1   Open the workbook **INS_SLS**. If the virus warning dialog box appears click the
    Enable Macros button.

If you don't have this workbook then use whichever workbook you used in the
previous activity.

2   Open the **Insert** menu and select **Name** followed by **Define**.

3   A dialog box appears; select the **Names in Workbook** box and type the name
    Auto_Open.

4   Select the **Refers to** box next. It must contain the name of the macro that you are
    calling.

    Type *=format_worksheet* then click **OK** .

5   Remove the formatting from the worksheet cells – see Task 4, Step 7.

    Save and close the **INS_SLS** workbook.

6   Now open **INS_SLS** again. If the virus warning dialog box appears click the
    Enable Macros button. The **format_worksheet** macro should run and the
    worksheet be formatted automatically. Reformat it if you wish.

    Close the workbook.

7   If you get an error message then check the following.

    Open the **Insert** menu, select **Name-Define** again and select the name *Auto_Open*.

    ■   Check the spelling and syntax of the entries in the dialog box; for the name
        Auto_Open to work correctly there must be no spaces and you must use the
        underscore (_), not the dash.

    ■   Now save and close the workbook and try again!

8   **Additional notes – information only**

    It is also possible to run a macro automatically when you close a workbook; use
    Steps 1–5, but in the **Name** box type a name that begins with *Auto_Close*.

    More than one macro can be run automatically from the same workbook.

    Each name must begin with *Auto_Close* or *Auto_Open*.

9   **Consolidation**. Open the workbook **HELPERS.XLS**.

    Using the above operations, make the macro **print_helpers** run automatically
    when the worksheet is opened.

If you don't have this workbook then any workbook containing worksheet data will
do.

Summary of commands

 Menu commands show the menu name first, followed by the command to choose from the menu, e.g. **Edit-Clear** means open the **Edit** menu and select the **Clear** command.

Keyboard commands

Ctrl/[letter]	Run macro using shortcut key
Ctrl/[select]	Select screen button

Menu commands

Format-AutoFormat	Select automatic worksheet format
Format-Cells-Number	Format a date or number
Format-Control	Format a selected object, e.g. a button
Insert-Name-Define	Assign a name to an object, e.g. a macro
Tools-Customize	Customise toolbars or menus
Tools-Macro-Macros	Run, edit or delete a macro
Tools-Macro-Record New Macro	Record a new macro
View-Toolbars-Forms	Display/hide Forms Toolbar
Window-Hide	Hide a workbook window
Window-Unhide	Show a hidden workbook window

Designing a user application

Important note

Units 12–17 form a unified development task – they all need to be completed in order for the purchase order application to work. Unlike previous units, there is no point in doing any one unit in isolation from the others – they all build on each other.

What you will learn in this unit

By the end of this unit you will be able to:

- name cells
- use the Drawing Toolbar
- display the Formula Bar
- hide the Formula Bar
- display gridlines
- hide gridlines
- record a macro
- run, test and view a macro
- group objects
- display scrollbars
- hide scrollbars
- delete worksheets
- display sheet tabs
- hide sheet tabs
- display the status bar
- hide the status bar
- create a text box
- display toolbars
- hide toolbars.

What you should know already

Before you start this unit, make sure that you can do the following:

Skill	Covered in
Basic mouse, menu and Windows operations	Unit 1
Using formulae	Units 1 and 2

What you need

No previously created worksheets are required for this unit.

Introduction

In the previous unit you created some simple macros that automated small tasks such as printing a worksheet. In this unit you are going to use macros to automate a whole application – purchase orders. Every time a company orders some goods it sends out a purchase order to a supplier, so it needs to maintain records of them using a database. Purchase order records will need to be added to this database, as well as being edited, saved and printed.

The application may well be used by people unfamiliar with Excel, who cannot be expected to use the normal menus, commands etc. Macros are the binding material that will hold the parts of the system together and present it to the user in a simple way. You will find that building a complete application is a lengthy, painstaking process, inevitably involving much testing and some frustration. Some of this can be avoided if you plan the application properly before you start. Trial and error and experimentation can then take place within a structured framework.

Overview of the application

It is important to plan the application, at least in general outline, before starting on the worksheet and macros. Use this section to understand the various parts of the system before you start on the first activity.

1   The first screen that the user will see is a specially designed title screen – see FIGURE 12.8. This will eventually offer a custom menu at the top of the screen that replaces the standard menus. Several macros are used to display this screen, e.g. to turn off normal screen defaults such as gridlines and tool bars.

2   A user form is also designed for the user to enter purchase order details, e.g. Supplier Name, Quantity, Product, Price – see FIGURE 13.1.

3   The data entered in this user form are transferred to a database using a macro.

4   Users will be able to edit the data records where necessary using a standard data form – see FIGURE 16.1. This too can be called by a macro.

5   Many of the items ordered from suppliers are standard; they are stored in a products list – see FIGURE 12.10.

6   The application can thus be divided into four main parts – the first three are shown much reduced in FIGURE 12.1.

■   Part 1 is the title screen.

■   Part 2 is the database of purchase orders.

■   Part 3 is the list of products.

■   Part 4 is the user form – see FIGURE 13.1.

■   The fifth element is invisible to the user – this is the macro module sheet that will contain all the Visual Basic commands to run the application.

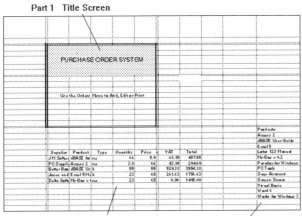

Part 1   Title Screen

Part 2.   Purchase Order Database   Part 3.   List of Products   FIGURE 12.1

Such an application can look daunting, but don't worry: it can be built up and tested piece by piece. At the end you will have a worthwhile application that can be added to as needs demand.

Programming in Visual Basic

Non-programmers need not worry unduly about the programming skills required.

Rather than start with a large section of indigestible theory, programming concepts will be introduced as we go on. Space will not allow us to explore every element of Visual Basic (VB for short), which in any case is well covered in the Excel Help text.

 If you have developed applications in Excel versions 5 or 7 you will find that some of the Visual Basic commands have changed and that there are some new development features. These will be dealt with as they arise. Briefly, they are:

- Generally, all the Microsoft Office products – Excel, Access, Word etc – have been given a common interface, similar to that of Microsoft's standalone Visual Basic version 5.0.

- Every workbook has an associated project that keeps track of all the worksheets, forms, macros etc.

- The Project Explorer helps you keep track of these elements.

- Macro sheets are accessible via an improved Visual Basic editor; they are no longer stored in a special macro sheet.

- The Properties Window allows you to set the properties of objects used in the application, e.g. menus, buttons or text boxes.

- New utilities replace the Menu and Dialog Editors.

Task 1: Creating user screens

In this task we will create the three parts of the purchase orders system:

- the title screen – see FIGURE 12.8

- the orders database – see FIGURE 12.9

- the list of products – see FIGURE 12.10.

1 Open a new workbook and maximise the worksheet if necessary.

   Check that the Drawing Toolbar is displayed at the bottom of the screen; if not open the **View** menu and select **Toolbars**. Select the Drawing Toolbar.

2 Move the cursor onto the Drawing Toolbar. A screen tip explains the function of each button – see the key at the end of this unit if necessary.

   Click the **Text Box** button (next to the oval shape).

   Now drag the mouse pointer to draw a text box that covers the cell range B2–H14. The exact size is not important.

 A text box may be moved or resized in the usual way – first click the border to select it. The box may then be resized by dragging a selection 'handle' or moved by dragging the border. To delete a selected box press the *Delete* key.

3   Double click the text box border – a dialog box appears.

Click the **Font** tab. Choose size **14** and **bold** for the text – see FIGURE 12.2.

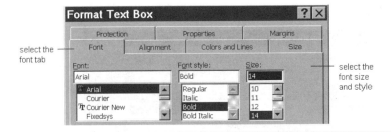

FIGURE 12.2

4   Click the **Colors and Lines** tab. Click the down arrow on the **Fill Color** box.

Select the **Fill Effects** option – see FIGURE 12.3.

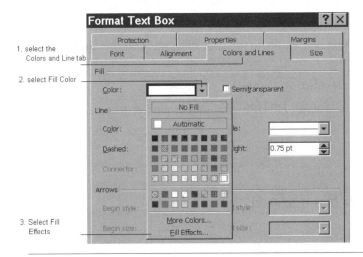

FIGURE 12.3

5   The **Fill Effects** dialog box is displayed. Click the **Patterns** tab – see FIGURE 12.4.

Select a suitable pattern/colour for the text box.

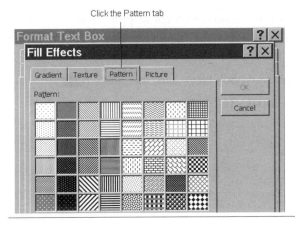

FIGURE 12.4

169

6 You are returned to the **Format** dialog box. Click the **Alignment** tab.

Centre the text horizontally and vertically – see FIGURE 12.5.

Click the **OK** button.

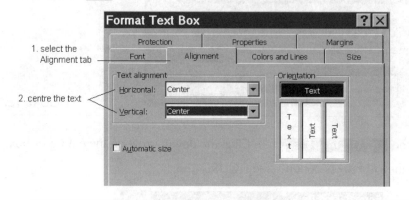

FIGURE 12.5

7 Click inside the text box and type the user message *Use the Orders Menu to Add, Edit or Print*.

Click outside the text box to deselect it.

Compare your results with FIGURE 12.6 and amend if necessary.

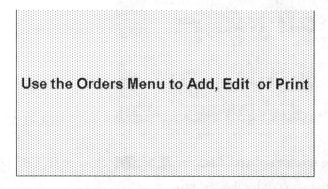

FIGURE 12.6

8 For a complex application it is useful to document its purpose in a summary box when you save it. Open the Tools menu and select Options. Click the **General** tab.

Select the option Prompt for Workbook Properties, then click **OK**.

Now save the workbook as **ORDENTER.XLS**.

A **Properties** dialog box appears; complete the summary box as shown in FIGURE 12.7 and click **OK**.

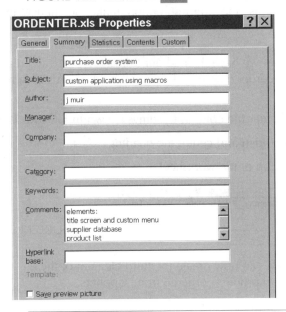

FIGURE 12.7

9 Click on the **Text Box** button again and draw a second text box on top of the first – see FIGURE 12.8.

Format the text in the box to 18 point bold and centre it as before.

Right click the second text box. Select **Order** and **Bring to Front** from the the popup menu (this ensures that the second box always overlays the main box).

10 Enter the text **PURCHASE ORDER SYSTEM**.

Your screen should now resemble FIGURE 12.8.

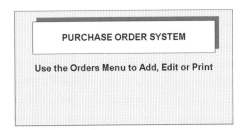

FIGURE 12.8

With the text box still selected, click the **Shadow** button on the Drawing Toolbar and select a suitable shadow effect.

11 **Grouping objects**. We want the two text boxes to retain their relative positions if either of them are moved.

Hold down the *Shift* key and click the borders of both boxes – they are both selected.

171

On the left of the Drawing Toolbar is a button marked **Draw** . Click this button and select the **Group** option. Both objects now form a group – if you need to change their relative positions, use the **Ungroup** option, make the change, then use the **Regroup** option.

12 **The orders database**. Now that we have defined our title screen we can create the headings for the purchase order database. These will hold records of items supplied.

Scroll down to cell L56 and enter the column headings shown in FIGURE 12.9.

Widen the columns and embolden and centre the headings.

Press *Ctrl/Home* to go to the top of the worksheet.

	L	M	N	O	P	Q	R	S
56	Supplier	Product	Type	Quantity	Price	Date	VAT	Total
57								
58								

FIGURE 12.9

13 **Creating the products list**. We can now create the third element of the application, the list of standard products ordered from suppliers.

Select Column U and widen it to about 20.00.

Enter the list of software products shown in FIGURE 12.10 in cells U21–U33.

	S	T	U	V	W
20					
21			**Products**		
22			Encarta 97		
23			Autoroute 5		
24			Excel 97		
25			Corel Draw		
26			Procomm Plus		
27			MS Office Manual		
28			MS Works 4		
29			Delphi Developer		
30			Visual Basic Manual		
31			Internet Guide		
32			Sage Accounts		
33			Norton Antivirus		
34					

FIGURE 12.10

14 **Naming the cell range**. We need to give the range of cells holding the products a name.

Select cells U22–U33.

Open the **Insert** menu and choose **Name-Define** – a dialog box appears.

Enter the name **PRODUCT_LIST** and click **OK** .

15 Double click on the **Sheet1** tab.

Rename the worksheet **ORDER SCREENS**.

Task 2: Macros which format screens

We now have the title screen, the orders database screen and the products list. The next step is to record macros to control them. We will create a number of small macros, each of which carries out a simple task, such as turning off menus or displaying a screen. As the macros only apply to the **ORDENTER** workbook they will be stored on a module sheet within the workbook, rather than in the general macro sheet **PERSONAL** (see Unit 11 if necessary).

We will use the same recording techniques that we used in the previous unit.

Remember the basic steps in creating a macro:

- Activate the worksheet that the macro will control.

- Open the Tools menu and select the Macro-Record New Macro option.

- Complete the dialog box, i.e. name the macro and allocate the shortcut letter.

- Record the macro actions.

- Click the **Stop Macro** button.

1 Make sure that the workbook **ORDENTER** is still open and the worksheet is currently displaying the title screen. Press the *Ctrl/Home* keys if necessary to return to the top of the worksheet.

 First make sure that neither the Excel application window nor the **ORDENTER** document window is maximised; if they are, press the **Restore** button(s) – the window size doesn't matter at the moment.

 If you're not sure of the position of these buttons, now is the time to check and experiment – not when you are recording the macro!

2 **The title screen macro.** This macro will turn off certain standard settings.

 Open the Tools menu and select Macro-Record New Macro.

 Using FIGURE 12.11 as a guide, complete the dialog box as follows:

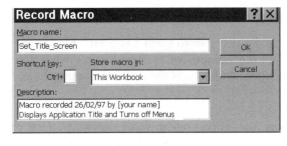

FIGURE.12.11

Name the macro *Set_Title_Screen*.

Complete the description box.

Make sure that the This Workbook option is selected.

Do not allocate a shortcut key.

Click **OK** .

From now on your actions are being recorded!

3 Click the **Maximize** button on both the Excel application window and the **ORDENTER** document window.

Click the sheet tab for the **ORDER SCREENS** worksheet.

Press down the *Ctrl* and *Home* keys together – the cursor moves to cell A1.

Open the Tools menu and select Options.

Click the **View** tab (even if it is selected).

Now click on the following options in turn to deselect them:

Formula bar

Status bar

Gridlines

Row & column headers

Horizontal scroll bar

Vertical scroll bar

Sheet tabs

Click **OK** .

4 Open the View menu and select Toolbars.

Click the **Standard** and **Formatting Toolbar** boxes to deselect them (and the Drawing Toolbar if selected) – don't deselect the **Stop Recording** box.

You will need to select the View menu several times to carry out this step.

Click **OK** .

5 Now click the **Stop Recorder** button.

The first macro is recorded and a new macro sheet has been added to the workbook. Most of the usual Excel features are removed from the title screen – the user will not be needing them and it gives the opening screen a tidier appearance.

6 **Restoring the screen defaults**. The second macro will reverse the effects of the first one, i.e. it will restore the normal screen defaults before the database screen is displayed. This is simply a matter of recording the macro again to reselect the options.

Open the Tools menu and select Macro-Record New Macro.

Name the macro ***Restore_Title_Screen***.

Complete the description box, e.g. **restores the normal screen defaults**.

Make sure that the **This Workbook** option is selected.

Click **OK** .

From now on your actions are being recorded!

7   Open the **Tools** menu and select **Options**.

Click the **View** tab (even if it is currently selected).

Now click on the following options in turn to select them – an 'x' will appear in each:

Formula bar

Status bar

Gridlines

Row & column headers

Horizontal scroll bar

Vertical scroll bar

Sheet tabs

Click **OK** .

8   Open the **View** menu and select **Toolbars**.

Reselect the **Standard** and **Formatting Toolbar** boxes (and the Drawing Toolbar if necessary).

Click **OK** .

9   Now click the **Stop Recorder** button.

The second macro is recorded and the Excel screen is returned to its normal appearance.

10 Save the workbook.

Task 3: Testing macros

1   To make it simpler to view macros we will remove all the other sheets from the workbook.

Click the **Sheet2** tab to select it.

Open the **Edit** menu and select **Delete Sheet**. A dialog box appears.

Click **OK** .

Continue to delete the other blank sheets in the workbook – you can select several sheets at once if you hold down the _Ctrl_ key.

175

If you accidentally delete the wrong sheet open the **File** menu and select **Close**. Close the workbook without saving it, then open it again.

2 **Running the macros**. Open the **Tools** menu and select **Macro** followed by **Macros** – a dialog box appears. Select the macro **Set_Title_Screen** and click the **Run** button. Check that the macro is setting off all the defaults.

Next, run the **Restore_Title_Screen** macro and check that it is working correctly.

3 **Viewing a macro**. Open the **Tools** menu and select **Macro** followed by **Macros** – a dialog box appears. Select the macro **Set_Title_Screen** and click the **Edit** button.

Check that the window **ORDENTER.xls – Module1 (Code)** is displayed. If not, use the Windows Taskbar at the bottom of the window to display it – see FIGURE 12.12.

FIGURE 12.12

The Visual Basic code is fairly easy to understand in this simple macro – **False** indicates that a setting such as a scroll bar is turned off.

To view the second macro click the down arrow on the procedure box – see FIGURE 12.13.

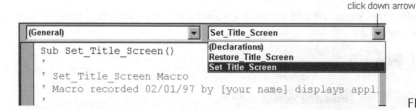

FIGURE 12.13

View the second macro, **Restore_Title_Screen** – it resets the default settings to True. Later on we will be adding comments to more complex macros in order to document them.

Use the procedure box to select the **Set_Title_Screen** macro again.

4 **Stepping through a macro**. It is possible to execute a macro one step at a time; this is useful for testing and debugging. To see it happening, both the worksheet window and the VB editing window must be visible.

First, click the **Excel** button on the Taskbar – see FIGURE 12.12 – the worksheet screen is displayed. Reduce the size of the whole Excel window until it fills about the top third of the screen.

Return to the VB editing window using the Taskbar and reduce its size so that it fills the bottom part of the screen – see FIGURE 12.14.

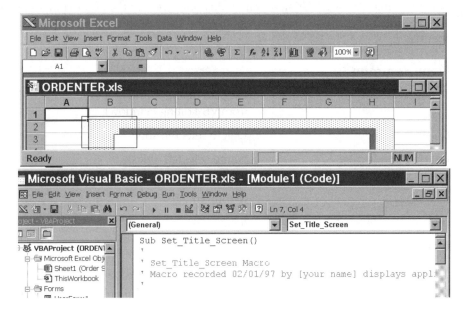

FIGURE 12.14

5   Open the **Debug** menu at the top of the VB Editing Window and select the **Step Into** option. The first line of the macro executes and the next line is selected.

Now keep repeating the **Step Into** command (or press the *F8* key) and notice the effect of each macro command on the worksheet settings; eventually you will step through the whole macro until you reach the final line: **End Sub**.

6   You can now step through the **Restore_Title_Screen** macro. Select the macro – see FIGURE 12.13 – and issue the **Step Into** command again until the entire macro has executed. The title screen will return to its previous appearance.

7   Close the VB Editing Window and restore the size of the workbook window.

8   `Save and close the workbook.

Summary of commands

Menu commands show the menu name first, followed by the command to choose from the menu, e.g. **Edit-Clear** means open the **Edit** menu and select the **Clear** command.

Menu commands

Debug-Step Into	Execute macro a line at a time (only available from VB Editing Window)
Edit-Delete Sheet	Delete selected sheet
Insert-Name-Define	Name selected cell(s)
Order-Bring to Front	Arrange one object on top of another (popup menu)
Tools-Macro-Macros	Select a macro to run, edit, delete etc
Tools-Macro-Record New Macro	Record new macro
Tools-Options-General	Document workbook features
Tools-Options-View	Turn on/off features of current worksheet
View-Toolbars	Hide/show toolbars

The Drawing Toolbar

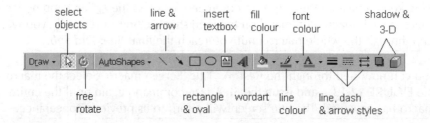

Further application development – user forms

Important note

Units 12–17 form a unified development task – they all need to be completed in order for the purchase order application to work. Unlike previous units, there is no point in doing any one unit in isolation from the others – they all build on each other.

What you will learn in this unit

By the end of this unit you will be able to:

- add buttons
- create a check box
- name cells
- create a combo box
- add labels
- record a macro
- step through a macro
- use the Properties window
- create a text box
- create a user form
- view VB projects.

What you should know already

Before you start this unit, make sure that you can do the following:

Skill	Covered in
Basic mouse, menu and Windows operations	Unit 1
Using formulae	Units 1 and 2

Introduction

This unit continues the development of the purchase order application begun in Unit 12. It creates further macros, and shows you how to create a form for the user to enter purchase order details.

Task 1: Macros that position the screen

As the Set_Title_Screen macro turns off the scroll bars, users will need each part of the **ORDER SCREENS** worksheet positioned for them. We therefore need two more macros to position the title and the database screens.

1   The workbook **ORDENTER** must be open, with the sheet **ORDER SCREENS** currently displaying the title screen.

First make sure that neither the Excel application window nor the **ORDENTER** document window is maximised; if they are, press the Restore button(s) – their size doesn't matter at the moment.

If you're not sure of the position of these buttons, now is the time to check and experiment – not when you are recording the macro!

2   Open the Tools menu and select Macro-Record New Macro.

Name the macro *Position_Title_Screen*.

Complete the description box appropriately.

Make sure that the This Workbook option is selected.

Click OK .

From now on your actions are being recorded!

3   Click the Maximize button on both the Excel application window and the **ORDENTER** document window.

Press down the *Ctrl* and *Home* keys together – the cursor moves to cell **A1** – the 'home' Position.

Click the Stop Recorder button now.

The third macro is recorded.

4   Test the macro as follows:

    ■ Scroll down the worksheet screen so that the title is no longer in view.

    ■ Open the Tools menu and select Macro-Macros.

    ■ Select the macro Position_Title_Screen from the list and click the Run button.

5   We now need a fourth macro to position the database screen.

As before, make sure that neither the Excel application window nor the **ORDENTER** document window is maximised; if so then press the Restore button(s).

 You may wish to try out the series of actions in Step 7 before you record them.

6   Open the Tools menu and select Macro-Record New Macro.

Name the macro ***Position_Database_Screen***.

Complete the description box.

Make sure that the This Workbook option is selected.

Click OK .

From now on your actions are being recorded!

7   Click the Maximize button on both the Excel application window and the **ORDENTER** document window.

Press down the *Ctrl* and the *Home* keys together – the cursor moves to cell **A1.**

Scroll down until row **56** appears at the top of the screen – the row containing the database titles.

Scroll *across* the worksheet until column **L** is the leftmost column; all the headings should be displayed now – see FIGURE 12.9 if necessary.

Make any final adjustments to the position and click in cell **L56**.

Click the Stop Recorder button now.

The fourth macro is recorded.

8   **Consolidation**. Now use the Tools-Macro-Macros menu to run the four macros in the following order:

   ■   Position_Title_Screen – the title box is positioned on the screen.

   ■   Set_Title_Screen – the title screen is set up.

   ■   Restore_Title_Screen – the normal Excel screen defaults are restored.

   ■   Position_Database_Screen – the database headings are positioned on screen.

This sequence should give you an idea of the way in which the completed system will call the macros.

 Troubleshooting – stepping through a macro (information only)

 It is possible to execute a macro one step at a time; this is useful for testing and debugging – see Unit 12, Task 4.

Open the Tools menu and select Macro-Macros.

Select the macro Position_Title_Screen from the list.

Click the **Step Into** button.

The Visual Basic Editing window appears at the bottom of the screen – the first line of the macro should be highlighted.

If necessary, drag the window and resize it so that you can see the worksheet screen as well.

Open the **Debug** menu at the top of the Visual Basic Editing window and select the **Step Into** option.

The first line of the macro executes and the next line is selected.

Now keep pressing the *F8* key and notice the effect of each macro command on the worksheet settings; eventually you will step through the whole macro.

Close the Visual Basic Editing window.

Task 2: Creating a user form

We have designed our opening screens and four macros to control them.

The next step is to design a special 'custom' user form to allow the user to enter records into the orders database. It will use typical Excel features such as buttons, check boxes and drop down lists.

FIGURE 13.1 shows the completed form.

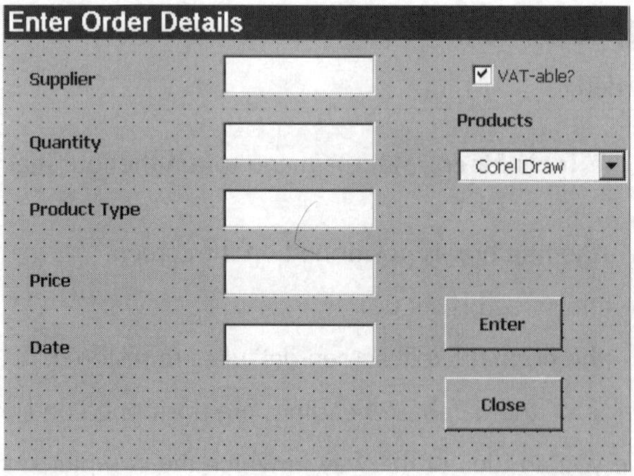

Enter Order Details
Supplier
Quantity
Product Type
Price
Date
☑ VAT-able?
Products
Corel Draw
Enter
Close

FIGURE 13.1

The user form will be controlled by a macro, created in the next unit.

1 **Opening a user form**. Open the **Tools** menu and select the **Macro** option.

   Select the option **Visual Basic Editor**.

   The Visual Basic Module opens, overlaying the worksheet. Maximise this window so that it fills the whole screen.

   Open the **Insert** menu and select **User Form**.

2   The window should display a blank form and the Toolbox – see FIGURE 13.2.

If the Toolbox is not open, select it from the **View** menu.

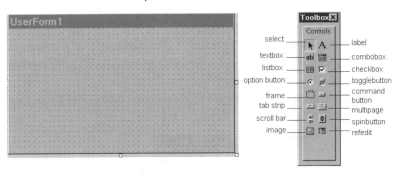

FIGURE 13.2

3   **Identifying VB project components**. The user form, together with the VB code
modules and the worksheet itself, form an overall VBA project. A Project Explorer
window allows you to view any hidden project component and work on it.

Let's try this.

■   First of all, display the Project window – see FIGURE 13.3. If you can't see it
then open the **View** menu and select **Project Explorer**. Check the listed
components against FIGURE 13.3.

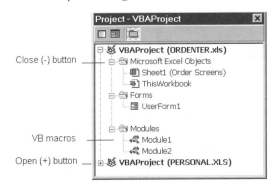

FIGURE 13.3

■   Double click the first two components, **Sheet1 (Order Screens)** and
ThisWorkbook and you will see that they are blank. They are intended to hold
the VB code that controls the workings of the worksheet or the workbook as a
whole. Close these windows again using the **Close** button.

■   Double click **UserForm1** – the form should already be displayed. Double click
Module1 (and **Module2** if present) – the VB code for the macros created in
Unit 12 is displayed. Close these windows again.

■   Experiment with the **Open** and **Close** buttons on the project window;
these are useful in hiding components. A large project could contain multiple
forms and worksheets/books.

■   Notice that the **PERSONAL** workbook may also be displayed as a separate
project (see Unit 11).

183

4   Finally, make sure that **UserForm1** is displayed and close the project window.

5   Click the edge of the user form – a selection border appears.

Move the screen pointer onto the bottom right-hand corner of the blank box and drag to enlarge it by about 30% – don't worry about exact sizes at this stage – all boxes and toolbars can be moved and resized by the usual dragging method.

6   **Viewing the Properties window**. Open the **View** menu and select **Properties Window**. The window opens – see FIGURE 13.4.

change the Name and
the Caption properties

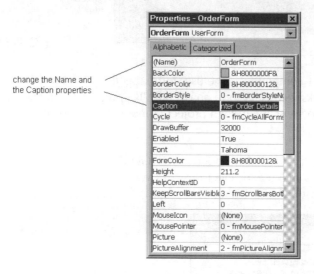

FIGURE 13.4

The **Properties window** is your major way of modifying the properties of the various objects that can appear on a form – buttons, text boxes and the form itself. Unfortunately, yet another open window all adds to the appearance of clutter on screen! If this hinders your work then you should get into the habit of only keeping those windows open that you are currently using – remember that it is easy to open them again using the **View** menu. You can also drag windows out of the way.

 If the Properties window suddenly changes size when you are moving it and 'squashes' the user form it can be dragged back to its normal shape.

7   **Adding a title**. At the moment the default title of the user form is **UserForm1**.

Select the Properties window and scroll down to the property **Caption** and change it to **Enter Order Details**.

Similarly, amend the form name from **UserForm1** to **OrderForm** – see FIGURE 13.4.

Close the Properties window.

 Don't confuse an object name with its caption; the caption is merely something that labels it for the user, but the name is used to identify the object to the rest of the project and has to be unique.

8 **Adding labels**. Move the screen pointer onto the Toolbox and click the **Label** button (see FIGURE 13.2).

Now move the pointer back onto the user form and drag to create a small label box.

Use FIGURE 13.5 as a rough guide; the size and position can be adjusted later.

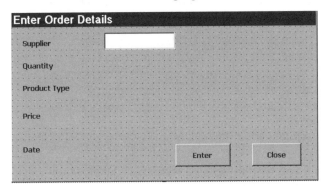

FIGURE 13.5

Now right click the label and select the **Properties** option from the popup menu.

The Properties window opens again (see FIGURE 13.4). Select the **Caption** property and amend it to *Supplier*. You have created your first field label; we will add the text box itself in Step 10.

9 **Labels and font styles**. Now repeat Step 8 to create labels for:

Quantity

Product Type

Price

Date

Use FIGURE 13.5 as a rough guide to their positioning. Again, change their captions as before – don't worry too much about their sizes and positions.

To alter the text size or style of a label (e.g. to bold) make sure that the Properties window is still open and that the correct label is selected.

Click on the **Font** property – a small ellipsis box opens (marked with three dots).

Click this box and the **Font** dialog box opens, allowing you to make the selection.

 If you double click an object by mistake then a VB module window may appear; if so, close the window and resume.

10 **Adding text boxes**. We need to add text boxes next to the labels so that the user can enter the order details.

Click on the **Text Box** tool (see FIGURE 13.2).

Move the pointer back onto the user form and drag to create a text box next to the **Supplier** label – see FIGURE 13.5.

Now right click the text box and select the **Properties** option from the popup menu.

The Properties window opens. Select the **Name** property and amend it to *TbSupplier* (the name property is listed at the top of the Properties window).

11 Now repeat Step 10 to add text boxes with the following names next to the other labels that you have created (refer to FIGURE 13.1 for guidance if necessary):

TbQuantity

TbType

TbPrice

TbDate

Again, don't worry too much about their sizes and positions.

12 **Correcting mistakes**. If you wish to delete a text box or label, simply click it to select it and then press the *Delete* key.

13 **Adding a check box**. We need to enter a check box so that the user can enter whether VAT is due on an item. As most items are VAT-able an 'X' will appear in the box by default; if the user deselects it then VAT is not payable.

Click on the **Check Box** tool (see FIGURE 13.2).

Move the pointer back onto the user form and drag to create a check box next to the **Supplier** box – see FIGURE 13.1 for guidance.

With the check box still selected, right click to open the Properties window if necessary.

Change the name property to *CbVat*.

Change the caption property to *VAT-able?*.

Change the value property to True.

14 **Adding a combo box**. The combo box will contain items of stock that can be added to the database.

Click on the **Combo** tool (see FIGURE 13.2).

Move the pointer back onto the user form and drag to create a check box below the VAT-able box – see FIGURE 13.1 for guidance.

A combination list/edit box (combo box) appears on screen. The scroll bars on the box will allow you to find and select the stock item you want. The edit box is to add a new stock item.

Name the combo box *CbProducts*.

15 **Labelling the combo box**. A label over the combo box will clarify its use for the user – see FIGURE 13.1 above. Click on the **Label** tool (see FIGURE 13.2).

Move the pointer back onto the user form and drag to create a label above the combo box. The name of the label is unimportant in this instance. Select the Caption property and amend it to **Products**.

16 **Linking the combo box to the product list**. If the Properties dialog box is not open then right click the combo box. Select the Properties option from the popup menu that appears. With the combo box still selected, select the Row Source property and key in the cell reference **U22:U33** – cell range U22–U32 on the **ORDER SCREENS** worksheet holds the list of computer products that the company buys from suppliers (see Unit 12, Task 1, Step 13).

Close the Properties box. When you return to the user form the list of products appears in the list box – click the down arrow and scroll through it if necessary.

17 **Adding command buttons**. Use the CommandButton tool on the Toolbox to add a button in the bottom left-hand corner of the form – see FIGURE 13.1.

Use the Properties dialog box to name it **btnEnter**.

Alter the caption property to **Enter**.

18 Create a second button below the first – see FIGURE 13.1.

Use the Properties dialog box to name it **btnClose**.

Alter the caption property to **Close**.

19 **A note on object naming**. It is good development practice to use consistent, clear names for objects and to identify the type of object with a prefix, as we have done above; e.g. all button names start with 'btn', text boxes with 'tb' etc. When we are creating VB code in the next unit it will make them easy to identify.

20 Now reposition all the elements in the completed screen to achieve a neat layout, using FIGURE 13.1 as a guide. First click the element to select it, then move the screen pointer onto the border to move it, or onto a selection handle to resize it. You can alter the size and position of a component more precisely by amending the Width, Height, Top and Left properties in the Properties dialog box.

21 Save the workbook.

Task 3: Naming the cells in the database

We are going to create a macro that transfers the order details from the user form into the database held in the worksheet. The macro will also multiply price by quantity to calculate the total price of the order and apply VAT.

1 Open the **ORDER SCREENS** worksheet and scroll so that L52 is at the top left-hand corner – see FIGURE 13.6.

	L	M	N	O	P	Q	R	S
52								
53								
54								
55								
56	Supplier	Product	Type	Quantity	Price	Date	VAT	Total
57								
58								

FIGURE 13.6

We are going to name a number of cells that will hold the order details when they are first transferred into the worksheet.

2 **Naming the database cells.** Click cell L52 then open the **Insert** menu and select **Name** followed by **Define**.

Enter the name **WSSUPPLIER** and click **OK** . This cell name is easier to remember and can now be used in a macro instead of a cell reference.

3 Name the following cells in a similar way:

Give cell **M52** the name **WSPRODUCT**

Give cell **N52** the name **WSTYPE**

Give cell **O52** the name **WSQUANTITY**

Give cell **P52** the name **WSPRICE**

Give cell **Q52** the name **WSDATE**

Give cell **R52** the name **WSVAT**

Give cell **S52** the name **WSTOTAL**

4 The 'WS' prefix to the cell names will identify them as worksheet names. This will distinguish them from the names used for text boxes (prefixed with 'Tb') in the previous activity.

5 Using the **Format-Cells-Number** command, format the cell **WSDATE** to a suitable date format, the cell **WSQUANTITY** to 0 decimal places and the cells **WSPRICE**, **WSVAT** and **WSTOTAL** to two decimal places.

6 Save and close the workbook.

Summary of commands

 Menu commands show the menu name first, followed by the command to choose from the menu, e.g. **Edit-Clear** means open the **Edit** menu and select the **Clear** command.

Worksheet commands

Insert-Name-Define	Name a selected object, e.g. cell(s)
Tools-Macro-Macros	Select a macro to run edit, delete etc
Tools-Macro-Visual Basic Editor	Call up a macro module, user form etc
Tools-Record Macro-New Macro	Record new macro

VB Editor commands

Debug-Step Into	Execute a macro a line at a time
Insert-User Form	Create custom user form
View-Project Explorer	View components of a project
View-Properties Window	View/amend the properties of an object
View-Toolbox	Display the toolbox button bar

Controlling a user form

Important note

Units 12–17 form a unified development task – they all need to be completed in order for the purchase order application to work. Unlike previous units, there is no point in doing any one unit in isolation from the others – they all build on each other.

What you will learn in this unit

By the end of this unit you will be able to:

- attach a code to an object
- use calculations in subprocedures
- use the Project Explorer
- change the tab order
- open a user form
- enter Visual Basic commands
- run Visual Basic commands.

What you should know already

Before you start this unit, make sure that you can do the following:

Skill	Covered in
Basic mouse, menu and Windows operations	Unit 1
Using formulae	Units 1 and 2

Introduction

This unit continues the development of the purchase order application begun in Units 12 and 13. It shows you how to create a macro that will take the purchase order data from the user form created in the previous unit and store it in the worksheet. You will need to key in the VB code – it cannot be recorded as a macro.

Task 1: Creating a macro to control the user form

We want to program the **Enter** button in the user form so that, whenever it is clicked, it will run a macro that takes the record held in the user form and add it to the database. In Visual Basic this is called an event handler procedure – it handles or responds to the event of clicking a button. This activity will introduce some programming concepts in Visual Basic. They will be introduced as we go along, so take the time to read the explanations rather than just copying the lines of program code.

First some general theory.

Objects. Visual Basic is an object-oriented language, i.e. the program manipulates objects. Worksheets, windows, user forms, buttons, menus and ranges of cells are all examples of objects. Objects can contain other objects: e.g. a worksheet contains cells, which contain values.

Some objects, called collection objects, contain sets of objects: e.g. a user form contains buttons and edit boxes. To identify an object you often need to identify its container as well, e.g. the user form that contains the edit box.

Properties. All objects have properties that determine how they look or how they work, e.g. a TextBox object has a *Text* property – the text it contains – and a workbook can be active or not – the property *ActiveWorkbook*. Not all properties apply to all objects. We have already used the Properties window in the previous unit to modify the name and caption properties of objects on the form.

Methods. These are used to perform actions on objects. An object's properties determine what methods can be used with them, e.g. many objects can be opened, closed, copied or activated – worksheets, workbooks etc – but calculations can only be applied to certain types of numeric objects.

Syntax. Objects, methods and properties are separated from each other by full stops; to refer to the method you are applying to the object you use the syntax *Object.Method*, i.e. object name separated from method name with a full stop.

1 **Opening the user form**. If necessary, open the workbook **ORDENTER**.

   Open the Tools menu and select the Macro option.

   Select the option Visual Basic Editor.

The Visual Basic Module opens, overlaying the worksheet. Maximise this window so that it fills the whole screen. If the user form **OrderForm** that you created in the last unit is not visible then proceed as follows:

- First of all, select the Project window. If you can't see it then open the View menu and select **Project Explorer**.

- Identify the Forms folder in the Project Explorer. If necessary open it to display the form **OrderForm**.

- Double click on the **OrderForm** icon to display it. Resize the form if necessary. Your screen should now look like FIGURE 14.1.

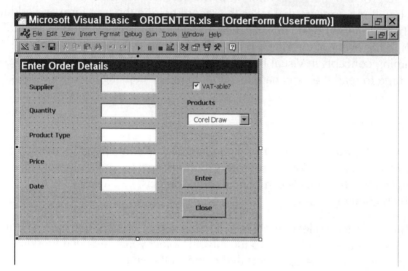

FIGURE 14.1

2 **Attaching code to an object**. A fundamental principle of object-oriented programming is that code can be attached to an object, such as a button, to control how it behaves.

Double click the **Enter** button on the user form.

A VB module sheet appears containing a code stub – the skeleton of a VB subprocedure. The first line – **Private Sub btnEnter_Click( )** – is simply the name that is automatically allocated to it; **sub** is short for subprocedure – part of the larger procedure or program – and **private** means that it only controls this button on this form.

End Sub marks the end of the subprocedure.

These two lines should not be deleted or changed.

The main statements (lines of code) in a program fit between the **Sub** and **End Sub** statements.

3 Position the cursor on the blank line between the two statements and carefully type in the following VB statements.

'Copy supplier name from user form to named cell in

'worksheet

Sheets("Order Screens").Range("WSSupplier") = _

OrderForm.TbSupplier.Value

4   **Tips on entering VB code**

■   Blank lines can also be inserted for readability.

■   You may enter the statements in upper- or lower-case.

■   A single quotation mark at the start of any line means that it is a comment. It is there to document or explain the program and will be ignored by it.

■   Press *Enter* after entering each line; it will automatically be checked and formatted for you. Any errors will be highlighted and an error message appear. Usually they are simple typing errors, but ones to check especially are:

   – When you split a long statement over two lines you must add a space followed by an underscore (_) character to the end of the first line – miss the space or use the wrong character and it won't work.

   – Use the double quotes " " and round brackets ( ) as shown, for example in *("Order Screens")*.

   – Don't include spaces around the full stops, for example in *OrderForm.TbSupplier.Value*.

■   **Help on VB code**. Locate the cursor on the word and press the *F1* key. Help on that term is provided. You will find it provides examples of code as well.

5   **Explanation of the VB statements**

Sheets("Order Screens").Range("WSSupplier") = _
OrderForm.TbSupplier.Value

The **Range** statement continues over two lines. It identifies a cell range called **WSSupplier** in the worksheet **ORDER SCREENS** and makes its value equal to the text box **TbSupplier** on the user form named **OrderForm**. This is an effective way of copying the supplier name from the user form into the worksheet (you will recall that **WSSupplier** is the name we gave to cell L52 – see Unit 13).

6   **Testing your first line of code**. The complete macro should look like this now:

Private Sub btnEnter_Click()

'Copy supplier name from text box in form to named cell in

'worksheet

Sheets("Order Screens").Range("WSSupplier") = _

OrderForm.TbSupplier.Value

End Sub

Open the **Run** menu and select the **Run Sub/User Form** option. The user form is displayed (notice that it has no dotted grid on it – this is only displayed when you are designing the user form, not when you are running it).

Click on the **Supplier** edit box to select it and enter any name.

Click the ▐Enter▐ button and then close the form using the ▐Close▐ button at the top of the form window (not the special ▐Close▐ button on the form – this has not been programmed yet). The subroutine **btnEnter_Click** is stopped and the form is displayed with its dotted grid again.

Activate the worksheet **ORDER SCREENS** (use the Taskbar at the bottom of the window – see FIGURE 14.2).

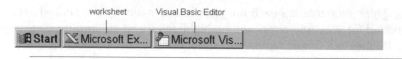

FIGURE 14.2

7 Check cell L52 – it should contain the data entered into the **Supplier** text box on the user form.

 If nothing has happened, or you get an error message, don't worry. Return to the user form and double click the ▐Enter▐ button on the form to display the VB module again and check:

the spelling of the code

the names of the user form, the worksheet, the cells and the text boxes.

If the program crashes and you get an error message, check whether the form is still running (it will not be displaying a dotted grid). If it is still running do not edit the VB code yet; open the **Run** menu and select **Reset**.

8 Now enter the rest of the subroutine as shown below.

You may find it quicker to copy and paste the lines, and then modify them.

> **Private Sub btnEnter_Click( )**
>
> *'Copy supplier name from text box in form to named cell in*
> *'worksheet*
> *Sheets("Order Screens").Range("WSSupplier") = _*
> *OrderForm.TbSupplier.Value*
>
> *'Copy product name from combo box in form to named cell in*
> *'worksheet*
> *Sheets("Order Screens").Range("WSProduct") = _*
> *OrderForm.CbProducts.Value*
>
> *'Copy product type from text box in form to named cell in*
> *'worksheet*
> *Sheets("Order Screens").Range("WSType") = _*
> *OrderForm.TbType.Value*

'Copy quantity from text box in form to named cell in
'worksheet
Sheets("Order Screens").Range("WSQuantity") = _
OrderForm.TbQuantity.Value

'Copy unit price from text box in form to named cell in
'worksheet
Sheets("Order Screens").Range("WSPrice") = _
OrderForm.TbPrice.Value

'Copy order date from text box in form to named cell in
'worksheet
Sheets("Order Screens").Range("WSDate") = _
OrderForm.TbDate.Value

End Sub

9 Now test that the user form is working correctly as before – see Step 6. You will need to enter some test data in the text boxes on the user form – use the mouse or the *Tab* key to select each box – see Step 13 to change the tab order.

Debug as before if necessary.

10 **Checking and calculating the VAT**. If the check box is checked then we want to add the current rate – 17.5% – to the total value of the order and transfer this to the worksheet cells we have designated – see Unit 13 if necessary.

The VAT calculation is simply the quantity multiplied by the item price multiplied by 0.175.

If no VAT is payable, then VAT is set to 0.

The VAT rate is held in a variable called **Vatrate**; this saves entering the rate for every order and makes it easy to amend if the VAT rate changes.

Insert a blank line before the **End Sub** line and insert the following VB statements:

'Calculate the VAT rate at 17.5% if check box is on
Vatrate = 0.175

If OrderForm.CbVat.Value = True _
Then
    *Sheets("Order Screens").Range("WSVat") = Vatrate * _*
    *Range("WsQuantity").Value * Range("WsPrice").Value*
Else
    Sheets("Order Screens").Range("WSVat") = 0
End If
*'Calculate the order total = (price * quantity) + vat*
Sheets("Order Screens").Range("WSTotal") = _
*(Range("WsQuantity").Value) * (Range("WsPrice").Value) _*
    + Range("WsVat").Value

11 Make sure that ***End Sub*** finishes the subroutine.

- The Excel property for a check box being set on is True.
- * is the multiplication sign.
- The VB syntax checker puts the ***If-Then-Else-End*** statement in blue.
- It places incorrect statements in red – this may merely be because a statement is incomplete and will disappear when you finish. If it remains red check it again – see Step 4.

12 Test the user form again with the check box on and off. Check that the VAT has been calculated and copied correctly to the worksheet cells R52 and S52. If it works then congratulate yourself – your first efforts at typing in VB commands can be fiddly, error-prone and frustrating. It will get easier as you practice!

If nothing has happened, or you get an error message, don't worry. Return to the module sheet containing the macro code and check:

- the spelling of the code and the other characters – especially brackets, the double quotation marks, the full stops and the space and underscore used to join the parts of a line
- the names – see Step 7.

13 **Changing the tab order (optional)**. If you were moving between boxes in the user form using the <u>*Tab*</u> key you may have noticed that the edit boxes were not selected in any particular sequence.

If the code module is showing open the **View** menu and select **Object**.

Open the **View** menu and select the **Tab Order** option – a user form appears.

Select an edit box from the list, then click the up or down arrow buttons to change its position.

When you are finished click **OK** .

14 **Independent activity – programming the Close button**. At the moment we have to use the standard window Close button at the top of the form. When the user clicks the custom Close button (next to the Enter button) on the user form we want the subroutine to end and the form to close.

Double click on the Close button at the bottom of the user form. Provided that you are in design mode (i.e. the subroutine ***btnEnter_Click*** is not running and the form shows a dotted grid) a VB module sheet opens ready named. Simply insert the following commands:

Application.Run "Set_Title_Screen"
Application.Run "ORDENTER.xls!Position_Title_Screen"
End

Run and test the Close button. It should set up and position the title screen and then close the form.

15 Save and close the workbook.

Summary of commands

Menu commands show the menu name first, followed by the command to choose from the menu, e.g. **Edit-Clear** means open the **Edit** menu and select the **Clear** command.

Worksheet commands

Tools-Macro-Visual Basic Editor   Enter VB Editor

VB Editor commands

Run-Reset   Reset a VB macro/program after crashing

Run-Run Sub/User Form   Run a VB macro, program or user form

View-Project Explorer   View components of a project

View-Tab Order   Change order edit boxes selected

Further macros

Important note

Units 12–17 form a unified development task – they all need to be completed in order for the purchase order application to work. Unlike previous units, there is no point in doing any one unit in isolation from the others – they all build on each other.

What you will learn in this unit

By the end of this unit you will be able to:

- use conditions
- add records to a database
- define a database
- test a macro
- create a message box
- insert rows
- hide and show a user form
- run a user form.

Introduction

This unit continues the development of the purchase order application begun in Units 12–14. It uses the **If** condition to let the user either continue using the user form or quit.

Task 1: Adding the records to a database

The procedure **btnEnter_Click( )** transfers the data from the user form to a cell range in the worksheet **ORDER SCREENS**. The next macro will transfer it from this cell range to a database held in the **ORDER SCREENS** worksheet.

This is a fairly simple macro to record. It involves:

- defining a cell range as a database
- copying and pasting the values into it
- inserting a blank row into the database for the next record

1 Open the workbook **ORDENTER**.

If necessary open the worksheet **ORDER SCREENS** and scroll so that cell **L52** is in the top left-hand corner of the window. As you have been testing the user form in the previous unit, cells L52–S52 will probably contain some test data; if not, create some – see FIGURE 15.1.

	L	M	N	O	P	Q	R	S
52	JM Software	Access Manual	textbook	10	24.5	02-Apr-97	42.88	287.88
53								
54								
55								
56	Supplier	Product	Type	Quantity	Price	Date	VAT	Total
57								

FIGURE 15.1

First we need to define certain cells as a database area. We can then record a macro that adds records to it.

Select the eight field names (cells L56–S56), plus the two rows of eight cells directly underneath. You have now selected the cell range L56–S58.

Open the Insert menu and select the Name-Define option.

A dialog box appears. Enter the name **DATABASE** then click OK .

2 Open the Tools menu and select the Macro-Record New Macro options.

A dialog box appears.

Name the macro **Add_Order** and complete the Description box; e.g. **adds record to database**.

Make sure that the option This Workbook is selected.

Click OK .

You are now recording.

3 Click the row designator number for row 57 – the whole row is selected.

Open the **Insert** menu and select **Rows** – a blank row is inserted.

Select the record in row 52 (cells L52–S52).

Open the **Edit** menu and select **Copy** – the record is framed by a dotted box.

Click cell L57.

Open the **Edit** menu and select **Paste** – the record is copied to the database.

Press the *Esc* key to remove the dotted box.

Click the **Stop Recorder** button.

4 Whenever this macro is run a blank row will be inserted into the database area and the new record will be copied from row 52 – see FIGURE 15.2.

	L	M	N	O	P	Q	R	S
49								
50								
51								
52	JM Software	Access Manual	textbook	10	24.5	02-Apr-97	42.88	287.88
53								
54								
55								
56	**Supplier**	**Product**	**Type**	**Quantity**	**Price**	**Date**	**VAT**	**Total**
57	JM Software	Access Manual	textbook	10	24.5	02-Apr-97	42.88	287.88

FIGURE 15.2

Amend the data in row 52; then run the macro using the **Tools-Macro-Macros** command – the row will be copied again.

5 **Viewing the module sheets**. Open the **Tools** menu and select the **Macro-Macros** option.

Select **Add_Order** from the list of macros and click the **Edit** button. You are taken to the correct module sheet to see the macro code.

Now check the name of the module sheet – Excel may have placed this macro on a new module sheet. As you can always locate the macro by using the **Tools** menu it does not matter.

6 **Testing the macro**. Maximise the module sheet window so that it fills the whole screen. If the user form *OrderForm* is not visible then proceed as follows:

▪ First of all select the Project window. If you can't see it, then open the **View** menu and select **Project Explorer**.

▪ Identify the **Forms** folder in the Project window. If necessary open it to display the icon for the form *OrderForm*.

▪ Double click on the *OrderForm* icon to display it. Resize the form if necessary.

▪ Close the Project window.

7 Open the **Run** menu and take the **Run Sub/User Form** option. The form should now be running – the dotted design grid on the form should not be visible.

Type in a new record, using data of your own,

Click the ███**Enter**███ button to complete entering the record.

Close the form using the ██**Close**██ button.

8 Open the **Tools** menu and select the **Macros** option.

Select **Add_Order** from the list of macros and click the ██**Run**██ button.

The new record should have been copied into the database. Open the worksheet **ORDER SCREENS** to check this.

You may need to adjust the column width of some of the database columns to accommodate the field lengths.

Task 2: Macros that call macros

We now need a macro to combine the activities of using the user form and adding the record to the database. We will also create a procedure that gives users the option to use the form more than once so that they can continue adding more records.

1 Display the user form as before, making sure that it is in design mode, not running (i.e. the dotted grid on the form is showing).

2 Double click on the ██**Enter**██ button on the form to call up the procedure *btnEnter_Click()* created in the previous unit.

Scroll to the end of the procedure and type the following statements just before the **End Sub** command:

'Hide the Order Form
OrderForm.Hide

'Run the Add_order macro to add record to the database
Application.Run "ORDENTER.xls!Add_Order"

3 This will close the user form and automatically run the **Add_Order** macro created in the previous activity, which will add the record to the database.

4 We now need to modify the **Add_Order** macro itself so that it prompts the user to add another record. Open the **Tools** menu and select the **Macros** option.

Select the **Add_Orders** macro and take the **Edit** option. The module sheet opens, showing the VB code for this macro.

Scroll down to the end of the code and insert a blank line before the **End Sub** statement, then type the following:

```
'Set up variable called reply to hold user response to
'message box
Dim reply

'Display a message box prompting the user to add
'another order
reply = MsgBox("Enter another order?", vbYesNo, _
"Purchase Orders")

'If the yes button on the message box is clicked
If reply = vbYes _
    Then
            OrderForm.Show 'Show the Order Form
    Else
            OrderForm.Hide 'Hide the Order Form
            'Return to the title screen on worksheet
            Sheets("Order Screens").Select
            ActiveWindow.WindowState = xlMaximized
            Application.Run "Position_Title_Screen"
            Application.Run "Set_Title_Screen"
End If
```

5 **Explanation of macro**. If you are new to programming then read this explanation carefully. It introduces some fundamental programming concepts. You should find that the comments in the macro explain each line fairly fully; however, some additional explanations and hints are given below.

Conditions. A macro can be designed to offer the user a choice, in this case to continue or quit, using an *If* condition. The macro can then branch, i.e. take alternative actions, depending on user choice, using *Else*. Every *If* condition needs an *End If* to show where it ends.

vbYes and *vbNo* are special Visual Basic constants generated by clicking a `Yes` or `No` button. A variable *Reply* is set up to hold the response.

MsgBox creates a small message box with a title, message and `Yes/No` buttons.

An *If* condition tests for a *Yes* response to the message and redisplays the user form.

The *Else* condition tests for the only other alternative – the user clicking the `No` button on the message box. The worksheet **ORDER SCREENS** is displayed and the macros Position_Title_Screen and Set_Title_Screen are called to display the start-up screen.

6 **Creating a macro that calls the order form**. Use the Windows Taskbar to return to the Excel worksheet screen.

Open the Tools menu and select the Macro-Record New Macro options.

A dialog box appears.

Name the macro Call_Order_Form and complete the Description box.

Make sure that the option **This Workbook** is selected.

Click **OK** .

You are now recording.

Now click the **Stop Recorder** button – you now have a macro that contains no commands.

Open the **Tools** menu and select the **Macro-Macros** options.

Select the **Call_Order_Form** macro and take the **Edit** option.

The module sheet opens showing the VB code for this macro – all that you need to do is to add the **OrderForm.Show** command as shown below.

Sub Call_Order_Form( )
'

' Call_Order_Form Macro
' Macro recorded 06/02/97 by j muir
'

OrderForm.Show
'

End Sub

Close the module sheet and return to the Excel worksheet.

7 **Testing the macros**. When you have typed in the code save the workbook.

To run the user form again open the **Tools** menu and select **Macro-Macros**.

Select the macro **Call_Order_Form** from the list and click the **Run** button.

If it runs do the following:

■ Enter a new record in the user form and click **Enter** .

■ The message box should appear. Click **Yes** and the order form appears again.

■ Repeat the two preceding steps, but this time click **No** instead of **Yes** .

■ The title screen should appear – if not you will need to run the **Restore_Title_Screen** macro to restore the screen defaults.

■ Check that the records are being added to the database.

8 **Debugging the macro**. If you get a mysterious-looking error message don't worry. Often the incorrect VB command is highlighted by the debugger. Return to the macro and check the following:

■ Does the *If* have an *End If*?

■ Check that *Then* is on the same line as *If*, or as I have done, joined to the previous line by an underscore preceded by a space.

■ Check that *Else* and *End If* are on separate lines.

- Check that you have spelt the commands, the worksheet and the macro names correctly.

9 Save and close the workbook.

Summary of commands

Menu commands show the menu name first, followed by the command to choose from the menu, e.g. **Edit-Clear** means open the **Edit** menu and select the **Clear** command.

Worksheet commands

Insert-Rows	Insert a new row into a worksheet
Insert-Name-Define	Name a selected object, e.g. database cells
Tools-Macro-Macros	Select a macro to run, edit, delete etc.
Tools-Macro-Record New Macro	Record a new macro
Tools-Macro-Visual Basic Editor	Enter VB Editor

VB Editor commands

Run-Run Sub/User Form	Run a VB macro, program or user form
View-Project Explorer	View components of a project

Creating a data form and a custom menu

Important note

Units 12–17 form a unified development task – they all need to be completed in order for the purchase order application to work. Unlike previous units, there is no point in doing any one unit in isolation from the others – they all build on each other.

What you will learn in this unit

By the end of this unit you will be able to:

- attach a custom menu to a workbook

- create a custom menu

- edit and test a custom menu

- call and use a data form

- assign a macro to a menu

- document a macro

- write a macro for printing

- write a macro for saving and quitting

- test a macro.

Introduction

This unit continues the development of the purchase order application begun in Units 12–15. It creates a data form so that purchase order records can be edited or deleted and creates a custom menu that will call various macros.

Task 1: Using a data form

Excel provides a standard form for you to add, delete or edit records – see Unit 5, Task 4. This will form one of the options in our application and be called by a macro Call_Data_Form.

1   If necessary, open the workbook **ORDENTER** and make sure that the worksheet **ORDER SCREEN** is displayed.

Open the Tools menu and select Macro-Record New Macro. A dialog box appears.

Name the macro Call_Data_Form and complete the Description box; e.g. *uses data form for editing*.

Make sure that the This Workbook option is selected.

Click **OK** .

You are now recording.

2   Click on the sheet tab for **Order Screens** to activate it (even if already selected).

Open the Tools menu and select the Macro-Macros options.

Run the macro Position_Database_Screen – the database cells should now be displayed.

Click anywhere on the database, e.g. on one of the heading cells in row 56.

Open the Data menu and select Form – a data form is displayed – see FIGURE 16.1.

Click the **Close** button on the form.

Open the Tools menu and select the Macro-Macros options.

Run the macro Set_Title_Screen.

Open the Tools menu and select the Macro-Macros options.

Run the macro Position_Title_Screen.

The title screen appears.

Click the **Stop Recorder** button.

Order Screens

Supplier: DP Publications   1 of 4

Product: Internet Guide   New

Type: textbook   Delete

Quantity: 12   Restore

Price: 8.99

Date: 3/8/1997   Find Prev

VAT: 18.879   Find Next

Total: 126.759   Criteria

Close

FIGURE 16.1

3 **Testing the macro**. Open the Tools menu and select the Macro-Macros options.

Run the macro Restore_Title_Screen to restore the screen defaults if necessary.

Now run the macro Call_Data_Form.

The data form is displayed. Click the **Close** button. The Set_Title_Screen macro will be called next and the macro will end.

Run the macro Restore_Title_Screen again.

 4 If your macro doesn't work, try deleting it (use the Tools-Macro menu) and re-recording the above steps.

 If it still doesn't work, check that the database is still defined – see Unit 15, Task 1, Step 1. If not, redefine it and try the macro again.

5 **Documenting the macro**. Designing macros can become complex in a large-scale application; macros contain many Visual Basic commands and call other macros in a variety of ways. It is therefore important to keep track of the project by using comments. They will also act as reminders if the application is modified in the future. Open the Tools menu and select the Macro-Macros options.

Select the macro Call_Data_Form and click the **Edit** button.

Your macro should resemble the following. Add the comments shown.

Sub Call_Data_Form( )
'

'Call_Data_Form Macro
'Macro recorded 07/02/97 by j muir
'uses data form for editing
'

207

Sheets("Order Screens").Select

'Run the macro to show the database cells
Application.Run "ORDENTER.xls!Position_Database_Screen"

'Select a cell in the database
Range("L56").Select

'Call the data form
ActiveSheet.ShowDataForm

'Run the macro to set up the title screen
Application.Run "ORDENTER.xls!Set_Title_Screen"

'Run the macro to position the title screen
Application.Run "ORDENTER.xls!Position_Title_Screen"

End Sub

Close the module sheet and return to the Excel worksheet.

Run the macro Restore_Title_Screen again.

Task 2: Printing, saving and quitting macros

We will write two short macros – one to print the database and one to save and quit the workbook. Turn on the printer for this activity (you can still carry out these activities without a printer).

1   **The print macro.** Open the Tools menu and select Macro-Record New Macro. A dialog box appears.

Name the macro Print_Database and complete the Description box; e.g. ***Prints database records***.

Make sure that the This Workbook option is selected.

Click OK .

You are now recording.

2   Click on the sheet tab for Order Screens to activate it (even if already selected).

Open the Tools menu and select the Macro-Macros options.

Run the macro Position_Database_Screen.

The database cells should now be displayed. Click cell **L56** – the first heading in the database.

Open the Edit menu and select Go To – a dialog box appears.

Click the Special button – the Go To Special dialog box appears.

Click the Current Region button then OK .The whole database area should now be selected.

3   Open the File menu and select Print – a dialog box appears.

Click the **Selection** button in the Print What section.

Click **OK** . Wait until the database has printed.

Open the Tools menu and select the Macro option.

Run the macro Set_Title_Screen then the macro Position_Title_Screen. The title screen appears.

Click the **Stop Recorder** button.

Run the macro Restore_Title_Screen to restore the screen defaults.

If the printout is not to your satisfaction then you may need to adjust the page setup. If so, delete and re-record the macro.

4   **Testing the macro**. Now run the Call_Order_Form macro to add another record.

Run the Print_Database macro to test the print macro.

Make sure that the full database is printed, including the new record.

Run the macro Restore_Title_Screen to restore the screen defaults.

5   **The save and quit macro**

The macro will save the whole workbook and then quit Excel.

Call the macro ***Save_Quit*** and start recording as before.

Save the workbook (**File-Save**) and then stop the recorder.

6   **Editing the** Save_Quit **macro**. Open the Tools menu and select Macro-Macros.

Select the Save_Quit macro from the list and then click the **Edit** button – the module sheet appears.

To complete this macro we need to insert a ***Quit*** method before the ***End Sub*** in order to quit Excel. Insert the line shown before the End Sub statement.

Sub Save_quit( )
'
'Save_quit Macro
'Macro recorded 07/02/97 by j muir
'Saves the workbook and exits excel
ActiveWorkbook.Save
Application.Quit
End Sub

7   Test the macro; it should save the workbook and then exit Excel.

8   Run Excel again and open the workbook **ORDENTER.XLS**.

Task 3: Creating a custom menu

We have created macros to run all the major database operations – adding records, updating and searching, printing the database and exiting. We now need to design a custom menu that offers these options; it will resemble a standard Excel menu in appearance and operation. It will open automatically when the workbook is opened and replace the standard Excel menus. It will look like FIGURE 16.9 when it is complete.

In Excel 97 the distinction between a toolbar and a menu has been dropped – they are both termed 'command bars' and are no longer treated as separate entities (although the menu/toolbar terminology is still used). Command bars can contain both toolbar buttons and menu items. They can either be 'docked' on the edge of a window or 'float' anywhere in the window. A custom menu is now created using the Customize dialog box rather than the Menu Editor.

1   Open the Tools menu and select Customize.

A dialog box appears. Click the **Toolbars** tab followed by the **New** button.

The New Toolbar dialog box appears. Name it **Orders** and click the **OK** button.

The new custom menu is displayed – at the moment it looks like a toolbar button – see FIGURE 16.2. The custom menu will be displayed on the worksheet while we are adding the options to it.

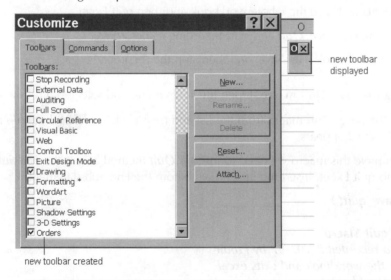

new toolbar displayed

new toolbar created

FIGURE 16.2

2   Now click the **Commands** tab on the Customize dialog box. Scroll down to the bottom of the Categories list and select the New Menu option. The New Menu option is now displayed at the top of the Commands list.

Move the mouse pointer onto the New menu command and drag it from the Commands box onto the custom menu – it will now resemble FIGURE 16.3.

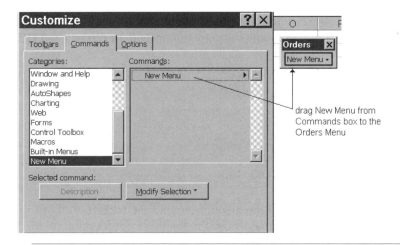

FIGURE 16.3

3   Now click the **Modify Selection** button on the **Customize** dialog box – a popup menu appears. Select the Name option from the menu and rename the menu *Purchase Orders*.

Press *Enter* – the custom menu will now resemble FIGURE 16.4.

FIGURE 16.4

4   Now click on the **Purchase Orders** option on the custom menu. An empty drop-down box appears – see FIGURE 16.5.

FIGURE 16.5

5   Now move the mouse pointer to the **New Menu** option in the **Customize** dialog box again. Drag it on top of the drop down box on the custom menu – it should now look like FIGURE 16.6.

FIGURE 16.6

6   Repeat Step 3 to rename this option *Enter an Order*. The custom menu should now resemble FIGURE 16.7.

FIGURE 16.7

7 Now repeat the above steps to drag a third menu option to the bottom of the **Enter an Order** option. Rename this new option ***Edit an Order*** – see FIGURE 16.8.

 If you make a mistake simply drag the menu item back onto the **Customize** dialog box to delete it.

FIGURE 16.8

8 Repeat the above steps until the menu resembles FIGURE 16.9. To insert lines between the groups of commands use the **Begin a Group** option on the popup menu.

FIGURE 16.9

9 **Assigning macros to the menu options**. We now need to assign the macros that we have already created to the menu options.

Right click the first menu option – **Enter an Order**. Take the menu option **Assign Macro** from the popup menu.

The **Assign Macro** dialog box appears. Select the macro **Call_Order_Form** from the list and click the **OK** button. This macro is now assigned to this menu option.

10 Now continue to assign the other macros to the menu option as follows:

Menu choice	*Macro*
Edit an Order	Call_Data_Form
Print Database	Print_Database
Restore Excel Screen	Restore_Title_Screen
Save and Exit	Save_Quit

11 **Attaching the custom menu to the workbook**. Click the **Toolbars** tab in the **Customize** dialog box. Make sure that the **Orders** menu is still selected in the **Toolbars** list and click the **Attach** button.

The Attach Toolbars dialog box appears – see FIGURE 16.10.

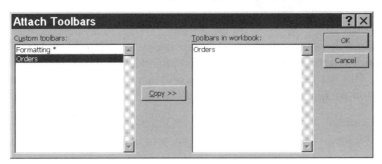

FIGURE 16.10

Make sure that Orders is selected in the left-hand Custom toolbars list; then click the **Copy** button – it is copied into the right-hand Toolbars in workbook section.

Click **OK**. The custom menu is now attached to the **ORDENTER** workbook.

12 Finally, drag the custom menu to the top of the workbook window and onto the main menu bar. It becomes a 'docked' command bar. Close the Customize dialog box. The custom menu should now occupy its own area at the top of the window – see FIGURE 16.11.

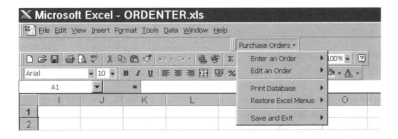

FIGURE 16.11

Be careful if you attempt to move the custom menu – it is all too easy to delete the menu options – see the note in the next task.

Task 4: Testing the custom menu

When the custom menu is opened it should look like FIGURE 16.11. If not, you will need to go back and edit it – see below.

This menu can be run whenever the workbook **ORDENTER** is opened and **ORDER SCREENS** is the active sheet.

Important cautionary notes: Editing the custom menu

When the menu is 'docked' at the top of the worksheet it is marked with a 'move handle' – two vertical lines on the left – see FIGURE 16.12.

213

vertical lines ——————||  Purchase Orders ▾
to move menu

FIGURE 16.12

Use this handle only to move the menu. Dragging any other part of the menu will delete the options. If this happens, then you will need to recreate them – see the previous task. This is an important point, as to edit menu options you will need to open the **Customize** dialog box and then move the menu bar so that it 'floats' on the worksheet.

1   Now test the menu options in turn, making a note of anything that does not work correctly.

■ **Enter an Order**. Take this option. The user form should appear.

Enter a new order and click the **Enter** button. The message box 'Enter another order?' should be displayed now.

Click the **Yes** button. You should be returned to the user form.

This time click the **Close** button. You should be returned to the special title screen.

■ **Edit an Order**. Take this option. The data form should be displayed.

First check that the record is added to the database.

Use the buttons and try editing a record then click the **Close** button. You should be returned to the special title screen.

■ **Print Database**. Make sure that the printer is turned on (if you have no printer press the **Cancel** button when the print message box is displayed).

Take this option and check that the new record is printed too. You should be returned to the special title screen.

■ **Restore Excel Screen**. Take this option. The default toolbars, gridlines etc are restored.

■ **Save and Exit**. The workbook should be saved and closed and you should exit Excel.

Start Excel again and re-open the workbook. Check that the new record was saved.

2   If any of the above operations don't work correctly make a full note of the problem. Don't worry – most applications don't work perfectly the first time! Notice that the custom menu options will respond automatically if the screen pointer is rested on an option – there is no need to click.

To edit the custom menu open the **Tools-Customize** menu. Remember that you can test individual macros a step at a time using the **Tools-Macro-Macros** menu – but see the important note above first.

3   If you are not going on to the next unit save and close the workbook.

Summary of commands

Menu commands show the menu name first, followed by the command to choose from the menu, e.g. **Edit-Clear** means open the **Edit** menu and select the **Clear** command.

Menu commands

Data-Form	Use a data form with a database
Edit-Go To	Go to selected cell(s)
File-Print	Print a worksheet
Tools-Macro-Macros	Select a macro to run, edit, delete etc
Tools-Customize-New	Create or modify a custom menu
Tools-Customize-Toolbars	Attach a menu bar to a workbook
Tools-Macro-Record New Macro	Record new macro

Completing the application

Important note

Units 12–17 form a unified development task – they all need to be completed in order for the purchase order application to work. Unlike previous units, there is no point in doing any one unit in isolation from the others – they all build on each other.

What you will learn in this unit

By the end of this unit you will be able to:

- back up an application
- run a macro automatically
- hide screen updating
- clear fields from a user form.

What you should know already

Before you start this unit, make sure that you can do the following:

Skill	Covered in
Basic mouse, menu and Windows operations	Unit 1
Using formulae	Units 1 and 2

Introduction

This unit completes the development of the purchase order application begun in Units 12–16. It tests the whole application and shows you how to make some final refinements.

Task 1: Enhancing the application

By now the purchase order application is up and running, but there are still some rough edges:

- If the user form is called a second time the previous record is still displayed.

- The worksheet **ORDER SCREENS** needs to open automatically whenever the workbook is opened and display the title screen.

- The Excel screen 'jumps' rather distractingly as the macro commands are executed.

We will put these problems right in the remaining activities.

1 **Backing up your application**

Open the workbook **ORDENTER** if necessary.

Before you start tinkering with the workbook make a copy of it as a backup.

Select **Save As** from the **File** menu.

Save the workbook under the new name **ORDENTER_BACKUP** – make sure that the correct drive is selected before you click **OK** . Close the backup and re-open the original version.

2 **Clearing the order form**. We need to clear out the contents of the order form so that it is blank when another order is added.

Let's recap on how the procedure **btnEnter_Click( )** transfers data from the order form to the database cells in the worksheet.

- The form was designed using the Visual Basic Editor – see Unit 13, Task 2.

- A macro was written to display the user form – see Unit 15, Task 2.

- When the **Enter** button on the form is clicked the user can enter a record, which is then stored in the worksheet – see Unit 14.

An example of the VB code that transfers the supplier name from the edit box in the user form to a named cell in the worksheet **ORDER SCREENS** is:

Sheets("Order Screens").Range("WSSupplier") = _
OrderForm.TbSupplier.Value

3 Open the **Tools** menu and select **Macro-Visual Basic Editor**.

The Visual Basic Module opens, overlying the worksheet. Maximise this window so that it fills the whole screen. If the user form **OrderForm** is not visible then proceed as follows:

■ First of all, select the Project window. If you can't see it, then open the View menu and select **Project Explorer**.

■ Identify the **Forms** folder in the Project Explorer. If necessary open it to display the icon for the form **OrderForm**.

■ Double click on the **OrderForm** icon to display it. Close the Project window.

■ Double click on the Enter button on the form. This will call up the procedure **btnEnter_Click( )**.

4 Locate the code shown in Step 2, insert a blank line and add the final line shown below, so that the section of code now contains the third line shown.

Sheets("Order Screens").Range("WSSupplier") = _
OrderForm.TbSupplier.Value
OrderForm.TbSupplier.Value = ""

(The **= ""** has the effect of blanking the edit box after its contents have been transferred to the database.)

5 Now return to the **ORDER SCREENS** worksheet (use the Windows Taskbar).

Open the **Purchase Orders** custom menu and select **Add an Order**.

Enter a new record in the order form and press the **Enter** button.

When the message box 'Enter another order?' is displayed click the **Yes** button.

When you are returned to the user form check that the **Supplier** field is blank.

This time click the **Close** button. You should be returned to the special title screen.

Restore the Excel screen again.

6 **Consolidation**. You can now blank out all the text boxes in the same way.

Test the macro again as above.

  The amended version of the code for this and the other macros used in this application is shown in Appendix 2.

218

Task 2: Making a macro run automatically

We will create a special macro named **Auto_Open** that will automatically run when the workbook **ORDENTER** is opened. We will use it to call the macro **Set_Title_Screen**. This will have the effect of automatically setting up the title screen when the workbook is opened.

1   Open the **Tools** menu and select **Macro-Record New Macro**.

Name the macro **Auto_Open** and complete the **Description** box.

Make sure that the **This Workbook** option is selected.

Click **OK** .

You are now recording.

2   Click on the sheet tab for **Order Screens** to activate it (even if already selected).

Open the **Tools** menu and select **Macro-Macros**.

Run the macro **Set_Title_Screen**.

Click the **Stop Recording** button.

3   Test the macro by saving and closing the workbook and then opening it again.

The title screen and the custom menu should automatically be displayed.

Task 3: Turning off screen updating

Once you have the whole application working correctly you can hide from the user what is happening 'behind the scenes'. In several macros there is an appreciable delay while the screen is being updated; if you turn off updating until the end of the macro then it will work more quickly and smoothly. The command is ***Application.ScreenUpdating = False*** to turn off screen updating, and

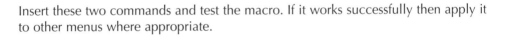

Application.ScreenUpdating = True to turn it on again. If you consult the list of macros in Appendix 2 you will see it applied to the macro **Set_Title_Screen**.

Insert these two commands and test the macro. If it works successfully then apply it to other menus where appropriate.

Summary of commands

Menu commands show the menu name first, followed by the command to choose from the menu, e.g. **Edit-Clear** means open the **Edit** menu and select the **Clear** command.

Worksheet commands

File-Save As	Backup a workbook under a new name
Tools-Macro-Macros	Select a macro to run, edit, delete etc
Tools-Macro-Record New Macro	Record new macro
Tools-Macro-Visual Basic Editor	Enter VB Editor

VB Editor commands

View-Project Explorer	View components of a project

List of Visual Basic commands used in the purchase order application

The commands listed below are, of course, only a small proportion of the complete VB command set. Similarly, the list only attempts to cover the main features of each command. For further information you are recommended to consult the Visual Basic online help features provided by Excel, or a specialised book on the subject.

Activating an object – the Activate method

Range("L57").Activate
Worksheets("Sheet1").Activate

Blanking the contents of a text box

'Blank the text box TbSupplier in a UserForm called OrderForm
OrderForm.TbSupplier.Value = " "

Conditions – the If-Then-Else-End If statement

Syntax:
If (condition) Then
  [statements]
[Else
  [elsestatements]]
End If
e.g.
'Calculate the VAT rate at 17.5% if check box CbVat is on
Vatrate = 0.175
If OrderForm.CbVat.Value = True _
Then
  *Sheets("Order Screens").Range("WSVat") = Vatrate * _*
  *Range("WsQuantity").Value * Range("WsPrice").Value*
Else
  Sheets("Order Screens").Range("WSVat") = 0
End If

Copying and pasting cell contents

Range("L52:S52").Select
Selection.Copy
Range("L57").Select
ActiveSheet.Paste

Copying from a text box to a worksheet cell

'Copy supplier name from text box named TbSupplier in a
'User Form to a cell named WSSupplier in a worksheet named
'Order Screens

Sheets("Order Screens").Range("WSSupplier") = _
OrderForm.TbSupplier.Value

Hiding and displaying a user form – the Hide and Show methods

OrderForm.Hide
OrderForm.Show

Hiding and displaying a standard data form

ActiveSheet.ShowDataForm
ActiveSheet.HideDataForm

Hiding and displaying toolbars – the Visible property

Application.CommandBars("Standard").Visible = True
Application.CommandBars("Standard").Visible = False

Hiding and displaying worksheet window objects – the Display property

With ActiveWindow
  .DisplayGridlines = True
  .DisplayVerticalScrollBar = True
  .DisplayWorkbookTabs = False
End With

Maximising and minimising windows

'Maximise the Application Window
Application.WindowState = xlMaximized

'Maximise the Workbook Window
ActiveWindow.WindowState = xlMaximized

'Minimise the Application Window
Application.WindowState = xlMinimized

'Minimise the Workbook Window
ActiveWindow.WindowState = xlMinimized

Message box – creating

A message box displays a message and buttons in a dialog box and records which button (Yes, No etc) is clicked. The syntax is:

MsgBox(prompt[, buttons] [, title] [, helpfile, context])

Notes:

A prompt is required, displayed as the message in the dialog box.

Buttons are optional. The VB help text lists common options – see the example below.

Title is optional, displayed in the title bar of the dialog box.

The *helpfile* is optional – see VB help.

Example:

Dim reply 'create variable to hold user response
reply = MsgBox("Enter another order?", vbYesNo, _
"Purchase Orders")

Quitting an application – the Quit method

Application.Quit

Running a macro – the Run method

Application.Run "Position_Title_Screen"

Saving a workbook – the Save method

ActiveWorkbook.Save

Screen updating – turning on and off

Application.ScreenUpdating = False
Application.ScreenUpdating = True

Selecting an object – the Select method

Rows("57:57").Select
Sheets("Order Screens").Select
Range("A1:C3").Select

List of macros used in the purchase order application

All the macros and procedures developed in Units 12–17 appear below and can be used to check your application. Remember that some details may differ from your application; you may, for example, have used different names for cells or text boxes.

Sub Add_Order( )
```
'

'Add_Order Macro
'Macro recorded 03/02/97 by j muir adds a record to the
'database
'

Rows("57:57").Select
Range("L57").Activate
Selection.Insert Shift:=xlDown
Range("L52:S52").Select
Selection.Copy
Range("L57").Select
ActiveSheet.Paste
Application.CutCopyMode = False

Dim reply
reply = MsgBox("Enter another order?", vbYesNo, _
"Purchase Orders")

If reply = vbYes _
Then
    OrderForm.Show          'Show the Order Form
Else
    OrderForm.Hide          'Hide the Order Form

    Sheets("Order Screens").Select
    ActiveWindow.WindowState = xlMaximized

    Application.Run "Position_Title_Screen"
    Application.Run "Set_Title_Screen"
End If
```

```
Sub Auto_Open( )
'
' Auto_Open Macro
' Macro recorded 26/03/97 by j muir

Sheets("Order Screens").Select
Application.Run "ORDENTER.xls!Set_Title_Screen"
End Sub

Private Sub btnClose_Click( )
Application.Run "Set_Title_Screen"
Application.Run "ORDENTER.xls!Position_Title_Screen"
End
End Sub

Private Sub btnEnter_Click( )
Sheets("Order Screens").Select

'Copy supplier name from text box in form to named cell in
'worksheet
Sheets("Order Screens").Range("WSSupplier") = _
OrderForm.TbSupplier.Value
'Then blank the text box
OrderForm.TbSupplier.Value = " "

'Copy product name from combo box in form to named cell in
'worksheet
Sheets("Order Screens").Range("WSProduct") = _
OrderForm.CbProducts.Value
OrderForm.CbProducts.Value = " "

'Copy product type from text box in form to named cell in
'worksheet
Sheets("Order Screens").Range("WSType") = _
OrderForm.TbType.Value
OrderForm.TbType.Value = " "

'Copy quantity from text box in form to named cell in
'worksheet
Sheets("Order Screens").Range("WSQuantity") = _
OrderForm.TbQuantity.Value
OrderForm.TbQuantity.Value = " "

'Copy unit price from text box in form to named cell in
'worksheet
Sheets("Order Screens").Range("WSPrice") = _
OrderForm.TbPrice.Value
OrderForm.TbPrice.Value = " "
```

```
'Copy order date from text box in form to named cell in
'worksheet
Sheets("Order Screens").Range("WSDate") = _
OrderForm.TbDate.Value
OrderForm.TbDate.Value = " "

'Calculate the VAT rate at 17.5% if check box is on
Vatrate = 0.175
If OrderForm.CbVat.Value = True _
  Then
            Sheets("Order Screens").Range("WSVat") = Vatrate * _
            Range("WsQuantity").Value * Range("WsPrice").Value
  Else
            Sheets("Order Screens").Range("WSVat") = 0
End If

'Calculate the order total = (price * quantity) + vat
Sheets("Order Screens").Range("WSTotal") = _
(Range("WsQuantity").Value) * (Range("WsPrice").Value) _
+ Range("WsVat").Value

'Hide the Order Form
OrderForm.Hide

'Run the Add_order macro to add record the database
Application.Run "ORDENTER.xls!Add_Order"

End Sub

Private Sub btnClose_Click( )
Application.Run "Set_Title_Screen"
Application.Run "ORDENTER.xls!Position_Title_Screen"
End
End Sub

Sub Call_Data_Form( )
'
'Call_Data_Form Macro
'Macro recorded 07/02/97 by j muir
'uses data form for editing
'
Sheets("Order Screens").Select
'Position the window to show the database
Application.Run "ORDENTER.xls!Position_Database_Screen"
'Select the database
Range("L56").Select
'Call the data form
ActiveSheet.ShowDataForm
```

```
'Run the macro to set up the title screen
Application.Run "ORDENTER.xls!Set_Title_Screen"
'Run the macro to position the title screen
Application.Run "ORDENTER.xls!Position_Title_Screen"

End Sub

Sub Call_Order_Form( )
'
'Call_Order_Form Macro
'Macro recorded 06/02/97 by j muir
'

OrderForm.Show

'

End Sub

Sub Position_Database_Screen( )
'
'Position_Database_Screen Macro
'Macro recorded 03/01/97 by j muir
'


'

Application.WindowState = xlMaximized
ActiveWindow.WindowState = xlMaximized
Range("A1").Select
ActiveWindow.SmallScroll Down:=55
ActiveWindow.SmallScroll ToRight:=11
End Sub

Sub Position_Title_Screen( )
'
'Position_Title_Screen Macro
'Macro recorded 03/01/97 by j muir
'


'

Application.WindowState = xlMaximized
ActiveWindow.WindowState = xlMaximized
Range("A1").Select
End Sub
```

```
Sub Print_Database( )
'

'Print_Database Macro
'Macro recorded 07/02/97 by j muir prints the database records
'


'

Sheets("Order Screens").Select
Application.Run "ORDENTER.xls!Position_Database_Screen"
Range("L56").Select
Selection.CurrentRegion.Select
Selection.PrintOut Copies:=1
Application.Run "ORDENTER.xls!Set_Title_Screen"
Application.Run "ORDENTER.xls!Position_Title_Screen"

End Sub

Sub Restore_Title_Screen( )

' Restore_Title_Screen Macro
' Macro recorded 02/01/97 by j muir restores
' the normal screen defaults

With ActiveWindow
  .DisplayGridlines = True
  .DisplayHeadings = True
  .DisplayHorizontalScrollBar = True
  .DisplayVerticalScrollBar = True
  .DisplayWorkbookTabs = True
End With

With Application
  .DisplayFormulaBar = True
  .DisplayStatusBar = True
End With

Application.CommandBars("Standard").Visible = True
Application.CommandBars("Formatting").Visible = True
Application.CommandBars("Drawing").Visible = True

End Sub
```

```
Sub Save_quit( )
'
'Save_quit Macro
'Macro recorded 07/02/97 by j muir saves the workbook and
'exits Excel

ActiveWorkbook.Save
Application.Quit
End Sub

Sub Set_Title_Screen( )
'
'Set_Title_Screen Macro
'Macro recorded 02/01/97 by j muir displays application
'title and sets off screen defaults
'
Application.ScreenUpdating = False
'
Application.WindowState = xlMaximized
ActiveWindow.WindowState = xlMaximized
Sheets("Order Screens").Select
Range("A1").Select
With ActiveWindow
   .DisplayGridlines = False
   .DisplayHeadings = False
   .DisplayHorizontalScrollBar = False
   .DisplayVerticalScrollBar = False
   .DisplayWorkbookTabs = False
End With
With Application
   .DisplayFormulaBar = False
   .DisplayStatusBar = False
End With
Application.CommandBars("Standard").Visible = False
Application.CommandBars("Formatting").Visible = False
Application.CommandBars("Drawing").Visible = False
Application.ScreenUpdating = True


End Sub
```

G	H	I	J	K
NCES - TERM 1				
Week 6	Week 7	Week 8	Week 9	Week 10
£ 495.00	£ 365.00	£ 235.00	£ 105.00	-£ 25.00
£ 495.00	£ 365.00	£ 235.00	£ 105.00	-£ 25.00
£ 60.00	£ 60.00	£ 60.00	£ 60.00	£ 60.00
£ 35.00	£ 35.00	£ 35.00	£ 35.00	£ 35.00
£ 15.00	£ 15.00	£ 15.00	£ 15.00	£ 15.00
£ 20.00	£ 20.00	£ 20.00	£ 20.00	£ 20.00
£ 130.00	£ 130.00	£ 130.00	£ 130.00	£ 130.00
£ 365.00	£ 235.00	£ 105.00	-£ 25.00	-£ 155.00

	A	E	F	G	H	I	J	K
1		PERSONAL FINANCES - TERM 1						
2								
3	INCOME	Week 4	Week 5	Week 6	Week 7	Week 8	Week 9	Week 10
7	Part Time Job				£ 20.00	£ 20.00	£ 20.00	£ 20.00
8	Parents					£ 30.00		
9	Total Income	£ 750.00	£ 615.00	£ 480.00	£ 385.00	£ 320.00	£ 225.00	£ 130.00
10								
11	EXPENDITURE							
12	Accommodation	£ 65.00	£ 65.00	£ 65.00	£ 65.00	£ 65.00	£ 65.00	£ 65.00
13	Food and Travel	£ 35.00	£ 35.00	£ 30.00	£ 30.00	£ 30.00	£ 30.00	£ 30.00
14	Books	£ 15.00	£ 15.00	£ -	£ -	£ -	£ -	£ -
15	Other	£ 20.00	£ 20.00	£ 20.00	£ 20.00	£ 20.00	£ 20.00	£ 30.00
16	Total Expenditure	£ 135.00	£ 135.00	£ 115.00	£ 115.00	£ 115.00	£ 115.00	£ 125.00
17								
18	CLOSING BALS.	£ 615.00	£ 480.00	£ 365.00	£ 270.00	£ 205.00	£ 110.00	£ 5.00

appendix 5

	A	B	C	D	E	F
1	Insurance Sales - First Quarter					
2						
3		Motor	Life	Property	Total	
4	Jan	1465	1243	2456	5164	
5	Feb	1345	1456	1987	4788	
6	Mar	1132	2310	1598	5040	
7						
8	Quarterly Average	1314	1670	2014	4997	
9	Quarterly Total	3942	5009	6041	14992	
10	% of Total	26.29%	33.41%	40.29%		
11						
12		This worksheet shows a sales analysis of				
13		the three major insurance categories				
14						
15						

appendix 6

	A	B	C	D	E
1	Order No.	Order Date	Co.Ref	Co. Name	Value
2	14005	11-Mar	955	Tilley Transport	1678.00
3	14003	11-Mar	1289	Marsden Products	4456.00
4	14009	12-Mar	1289	Marsden Products	1652.54
5	14007	09-Mar	1453	Wilson Garages	2654.00
6	14000	10-Mar	1453	Wilson Garages	3200.00
7	14002	11-Mar	1453	Wilson Garages	98.76
8	14008	12-Mar	2245	Goldfield Stables	123.85
9	14006	10-Mar	2375	Patel Kitchens	55.54
10	14001	08-Mar	2413	Patel Industries	1466.00
11	14004	10-Mar	2413	Patel Industries	567.00
12					

appendix 7

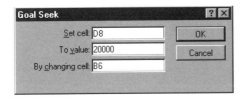

Goal Seek [?] [X]

Set cell: D8

To value: 20000

By changing cell: B6

OK

Cancel

231

appendix 8

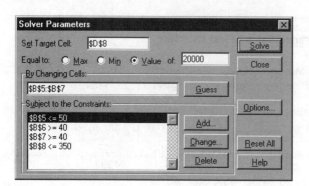

appendix 9

1(a)	**IPMT** function
1(b)	**RATE** function
2(a)	**ROUNDUP** or **ROUNDDOWN** functions
2(b)	**SUBTOTAL** function
3(a)	**COUNTBLANK** function
3(b)	**NORMDIST** function
4(a)	**REPLACE** function
4(b)	**TRIM** function
4(c)	**UPPER** or **LOWER** functions
5(a)	**TYPE** function
5(b)	**ISBLANK** or **ISERR/ISERROR** functions

Glossary

Active Cell	The cell currently selected and shown by a heavy border. In Excel 97, a cell can contain up to 32,000 characters
Address	Consists of two co-ordinates – the column letter followed by the row number (as in a street map)
Advanced Filter	Option that allows you to search on more than two fields, and offers a wider range of operators than those offered by a data form
Autoformat feature	Allows you to format your worksheets automatically, offering 17 built-in formats to choose from. Excel will automatically detect which worksheet areas should be headings, data, totals etc.
Autosum button	Offers the quickest way of adding a column of figures; it is on the Standard toolbar and is marked with the Greek letter sigma (Σ)
Box or cell	Where a column and a row intersect
Cell reference	Consists of two co-ordinates – the column letter followed by the row number (as in a street map)
ChartWizard	Allows you to create simple charts using four steps (see Unit 3); allows you to change the chart type and other parameters
Close buttons (an 'X')	These close either Excel or one of the workbooks. If you click one of these buttons by mistake you will need to open Excel and/or your workbook(s) again
Column and Row Headings	These contain the column references (letters) and the row references (numbers); jointly they give the cell reference or address, e.g. A1, D5.
Command bars	In Excel 97, the common term for a toolbar and a menu
Comparison operators	The following six operators can be used in searching the database: = equal to (not needed on its own); < less than; > greater than; <> not equal to; <= less than or equal to; >= greater than or equal to
Control Menu boxes	These offer commands such as resizing and closing the window

Cutting and pasting　　Cutting cells physically removes them from their original location so that they can be pasted to a new one; this is similar operation to copying

Doughnut chart　　Like a pie chart; it shows the relative contribution of various quantities to a total; however, unlike a pie chart it is not restricted to one data series

Drawing Toolbar　　This allows you to draw a variety of shapes on your worksheet – circles, rectangles, arrows etc.; it also allows you to add colour and text effects

Elevation　　In a 3-D chart, the height (in degrees) at which you view the columns; it can vary from 0 to 44 degrees in a column chart

Favorites folder　　Provides a shortcut or link to any folder that you need to find quickly; this is most appropriate when you have a large number of folders and subfolders on a hard drive

FORECAST* and *TREND　　These statistical functions allow you to predict future results based on past data; they are valuable tools in predicting many business trends, including share prices, sales figures and stockholding needs

Formula Bar　　This shows whatever is in entered in the active cell

Formulae　　Tell the spreadsheet to perform calculations, e.g. add the values in a column or work out a percentage

Goal Seek tool　　Can substitute various values for a variable in a formula; it cannot determine what the 'best' ones are for your purpose

Macro　　Lets you save commands in a special macro sheet – the commands can then be run automatically whenever one needs to use them; nearly any series of keystrokes, menu choices and mouse movements can be stored in a macro and used again when required

Maximize buttons (a square)　　These either increase the size of the Excel application window to fill the screen or increase the size of the document window so that it fills the whole of the application window

Methods　　In Visual Basic, these are used to perform actions on objects (qv); an object's properties determine what methods can be used with them, e.g. many objects can be opened, closed, copied or activated – worksheets, workbooks etc – but calculations can only be applied to certain types of numeric objects

Minimize buttons (a line)　　These either reduce Excel to a button on the Taskbar or the document window to a small icon within the application window

'My documents' folder
Provided for you to store current work. It is stored in the main or root folder on the hard drive. The first time that you use the Open or Save As commands in an Excel session it is offered as the default folder. If you share your PC with others this folder can soon get very full if it is used indiscriminately

Objects
Visual Basic is an object-oriented language, i.e. the program manipulates objects; worksheets, windows, user forms, buttons, menus and ranges of cells are all examples of objects. Objects can contain other objects: e.g. a worksheet contains cells, which contain values

Office Assistant
New to Excel 97 and supplements other Help features by answering questions typed in ordinary English

Paste Link command
Ensures that when the original workbook changes the copy also changes

Perspective
The three-dimensional depth of a 3-D chart (see Unit 4)

PivotTable
Allows you to rearrange the columns and rows of a database and summarise the data in new ways; it is quicker and easier than using formulae or queries

Properties
In Visual Basic, all objects have properties that determine how they look or how they work, e.g. a TextBox object has a Text property – the text it contains – and a workbook can be active or not – the property ActiveWorkbook; not all properties apply to all objects

Properties window
Your major way of modifying the properties of the various objects that can appear on a form – buttons, text boxes and the form itself

Reference Area
This shows the row and column number of the active cell

Restore buttons (overlapping squares)
These restore the individual windows to their original sizes

Rotation
Rotates a 3-D chart about its vertical axis

Scenario Manager
Allows you to save different combinations of variables as named scenarios and run and print them later

Sheet names
Each sheet is marked with a name tab – the name in bold indicates which sheet is currently selected or 'active'

Solver
Can solve certain types of problem; it will juggle with multiple values for variables and find the combination producing the optimum or target result, e.g. it can determine the most profitable mix of products, schedule staff to minimise the wages bill, or allocate working capital to its most profitable use

Spreadsheet   Is a grid of vertical columns and horizontal rows.

Status Bar   Displays information about the current command

Syntax   In Visual Basic, objects, methods and properties (qqv)are
                             separated from each other by full stops; to refer to the method
                             you are applying to the object you use the syntax
                             Object.Method, i.e. object name separated from method name
                             with a full stop

Trendline   Useful for emphasising relationships between different data series

Visual Basic
programming language   An 'object-oriented' programming language specially developed
                             for Windows applications

'What's This?' feature   Offers 'context-sensitive' tips, i.e. tips specific to the Excel feature
                             that you are currently using